# Popular Religion
# in China
## The Imperial Metaphor

# Popular Religion in China
## The Imperial Metaphor

**Stephan Feuchtwang**

CURZON

First Published in 2001
by Curzon Press
Richmond, Surrey
http://www.curzonpress.co.uk

© 2001 Stephan Feuchtwang

Typeset in Horley Old Style by LaserScript Ltd, Mitcham, Surrey
Printed and bound in Great Britain by
Biddles Ltd, Guildford and King's Lynn

*British Library Cataloguing in Publication Data*
A catalogue record of this book is available from the British Library

*Library of Congress Cataloguing in Publication Data*
A catalogue record for this book has been requested

ISBN 0–7007–1421–9 (hbk)
ISBN 0–7007–1385–9 (pbk)

# Contents

# Preface

This is a book about Chinese popular religion. A sensible reader will ask: What is that? What is its name? We have come to expect of religions that they can be named like identities of nations or cultures or at least that they can be understood as doctrines. But in this case, these sensible questions must be given a disconcerting answer, because it has no name. This is not a religion of a Book. Nor is it the named religion of China – Daoism. That religion, with Daoist philosophy at its heart, comes closer to the popular religion I shall be describing than do the other religions identifiable in China, such as the official imperial cults honouring Heaven and Confucius, or the denominations of Buddhism. The popular religion includes some elements of both Buddhism and the imperial cults, more of Daoism, but it is identifiable with none of them. In fact 'religion' here is simply a category, not a singular thing.

It is religion of the common people, not 'of the people' in the sense of a national population's mass culture, but in that it contains a crucial and political relation to official religion and to others with the power to define orthodoxy in China. It is also popular in the sense of being local and true of the China of the Han, or Chinese-speaking people, where every place had or has its local cults and the festivals peculiar to them. The institution of local festivals and temples is not so well known as that of ancestor worship and clan and lineage halls, but it is just as much a universal fact of Chinese life.

This book will show that it is a distinctive institution. Whether it is a recognisable religion, you will have to decide for yourself. There have been many articles and books on the gods and festivals of Chinese villages and towns. Standing alongside these studies[1] I hope this book will allow the institution to be better known. Its content is an imperial metaphor, which stands in relation to the rest of its participants' lives, politics and historical events as the poetry of collective vision theatrically performed, built and painted in temples, carved and clothed in statues. It is a metaphor at all times, including the times of imperial or dynastic rule, as well as during the more recent political history of republican China.

Some readers of the first edition of this book have mistaken my presentation of the imperial metaphor. They have understood it to be a parallel and confirming structure of imperial bureaucratic rule. But it is not. What this book shows instead is that the performance and imagery of local temple rites and festivals are sufficiently different to present a sense of place and of power which is a supplementary universe to that of ruling orthodoxy. For an argument about parallel and confirming structure to hold, the metaphor would have to change with changes in the structure of government. But in fact the nature of rule has changed over the centuries in a rhythm and with a drama greater and quite distinct from the histories of local cults of gods. Changes of dynasty were drastic events. Each claimed continuity from its predecessors or from a golden era of sage rulers, but in fact there were dramatic changes in the extent and nature of their rule. The most dramatic change of all has occurred in the twentieth century, a century of revolutions in China. The imperial metaphor has also changed, but not in the same way or at the same pace, nor has it ceased though the imperial regimes have gone.

There is of course a relation with imperial cults and their ideology. The time in which the imagery of local cults is set is the same cosmic time as the claims to legitimacy of the ruling dynasties. But local cults are created and disappear in a distinctive dynamic. They are constrained by government, but their dynamism does not confirm that of government. This is most dramatically to be seen in the twentieth century during which the cosmic claims of imperial dynastic rule have been eliminated, while those of local cults have remained. So this book definitely does not argue that the religion of local cults reflects and reinforces government. On the contrary, I think I have been able to demonstrate that even during the centuries of imperial rule the cosmology enacted in local cults was not that of centralised administration, but of linkages with many centres and with a distinctive character. Besides, local cults are embedded in a sense of place and its history which is not that of a dynasty or of a nation.

In China there was no self-evident and indisputable world of practice, classifying places, people and times in a hierarchy, and expressing its discontents as part of the same order reinforced by language, myth and rite, which Pierre Bourdieu names *doxa* (1977:

164–168). Instead there was an interplay between orthodoxies and heterodoxies, both of them in the plural, each reflecting upon the other. But they did exist within limits that were themselves not challenged until the crises of the last, Qing dynasty and its confrontation with the states of industrial capitalism. Most of the direct observations of local cults which I shall use come from late Qing and the twentieth century. The changes which local cults have undergone will be an important topic of this book. But first, Chapter 1 makes as explicit as possible the terms in which I will describe this institution of popular religion.

Chapter 1 raises a contentious issue of interest to historians and social scientists: how to describe others' beliefs in gods without resorting to them yourself, but still remaining faithful to what people say and do. I outline the basically political and historical perspectives in which I think they can be best understood and describe the operations of identification and representation of which I think they are examples. It also introduces the imagery of Chinese gods and demons and the rituals which address them. It starts off an inquiry into how they constitute a transcendental and archaic metaphor and goes on to develop a concept of religion that may well be of more general validity. It is most worked out in the concluding section of Chapter 5.

Chapters 2–7 describe the institution of local cults, their festivals and their gods in the political and religious context of imperial and republican China. The imperial official cults, the nature and ideology of imperial rule, receive particular attention in Chapters 2 and 3. Chapter 2 shows that ritual authority was part of imperial rule and that popular versions of its cosmology turned it into a threatening and demonic one. Chapter 3 establishes the relation between imperial authority and local territorial cults. Chapter 6 is devoted to Daoism and the great rite of offering performed to inaugurate a new or rebuilt temple. Imperial cults and Daoism are the most immediate religious contexts of local cults, the most connected and also the contexts from which their distinctiveness is most contested.

The political culture of local temples and festivals themselves is described in detail in Chapters 4 and 5. In them I refer to both the imperial and the republican regimes under which they have flourished. The detailed description of local festivals and temple organisation in Chapter 4 is based on my own observations in Taiwan. But it follows a chapter in which I hope I have been able to establish with references to other regions, particularly to northern China, the ubiquity of the institution of territorial cults and their festivals in China.

Imagery and the operations of ritual representation are the particular concern of Chapters 5–7. I hope they will have shown what is distinctive about the institution of local festivals and territorial cults, and that it has to do with a representation of demonic power. What 'demonic power' and its representations mean will be clear by the end of Chapter 7.

Beside revising details in each chapter and clarifying its main points, for this new edition I have added a new, long chapter on the political and economic transformations which have affected popular religion in the mainland and Taiwan. For the mainland I take up the question whether the politics of mass mobilisation under the leadership the Chinese Communist Party and Mao-Zedong-thought are best described as 'religious'. Ritual and religion are always close, particularly when interpreted and analysed in a human science which is not a theology. But I think the appropriate term for the cult of Mao is 'political rituals'. It was a formation of selves in relation to the larger destiny of a people. A major subject of the chapter is the effect of rituals of mass mobilisation, which replaced, suppressed or destroyed all religious rituals. But the longest and last section of the chapter is about the revitalisation of local cults since the ending of the politics of mass mobilisation. To what extent do they contain the effects of preceding political rituals? The chapter also includes a comparison with developments in Taiwan. In both Taiwan and the People's Republic of China there has been a strong growth of what I call congregational religions and of religious practices concerned with individual lives and prospects. They are less locally rooted, but they co-exist with more traditional local cults. In both secular states there is great and varied religious life; in their turn, religious traditions and new religions have become subjects for the politics of community development, culture, tourism and the making of heritages.

## NOTE ON THE TRANSLITERATION OF CHINESE TERMS AND NAMES

With two exceptions, all Chinese names and terms are spelled in what has become the standard system: pinyin. Even where they refer to statements made in one or other of the dialect-languages of China, such as Southern Fujian, I have put them into the common language (putong hua). This should avoid confusion and it should also help reference between local practices and beliefs.

One of the exceptions is when directly quoting a text using another system of transliteration, usually the Wade-Giles system. There I have preserved the transliteration used in the original and inserted the pinyin transliteration after the Wade-Giles when it is not obviously apparent from the similarity of spelling. The other exception is where I have quoted direct speech in Southern Fujianese, or Amoy, the dialect also spoken in Taiwan. The system preserving that pronunciation is the one created for spoken Amoy speech by Bodman. Pinyin insertions and explanations are added for clarification.

# Acknowledgements

My own local study in Taiwan (1966–8) was financed by the Nuffield and Carnegie foundations through the now defunct London-Cornell Fellowship. A brief but productive visit to Beijing, Xiamen and Quanzhou in 1988 was financed by the China exchange scheme of the UK Economic and Social Research Council, the British Academy, the Chinese Academy of Social Sciences, and by the Spalding Trust. Visits to selected villages in five mainland provinces in 1990 and 1992 were financed by the Economic and Social Research Council of the UK, and a revisit to my original field in Taiwan in 1995 was financed by the Chiang Ching-kuo Foundation. I am very grateful to them all.

My debts to other local studies and analyses of Chinese ritual and religion are acknowledged in their proper places in the book. But a more general debt to mentors must be acknowledged here: to the late Maurice Freedman, the tutor with whom my sharp differences did not prevent affection and mutual respect; to G. William Skinner, whose local systems modelling has brought sense and inspiration to any attempt to generalise about China, including mine even if I do not make much of it here, and whose encouragement of my first publications on Chinese religion was invaluable; to Arthur Wolf for his introductions to Taiwan; and to Kristofer Schipper for his guidance and insights into Daoism. I owe the development of a lifelong interest to them.

Another kind of intellectual debt to be acknowledged is the one I owe to engagements in discussion and comprehension over many years with Beverley Brown, Mark Cousins, Paul Hirst and Homi Bhabha. Quite what I owe to them in this book cannot be specified, but that something is owed I do not doubt. And for encouragements to 'see him' warm thanks to James Hamilton-Paterson.

To the families of Gao Mingguo and Doctor Gao of Shiding, many of whom have become lifelong friends, I owe a special thanks for their initial hospitality and of course a continuing gratitude for the warmth of their welcomes. To David Chen I owe in addition thanks for the results of his very able assistance in my Shiding fieldwork and for the memory of his spiky chin in my shoulder as he rode the bumps on the pillion of my Honda 50cc down the winding road to Taibei.

# Chapter One

# History, identification and belief

People in the course of their lives are involved in rituals and conventional celebrations of many kinds. What sense of history would they find framed in these rituals? How would their own biographies be marked by such collective occasions?

Rituals may be disdained, others accepted as social obligation, some with wholehearted enthusiasm. The psychic attachment to each is a matter for the individual. But ritual occasions and their references also set social rhythms of historical identification. As anywhere else, people in China can experience several systems of ritual occasion framing their lives. Each system displays a different sense of history.

Start from the greatest scope of historical inclusion, and consider someone identifiable simply as Chinese, a nationalist, a socialist, a Christian, a Muslim, a Buddhist, a Daoist or a Confucian Chinese – or several of these. Each qualification of being Chinese is represented by ritual occasion and celebration – of the establishing of the republic, of leaders of revolution, of prophets and of founders. And each refers directly to a well defined textual tradition – the *Three People's Principles* by the Father of the Republic, Sun Yat-sen; the works called the *Thought of Mao Zedong* and the works of Marx, Engels and Lenin, establishing the ideology of the foundation of the People's Republic; the revealed Book (Koran or Bible); the sutras of the various schools of Buddhism; the liturgies in the canon of Daoism; the classics of Confucius and his disciples; and the most revered commentaries on each of the foregoing. 'Classical' is an appropriate name for these resources. Claims to all-inclusive Chineseness are made by reference to them. The classical traditions of Marxist atheism and its Chinese version, or the various Christianities, the various Islams, Buddhisms, Daoisms and Confucian teachings, are the usual sources according to which Chinese history and its institutions are described and included in larger histories.

1

Reference in this classical mode and its occasions is a reference to narratives which scholars can ascertain and argue about. They rely on writing and printing.

But in addition to these classical identifications, the Chinese person will also know about and have some obligations to attend, with his or her family, the days of birth, death and for celebrating immediate ancestors, or simply to acknowledge family completeness by gathering or communicating at the Spring Festival and lesser annual occasions. These entail another sense of history, another rhythm and division of time – that of family line and generation. They may be compatible with some, more than with others, of the classical frameworks and their ritual occasions. But they rely less on writing than on the rituals and the objects which mark the classical occasions.

Third, the place in which this person grew up will have had its own peculiar occasions, catastrophes and the exceptional ritual remedies sought for them. Regular festivals or fairs, theatrical performances and other displays and stories commemorate these occasions. They will include local variants on regular, China-wide annual occasions, such as the Spring Festival, or the Seventh Month festival of purification and propitiation of hungry ghosts. But they also include days not celebrated elsewhere, or else shared only by fellow followers of the cult of a certain deity and its localities. The founding moment of a cult would be its manifestation in some extraordinary event or person, possibly with some further backward reference to other origins. The repetition, annual, five-yearly, whatever, is then repetition of origination just as it is of an ancestor or an historical foundation and its anniversary. These occasions are even less reliant for their authority on written forms. Even more than familial rituals, their ritual repetition is itself the inscription of an origin and its renewal. But the stories they celebrate are part and parcel of the popular narratives of theatre and story tellers.

In this kind of rhythm, a local history and identification, differentiated from neighbouring localities, is marked. In the course of a lifetime moving from one to another an individual may link and be associated with a number of such local, historical identifications in addition to the identifications provoked by the other frames.

By historical identification, I mean that each one of these three kinds of occasion – the classical, the familial, and the local – marks out a dimension of time and a dimension of inclusion and exclusion. The time dimension is the rhythm of repetition and of (re)origination. It is a capacity to do the same as well as a cyclical memory, of years, of generations. Each repetition renews memories and calendrical markers of a narrative of origin, adding one more in which the repetition's significance is either reaffirmed or is tested by a new cyclical moment and its memories: the joys or disasters of the day or of the intervening period. In addition to this temporal rhythm there is a dimension of inclusion and exclusion in the extent and scope of the ritual occasion, its name and what it celebrates, by which a person can be identified with the occasion. For instance, the foundation of the republic, celebrated on 10 October, includes anyone who is a citizen of the republic – whether they choose to be so identified or not – and it excludes, as guests, as recent immigrants, or as enemies, those who are not. Its celebration is a renewal of the memory of its sovereign territory and its foundation, and with them of its subjects and their acceptance (or not) of its governmental representation. For another instance, the Spring Festival, which is a renewal of the lunar calendrical year, celebrates a Chinese tradition, the scope of inclusion being that of birth or marriage into a Chinese family. The excluded are guests and non-Chinese enjoying the external spectacle which marks the occasion, in Hong Kong, in London or San Francisco, and the relatively indifferent rest.

Within either of these most-inclusive identifications as being Chinese, the one distinctively territorial and political, the other distinctively familial and ethnic, are more restrictive inclusions. These include identifications of name and ancestry in clan and ancestral festivals such as the cleaning of graves at the other spring festival called Qing Ming, and the family households themselves at the turn of the year during the Spring Festival. They also include the festivals of the gods of local, territorial cults, which are the main subject of this book and to which I now turn.

## HISTORICAL SIGNIFICATION

The beings celebrated and pictured in Chinese local festivals are addressed as actual historical persons. We could appropriately call them heroes and heroines. In principle they can be traced to and identified with historically documentable biographies. Very often they are.

They might also be called saints for this reason. But saints include martyrs, historical individuals who sacrificed their lives for a faith. Their celebration is therefore as much an affirmation of that faith as of a particular biographical slant and speciality of that faith. The Eucharist and the relics of their own bodies also had a peculiar place in the Christian cults of saints, absent in the Chinese cults. The virtues exemplified by Chinese heroes and heroines are not accompanied by a belief in a supreme truth, nor by relics of their bodily existence. They were often martyrs, but to a loyalty, not a faith – loyalty to friends, loyalty to principles of behaviour, loyalty to an emperor or dynasty, loyalty to family line and its honour.

Apart from these important reservations, the term 'saints' might still be preferable to 'heroes and heroines'. For, like saints, Chinese gods are credited with a present effectiveness. It is not the effectiveness of faith or of intercession with a redeemer. But it is intercession in a hierarchy of gods and their underlings, having power to control malign and disorderly influences which are themselves also in principle historically identifiable individuals. I will have to qualify this eventually, and introduce the cosmology personified in popular cults. But I am concerned for now precisely with the personification itself which characterises the popular cults.

The similarities with the cults of saints in Christian Europe are profuse. Let me cite some of the conclusions drawn about them in which we could as well read 'the gods of local cults in China'.

'Once Christianity became established, every place came to have its patron saint or saints. These fulfilled the functions of the local gods or tutelary spirits found elsewhere in the world'. Protection was

> expressed and renewed via the annual saint's festival .... The festival usually involved special ritual, official and unofficial, in honour of the saint; a procession in which the saint's relics [in China, the god's image and incense] would be carried between significant points of the village territory, often marking its boundaries; and a banquet in which all the inhabitants participated, followed by further merrymaking.

Cures, exorcisms, and changes of fortune were sought from the saint's own powers at her or his shrine by means of vows with gifts and promises of actions. 'Moreover, the complementary practice of punishing saints who did not perform the required favours highlights the vow's "magical" and unsophisticated features as well as the element of bargaining and negotiation.' Saints were also believed to send the diseases which they cured, and were therefore offered gifts in fearful expectation as well as gratitude.

Beside being reputed with their own powers, saints might be seen

> as advocates pleading causes before a stern divine judge, as mediators, as go-betweens, as intriguers or wire-pullers at the

court of Heaven – all metaphors were used. It is significant also that the saints themselves were arranged in a hierarchy, in both the liturgy and official iconography, with the Virgin Mary as the arch- intercessor through whom petitions of other saints were directed. (Wilson 1983:22–9)

In China, the Goddess of Mercy, Guan Yin, and several others were intercessors. But none was arch-intercessor. Since the gods of Chinese popular religion can be traced to historically documented biographies, their cults could be held to be merely commemorative – the selection of biographies for whatever historical significance they have for those who celebrate them. Indeed, it is by insisting upon their gods as mere historical personages that state officials in both imperial and republican regimes have attempted to discredit popular cults. But this only draws attention back to the present efficacity with which the gods of popular cults are credited. As Wilson says of the cults of saints, they were

an important ingredient of a 'popular' religion which was conceived of as belonging to the 'people' as against the clergy [in China, officials and scholars of classical orthodoxies], or to the locality as against the outside world and its regulatory powers, and, as the bias of our evidence suggests, this feature seems to have become more prominent in the post-medieval period in Europe [post-Tang dynasty in China] in the face of changes which tended to marginalize certain regions and certain parts of the population. (Wilson 1983:40)

Suppose we look upon the cults as historicisation at odds with the archival documentation to which the officials resort. So posed, popular cults would become intelligible as part of a set of political relations. Such a proposition would also address the difference between the formalities of political relations and the performance of popular rituals. The latter seem to be analogies and rehearsals of the former, as Emily Martin Ahern has pointed out (Ahern 1981a). But as she also says, the differences between them are critical, if not also oppositional.

The cults indicate a process of historical signification, and its potency. Official histories, dissenting histories, and the myths, festivals, theatre, and ritual of popular gods are all open to being interpreted as operations of historical signification and its celebration.

Making something a past which will not recur is to give it historical significance. But this is a thoroughly ambiguous operation. When the significance is stressed for itself it attaches to something valued in the present. Yet when the historical is stressed, it is assigned to another time. Levenson, in his classical exposition (Levenson 1965:87) contrasts absolutist with relativist, by which he means modern, history. But both perform the operation of historical signification. The only difference is that relativist histories are written in the languages of movement rather than in the language of fixity.

'Modern Confucianists relativised Confucianism to Chinese history alone, and modem anti-Confucianists relativised it to early history alone' (Levenson 1965:95). Consignment to a past which is not present is, however, still placing it in a movement which is both past and present, though not a fixity. It tells 'how a certain people made history at a certain stage of a master-process' (Levenson 1965:100). In relativising Confucianism, the master process is a people's history. Modern historicisation may or may not indicate an encompassing, master process – the evolutionary dynamic or the laws of production and social formation. Its contrasting character with pre-modem does not depend so much on whether such a transcendent master-process is explicitly evoked. But the possibility of a master-process does bring home the fact of a continuing process, in which the past is consigned but remains in some present manner. And it is this assumption of continuing process which characterises historicisation. What distinguishes modern from absolutist historicisation is its plurality of identities which are the subjects of history. Consignment is at once a demarcation of a past and a selection of something as significant by placing it beyond that demarcation. Beyond the demarcation is where? In the past, or in the present? On the border between them? Or on the border between past and future, the future past? The 'people' continues, while its monuments are of its past.

The important point is the operation of making something past and thereby giving it a significance. Selection for significance involves an identification, a centring from which claims to authority are made. Modern historicisation involves the times of peoples, of collective human subjects in a history of humanity. Absolute historicisation identifies a centre and an authority of a world with its levels and its tributary edges.

'When the world (as seen from China) was a Chinese world, Confucian civilization was civilization in the abstract, not a civilization in a world with others' (Levenson 1965:108). Imperial and local histories, written by officials and local scholars, included biographies, geographies and several other categories of fact in a continuing landscape. Their temporality can be described as eternity subject to disruptions, and their spatiality as order or harmony subject to confusions. Historiography was a list of ordering or disordering occurrences and a detailing of local features. This was the recording of annals or chronicles. Beside listing, it was also a commentary upon the maintenance or deterioration of the old landscape. The conception of that absolute universe includes such variations as a backward perspective upon a golden age of the past, or an improvement of knowledge in a temporality which can be resolved or transcended into an eternity, or an occasionally achieved and achievable ideal state.

Imperially sanctioned histories were, as Levenson put it, absolute. 'Absolutism is parochialism of the present, the confusion of one's own time with the timeless.' Official and other Confucian historians were 'self-evident heirs' to that eternity. They did not historicise it as a tradition. Rather they upheld it, against encroachment or neglect. The past was simply other years of the same order: a series of reigns and their names, each succeeding the former and starting again with 'one'. It did register restorations of that order, and therefore beside eternity was its potential demise. But official history commented only upon restoration or maintenance. It was 'intrinsic classical learning, the exercise of divining from canonical historical records how men in general should make history for all time'. The canonical records were those of a late-Zhou dynasty China (400–200 BC), set apart as an intellectual mother-country, whose principles rose as the authority for alternatives even over atmospheres of polemical intensity (Levenson 1965:87–101).

What was the 'past' for a 'parochialism of the present'? The historian was the inheritor of what he recorded. The past signified the present as its superior antecedent. The past was an ancestor, history its genealogy.

Past was distinguished from present, venerated as a canon, to be rerealised, with ritual or other kinds of observance and knowledge improving upon those which had failed, and history was written as a commentary upon the past and these failures. The present was corrected by the measure of the past, and the more immediate, or failed pasts could be improved upon in the present, by commemorating what should not have been forgotten, by remaking the past.

This is the history of office, or aspiration to office. The past was a lesson of good conduct. The past was the record of sages and the exemplary statements and conduct of those who followed them. It was negative examples of those who departed from their way. And it was stories of the correct who suffered under negative examples of rule.

Historical signification here is an operation by which a past lends authority to a present in a continuing order. The past is demarcated and its pastness sanctified. The same one word, *sheng*, translates the English 'sage' and 'sacred', but in popular cults it can also be the word for effective power in the present.

A dissenting history, contemporary with absolutist history, could place the capacity for restoration or maintenance elsewhere than in the ruling dynasty. But restoration and maintenance were the criteria of significance for both official and dissenting histories with aspiration to office. Otherwise, dissent was anarchic, anti-historical or chiliastic.

An altogether rival historicisation would make demise of orders and the coming of new orders prominent, like a history of continuing revolution. It would make several 'pasts' and distinguish them as different orders, with different memberships and their own significance. It is possible to read a dissenting history, deeply embedded in the myth and ritual of late imperial Chinese popular religion. Is it merely dissenting, or does it approach rivalry with the official eternity? Or is it an altogether alternative form of historicisation?

We shall see. But if I am to describe ritual as a kind of history, I must first address the sacredness of its objects and occasions.

## BELIEF IN SPIRITUAL AGENCY

The rituals I shall describe are both religious and magic, they refer to spiritual beings which are efficaceous. So I shall not assume a basic distinction between religion and magic for description, nor do I need it for analysing or interpreting what I am describing.

In the description of ritual, it is common practice to refer to spirits or gods or ancestors as if they exist. For instance, historians and observers often find it convenient in their descriptions to write of 'relations between the living and the dead', when offerings are to be understood as 'transfers of food to the dead'. Reading such descriptions, in the English of the observer, we are expected to suppose that the description translates what might have been said by participants, who believed or at least suspended disbelief in their own description of the ritual relation. The dead or the gods were not evident. But straining to be faithful only to what was before the eyes of the observer would be pointless, because it would miss the context and the pretext of the activity described. It would miss what the offering or the incense addressed or the statue represented. But how should we translate such representation? The false naivety of reference to spirits as if they were equivalent to the participant actors is convenient. But it raises questions which usually go unanswered.

What is equivalent to what? How is the 'as *if*' to accomplish a description that does justice to the activities and statements of the participants and at the same time to the concepts and interpretative discourse of the language into which they are translated? What do we impute to the participants when we include the spirits and gods as interlocutors or agents of the activities we perceive and describe? What do we impute to them as producers of our translation?

Chinese and other so-called ritualistic cultures seem to offer a way of avoiding these questions. In them, correct, standard performance of rites is stressed. Contrasting this with religions stressing personal belief, James Watson contends that

> the proper performance of the rites, in the accepted sequence, was of paramount importance in determining who was and who was not deemed to be fully 'Chinese'. Performance, in other words, took precedence over belief – it mattered little what one believed about death or the afterlife as long as the rites were performed properly (Watson and Rawski 1988:4)

So the problem of belief could conveniently be avoided by bracketing off what are represented and concentrating on the rites and textual statements themselves. And this would be warranted by the participants' own cultural priority. But is the separation of belief and performance possible, and if it is, would a distinction between the two in fact be true to Chinese ritual and culture?

Giving priority to performance might describe processes of standardisation and control. These are processes of political culture and of cultural politics. They set up authority and identification with authority. In China, the identification of what is properly Chinese, and the means of claiming the authority to be so identified, have seldom in the long history of a unified polity been those of adherence to a dogma. 'Belief' in the sense of adherence to a dogmatic proposition of what is held to be true, is a key problem of Islam and of modern European, Western religion, theology and philosophy. It is not central in Chinese philosophical and religious authority and judgement. But acceptance of the authority of imperial or archaic orthodoxy of rites is also acceptance of an idea of an ordered universe. The synchronicity, or harmonics, of an organic universe, with no originator and no external will of creation has often been noted as the

9

key characteristic differentiating Chinese from other conceptions of the universe and of history. (For a summary of Chinese conceptions of time and history, see Needham 1965.)

Correctness and exclusive authority have in China been concerned with the ordering of social relations, the maintenance of that order and the observation of proper rituals. Propriety and impropriety (*zheng* and *xie*), order and chaos (*anping* and *luan*) or harmony and clash (*heping* and *chong*) in any activity, but particularly in ceremony and statement, have been central to Chinese problems of authority and of identification with that authority (belonging to a community, local or imperial). Both cults and texts are included in this concern with propriety.

Authority has in China been vested neither in a set of supreme propositions, such as the propositions of impossible – or mysterious – truth to be found in the Christian creed, nor, until recently, in the capacity of reason to make propositions of possible truth. Nor has the sanctity of personal belief and its separation from rites and institutions been characteristic of Chinese political culture until recently. But far from this being convenient because it means we can set belief aside, it is an admission that ritual performance and belief are not distinguished. It means that the separation of belief from performance is inappropriate.

Worse, to insist on such a distinction masks a major problem of translation, in the description of Chinese religious practices by a European language of religion replete with this inappropriate distinction between belief and performance, conscience and action, spirit and person.

On the other hand, if 'belief' is as vague as 'meaning', the whole interpretative enterprise must accept as a universal premise that anything identified as human social relations, and in particular when they are symbolising activities and statements, conveys 'beliefs'.

Recourse to the notion that Chinese religion is of the ritualistic type is no help here either. It is necessary to treat activities identified as being religious or as ritual, as representations. They signify. What do they represent, and in what set of resemblances and contrasts (in short, of categories)? These questions have to be answered in any description. The description must be an interpretative discourse and in another register if not also another language. Its adequacy is measured by its living up to the questions it necessarily sets up as a description. So we are back to the 'as if' of representations which refer to spiritual beings.

When I write that people made offerings to a god, I am describing a ceremony of reverence which has a definite object which I can name by translating the name given to me, or by describing what has been pointed out to me as its statue or picture. But I imply more. I am impelled to say what more that is, for the naming and the picturing are themselves indicative. It is no good being agnostic. That simply admits God or gods in by a backdoor as causative or real objects of representation.

An instructive example of agnosticism is provided by Ahern's discussion of this very question of what vocabulary we should use, as she puts it, to describe Chinese ritual. She decides that the appropriate vocabulary is interpersonal and transactional, because that is how the Chinese participants intend their rituals. Because the Chinese rituals resemble in many ways acts of deference, bribery and negotiation with political officials and their underlings, because the participants act in the belief that their actions will have bureaucratic efficacy, it is appropriate to describe them as transactive and interpersonal (Ahern 1981a: 4–11).

When we consider the organisation of religious rituals and the rituals themselves as an ordering of the participants, it may well be appropriate to describe them as social relations and the positions in them as social and more specifically as political persons. In that restricted case, what Ahem advocates is acceptable. But can gods and other spiritual 'beings' be included in this 'vocabulary'?

There are many reasons why they cannot be included. The first is that, as she admits, the participants themselves distinguish between the social world in which they act as persons and another in which the gods are persons. She describes this as an analogy.

'On analogy with everyday transactions, orders are issued, reasons given, demonstrations made, communications bracketed, attention drawn, and so on' in much Chinese ritual (Ahern 1981a:14). Thus she fully acknowledges participants' own distinction between what the convention of philosophical anthropology distinguishes as human and non-human agencies. Her detailing of participants' own accounts is particularly good in drawing out the selectiveness of the analogy: rituals addressing gods are like having access to high and upright officials who respond to our needs as good parents would (Ahern 1981a: 99). But she avoids the analogous belief in the agency of the ritually indicated 'beings'. Instead she treats the fact that they are analogous simply as a demarcation of performances, both equally performative.

11

On the one hand is performance addressing actual political persons – communications, instructions, mediations and blockages, of the imperial bureaucracy, or of republican officials, and between them and those they govern. On the other is a performance between actual persons and posited persons. What is performed between actual and posited persons she treats as a learning about what is performed between actual persons: a more or less accurate knowledge and rehearsal of what can be performed between actual persons; a more or less idealised, and therefore potentially critical, acting out of an actual, contemporary regime under which and within which the participants perform.

By treating both as performance, Ahem can demonstrate and specify parallels, showing ritual performance to be like political performance, and therefore likely to have political meaning and functions. But she avoids the institution of the analogy. She does not ask how it works, how it is constituted. To ask would be to confront the problem of belief in non-human agency which she needs for her demarcation. Instead she uses an agnostic vocabulary of performatives.

It comes from the work of John Skorupski (1976). She uses it (Ahern 1981a:11, 13–14) to describe the ritual analogy with authority and its effectiveness as an 'operative act'.

Her first reference is to the first page (p. 93) of his chapter devoted to this notion. Operative acts are ceremonial (customary and formal) action intended to bring about a consequence (pp. 93–4). Their consequentiality relies on their being performed in what is established as the proper manner and by the appropriate person. They therefore include the ceremony of establishing – enthroning, installing – after a passage between statuses. They give authority or establish new authoritative positions.

Skorupski's backdoor theism is all the plainer for being philosophical. In defining a category of 'operative acts', Skorupski identifies authorisation as a social fact and religious ritual as its performance. The authority is the ceremonial itself and may involve recognition of a non-human agency (p. 102). Note that operative acts are not merely repetitive. They 'are performed to set up new patterns of roles. Hence we can also say that they can establish people in new statuses or roles, and can set up new institutions' (p. 99). But now note how he sets up this category. It is one of a number of categories in the exhaustive class of consequential action. What an operative act performs and brings about cannot be simply the effect of factual conditions, or of other rules, or of natural causes. These are the other categories in the set. The outcome of an operative act like any other consequential action must be brought about by an agency, in this case by persons. 'This must be so, if we are dealing with an operative act: there cannot be an operative act which does not gain its operative force from the authority of some person or group of persons ... directly or indirectly' (p. 102).

This is where he introduces gods by the backdoor, for he says that these persons are not necessarily human nor naturally present. For instance, Skorupski describes as an example of an operative act the installation of the Shilluk king by the authority of God and no human actor (p. 108). Skorupski's class of operative action compels him to posit the operative force of non-human actors, even if he then gives himself a let-out by the qualification 'directly or indirectly'.

When we turn to the other page to which Ahern refers (p. 153) we find that she has taken up his hedged and hesitant suggestion that magical acts which work by symbolic identification and contagious transfer – that is, action directly upon what is taken to be part of the represented object – can be included in the scope of 'operative action'.

We see what this means for Skorupski a little later (p. 155). Such symbolic magic involves

> actions which are expected by the actors to produce a result through the mediation of a non-human agency, capable of understanding and action. The primary idea required here is ... that of a mode of understanding and acting on the world whose fundamental rationalising concept is the notion of *agency*. Such is the explanatory framework of those traditional or primitive cultures which anthropologists have studied. (p. 155)

To be called 'religious' such an explanatory cosmology must posit 'moral and emotional relationships between presumed agencies and believers' (p. 155).

The anthropological and philosophical vocabulary which describes religious agencies as 'presumed' and 'recognised' seems to establish an interpretative distance. Yet it recognises the presumed agencies as social actors.

How can I do better? I will start, as have so many before me, with Durkheim's and Mauss's concept of collective representations.[1] Acts of worship and statements of belief, positing objects in the sky or beneath the earth with earthly efficacy, or past lives with present efficacy, are all collective representations of a special kind. This may seem perverse to those who know how tellingly the concept has been subjected to criticism. Even so, disencumbered of its false assumptions, it remains indispensable.

Durkheim and Mauss said that religious and other symbolic actions and objects are collective representations in three ways: they represent the solidarity of the whole society; they represent the society to an individual as images or as significant others and his or her attachment to them; and they represent the system of representations of which they are part, as a word represents a vocabulary. Through collective representations, the individual is formed into a social, intellectual and communicative being.

Now consider that most trenchant critic of Durkheim and Mauss, Rodney Needham (1972). Needham is faithful to the British social anthropology of social structures. He retains the basic notion of structure as 'rules', and of rules as 'jural' – which is a cross between customary and lawful, or political in the broadest sense. He carefully points out that the 'relatively distinguishable realms of symbolism and jural organization can be studied together'. A concordance between them can be demonstrated. But this 'does not at all confirm the theory advanced by Durkheim and Mauss', and here is the main thrust of his criticism. It is quite wrong to claim, as Durkheim and Mauss do (in their essay on 'Primitive Classification') that social structure or solidarity must be what is represented. It is also wrong to claim that representations of the social structure form the minds of individual actors, for they must already have the categories of thought necessary if they are to recognise the representations which they experience.

Nevertheless, the idea of collective representations 'has the singular advantage of displaying the radical importance of those principles of order, expressed in cultural categories, which serve to articulate the system of thought and action' (Needham 1972:155).

Note the object: system of thought and action. Note the methodological principle: the same system for both thought and action, and that it is bound by principles of order. This is what is meant by social structure. Note, finally, that cultural categories 'express' this system. How far has Needham departed from Durkheim and Mauss? He has placed structure into the mental functions and motivating forces of actors, and has placed collective representations into an expressive relation to these, rather than as formative of individual minds. This amounts to interpreting or rather to resolving cultural manifestations and social actions into underlying principles of thought and of social system. Durkheim and Mauss analysed culture as a manifestation of social order and as the order of relations among

14

collective representations themselves. There is not much difference. Having distinguished the two realms of symbolism and jural rules, Needham dissolves both into an underlying conceptual order.

I will instead remain faithful to the radical impulse of his criticism of Durkheim and Mauss, and retain the concept of collective representations while abjuring an order underlying the three ways in which they represent. In other words, the images and motivations of an individual, social relations, and the relations among representations are all distinct orders and they are to be related to one another without reduction to any one of them nor to any other order. But that only gets me as far as saying that any social object or action is collective and representational. I still have to address the distinctiveness of religious collective representations.

Durkheim's conception of religion is: that which delineates occasions and places in which objects and actions are sacred because they are what mirrors the social to itself. I must reject the wholistic category of 'the social' as the ultimate truth of religion. We can never know what is this social essence whose binding solidarity is helped by being represented, to individuals or to itself. There is no good reason for us to say that something essential to a social being is represented in whatever is set apart for representation in a sacred language. A number of objects may be represented, any or all of them social. Why should anyone accept the anthropologist's assertions that they are 'the' social being, or 'the' ethnicity or culture designated? It is a strange assurance which over-takes the unsure setting of boundaries of a society and the dubious existence of a fundamental social or cultural essence in a cultural anthropologist such as Stephen Sangren or a social anthropologist such as Maurice Freedman.[2] Each in his own way asserts the existence in religious collective representations of a whole social being called China or Chineseness. Indeed they see this to be the compulsory object of their analysis, even if this time they may have only approximated it. I do not feel this compulsion.

I think that Durkheim's and Mauss's lasting legacy for the analysis of ritual and religion is their apparently simple stress on the fact that people set up spatial and time boundaries. What is achieved by these boundaries is the capacity to represent and to identify. 'Metaphoricity' we might call it, were it not for the fact that what is set apart and bounded is also linked with the other side. The boundary made is also crossed – by sacrifice and inspiration. Most importantly, this metaphoricity works by selection of objects from either side, making them doubles of each other, but not identical.

15

Each is thereby a reminder or an imaginary invocation of the other, the profane object of its sacred counterpart, and the sacred of the profane. But that is all very much too simple and clever, you must be thinking, for setting apart on its own says nothing about the reason for calling one side of the boundary 'ritual', 'religious' or 'sacred'. What kind of bounding is it which makes what is set apart from the rest privileged in its capacity to represent, what makes the sacred symbolise in a way which the profane does not?

Everything, every action in human relations can be imagined and can conversely be intended according to an image of which it is a realisation. Such a representation is an image/intention. But its results are predicted from the representation. Other images and intentions are drawn from it and focused upon it. Everything and every action in human relations is both the material effect and the interpretation. Every one stands for something else; indeed what it is, intrinsically, must always be problematic. There is nothing which is not also a representation and a disguise. An outcome is a realisation escaped from its image, interpreted as another. Can any representation be said to be specially representative, heightened, an institution of image-bearing things and acts? What could make it so?

Many answers have been given. They can be read as modern myth. Durkheim's and Mauss's myth goes like this: in the beginning was the social, and it was intelligent and impersonal; its representation wrote itself upon the diffuse representations in the life of the human animal where it was first experienced. Its original scene was a gathering. The overwhelming experience by individual members of their collectivity and at the same time its relation to other collectivities instituted the idea of a universe and its parts, or categories of being. That scene and the retained images of it, attached to the forms of real things and features found at it, were set apart by the overwhelming experience. Thereafter, they became reminders. Re-enactments of the original scene became the ritual through which the sentiments of wholeness and solidarity which it inspired re-appeared. They were occasions for the consciousness of symbolic representation itself, rehearsals of that which transformed ordinary language into human language.[3]

In short, the original experience of the social was also the origin of metaphor.

The mythic quality of this narrative is its circularity. The original scene does not need to have happened chronologically. It is always represented, and it is the truth of all representation. The important point is the simultaneity of the social with intelligent and intelligible representation by physical forms and sequences of action.

Language reminds us of our social being, though never of a truth, because while it is the trusted model of communication, it also always deceives and disguises, just because it represents. In Durkheim's myth, the origin of language is not speech. It is (as Gane points out) graphic, which is to say its forms are outside and not only those produced by the body of human beings. Their existence outside the human body is essential to Durkheim's empirical demonstration that they represent the social and the rest of the world from which they were set apart. They are of the natural world, but they represent. They are not the natural things themselves. So these external forms represent in three directions: they represent social being, they represent the natural world from which they are selected, and they represent the individual human experiences of both the social and the natural world. None of the original experiences or things, whether they are the presence of the social, or the feelings of the individual, or the things and movements of nature are present in their representation.

The presence assumed by representation is the power of a representation, but it is not its reality or its meaning. That is where the philosophical critique of representation and of epistemology has also been a critical corrosion of Durkheim's mythical assurance of the essence of religious, and therefore of all other human representations: the truth and presence of social being is a chimera.[4]

But it does not corrode one answer provided by Durkheim's myth to the question: what separation makes one side of the boundary a privileged representation, an institution of representation? It is whatever allows a claim in that culture to be made that what is represented is the presence of a totality: the world, the whole society, nature, the whole possibility of representation itself. The claims can all be interpreted without being accepted. They are intentions or images of wholeness. The way they are set apart and what is said about them and by their means should indicate this intention and imagery. They are also, by their similarities to and their differences from other representations, to be interpreted in relation to other representations, through observation and through participants' statements of similarity and difference.

In the concluding section of chapter five I suggest a concept of religion as a representation of fulfilled communication, the rituals of which are rhetorics of response. Here, the more obvious and preliminary point must be stated, that religious representations proclaim or gesture towards a more basic and ultimate unity. But that means that they also represent what is otherwise separated. The separations upon which I shall dwell are those of past from present and outside from inside.

Historical significance links past with present, uniting for a future what as its first premise must have been separated into times. Identification in time with a past or in space with others in a locality has a premise of exclusion; it is selective. But the boundaries it sets up are at the same time tense. They exclude what threatens to be included. Religious representation itself draws upon an encompassing vision, but is always located.

Religious historicism can be approached through local traditions: what people say they have always done, here. They join and they exclude. One of the joins is between past and present, other world and this world. On that join rest the claims to efficacity which others, by a firmer separation between them or between image and reality, deny.

## TRADITION AND ITS IMAGERY

'Tradition' indicates a practice that has always occurred, authoritative and socially compelling. A repetition – 'the way we do it' – which transmits something in time, implying the 'past' and 'future' of what is repeated. *Chuantong*, the Chinese word which translates 'tradition', emphasises the transmission aspect of this repetition. We might say that what is called 'tradition' is transmission in an eternal tense. We might then place the weight of attention either upon the repeated structure of tradition or upon invention within it. But in either case and even when the structure's own date of origin and history is investigated, anthropologists and historians assume in it the existence of an identifiable culture, or a set of essential myths, texts or practices. The task performed upon this assumption is to describe the substantive content of what is repeated. I want instead to start with the assumption of traditionality itself – its mood and tense, not its content. And just as there are many contents, many traditions, so might there be many traditionalities, each capable of conveying many themes and inventions.

Traditions are not just unconsciously motivated activities, they are set apart by some means. They are ritual, ceremonial, *cliché*, proverbial, fabulous, exemplary or precedential in style. Their repetition is therefore representative or figurative in relation to the

18

eventuality and variations of context in which they are repeated. So the work of any traditionality – of any mode of transmission which has the authority of tradition – must include this repeated distancing and abstraction from the individuality of its context such that it has a representative as well as an authoritative relation to the context in which it is performed. It has the authority of the sacred because it refers to the eternal, but it is historical sanctity.

In sum, the description of any traditionality, if it were to be complete, would have to include:

1  the work it does of abstraction and differentiation from its context such that its repetition is metaphorical;
2  its temporality of repetition and transmission;
3  what this poses as its content;
4  the work of social compulsion its performance entails.

It is frequently observed by writers on the traditions of celebrating gods in Chinese popular religion that their imagery is like the costume and ceremonial of the Chinese imperial court and its bureaucracy. The question this raises is what makes the imagery and ritual a metaphor, how is it sufficiently unlike its historical and secular derivation to take on a power beyond that of historical re-enactment.

Let me first establish this dissimilarity through an example. It is that of money. Paper money, or something like it, is burned to honour the gods. The burning, often accompanied by firecrackers, is a completion of an act of offering. It occurs after opening communication and welcoming the presence of the god, naming the place and persons to which the god is invited. It occurs again after food, memorial petition, and incense, as well as the money itself have been presented.

In fact the burnt sheets are rarely called 'money' (*qian*). They are usually called 'gold' (*jin*), a more generic name for money or wealth, if they are burned in offering to gods. And 'gold' is the character stamped on the wad of paper spirit money for gods wrapped in more ornamental sheets. 'Money' is the term used to refer to a distinct type of spirit money, reserved for offerings only to the newly dead and to orphan souls and their purgatorial guardians in the courts of hell. 'Silver' (*yin*) on the other hand is used only for offerings to ancestors, but may also be used indistinguishably from 'money' for the newly dead, orphan souls and the propitiation of demons. There are various gradations of 'gold' and of 'silver', each with their proper use in a graded hierarchy of address to gods and spirits, which commentators like Gary Seaman have likened to the spheres of exchange in imperial Chinese transactions (Seaman 1982).

First of all, it is worth pointing out the obvious, that only the most extravagantly demonstrative of their wealth burn money recognised as currency for purchase. Secondly, when actually compared there is little similarity between the spirit money and money. There are some similarities in appearance. The official seal on imperial currency has a remote equivalent in the central motif of modem spirit money – the circular figure of double blessings (*shuang xi*), also to be found on plates in Chinese restaurants.

The portrait on a Taiwanese bank-note of 1964 has its equivalent in the central, if not the side figures on sheets of spirit-money in the same year. It could be the central one of the three standard blessings portrayed on spirit-money: the blessing of wealth by salary and an official's career. The other two blessings are health (and long life) and happiness (including progeny). The same three figures are depicted on the scroll which was most often bought to adorn the wall behind the incense-burner for ancestors on domestic altars in the town I studied. It is headed 'ancestral virtue, flowing and fragrant' (*zu de liu fang*).

An emblem of office, power and wealth repeated on this scroll and on a sheet of spirit money for gods is the winged hat of an imperial magistrate. Another is the top-knot in the head-dress of an imperial prime minister, repeated in the flamed head-dress of the stove god on the scroll which often went behind the incense-burner for gods on domestic altars. Both prime ministers and stove god are intermediaries to higher powers. Indeed, on closer attention to spirit-money we find that it is an abbreviated form of petition for the favours depicted, including that for which 'gold' itself stands.

Emblems of authority are simply that, repeated on bank-notes, official dress, or the costume of temple figures and altar hangings. Ahern rightly observes that the parallels between signs of imperial power and the signs of authority in ritual goods 'might well have enhanced the authority of gods' (1981a: 88 on the parallel between imperial warrants and a form of divination; see also pp. 36 and 39 for further observations on parallels between command and magic, as well as on money for gods).

But we could not speak of parallels without there being differences and they are great differences. What is repeated in the religious rituals is only remotely like and repeats only some of the objects and manners of imperial rule. It is the difference which makes the repetition timeless or traditional, and it is also what makes of the similitude another, parallel (invisible, religious) authority, or else a superstitious and empty chicanery, according to whom you ask.

I asked many people in the small town of Mountainstreet what was the meaning of 'burning gold' (*xiao jin*). Some of the answers referred to the legendary inventor of paper – Cai Lun, a eunuch in the court of the Han emperor He (89–106 AD). The more dismissive answers told of Cai Lun finding a clever way of increasing sales of his invention or of the trimmings from his sheets of paper by a deception plotted with the help of his wife. After sticking little bits of gold and silver on to pieces of paper he pretended to be dead, lying in a coffin. His wife spread news of his death and when neighbours came to pay respects, she burned the prepared paper. As it burned Cai rose as if saved from death, saying his reprieve from hell had been bought by the gold. Less dismissive versions also refer to intercession on behalf of the dead in the courts of purgatory achieved by the journey to hell of the founder of the Tang dynasty, Li Shimin. Whether or not dismissive, these are stories based precisely on difference from the real thing.

But it is not enough to note discrepancies and similitudes as I have done so far. They raise questions. One question, to which I shall return, is about the quality of the dissimilarities, what do they convey? Two other questions are about the creation of dissimilarities between the political and the godly, between the historical and the traditional. Is the dissimilarity constantly re-made in the repetition? What work of ritual does this?

I am not asking why mistakes have been made in the exact reproduction of imperial money. I am trying to grasp the significance of a discrepancy that can be observed, not point to error. There is a process by which a ritual, which includes a deliberate and self-evident statement of historical origin and at the same time is performed with contemporary relevance, is made significant by being demonstrably neither historic nor contemporary. I assume this process to be something like erasure, a disjoining of the historic continuity. The gods and the ritual of their address are and are not historically derived; they are and are not re-enactments. The obliqueness between 'are' and 'are not' constitutes the power of traditionality and possibly also of that something else which makes it 'religious' ritual. So I am asking whether there is a repeated process of erasure which inscribes this oblique power.

Perhaps the story of Cai Lun's counterfeit is a clue. His paper was necessarily not-money. It was to be burned on behalf of the not-living by the living. In short, spirit-money for the dead is partially of the

21

living. The not-living do not have a purely separated imagery. Purely separated their having lived would not be represented, and in any case they would be unimaginable. On the other hand, the partial likeness creates a capacity to reflect the living, by not being of them. Like Li Shimin, the spirit-money crosses between what are separated as living and not-living. By this materialisation, the substantial image of commerce made from the scourings of paper for writing helps re-create the not-living as precisely an imagery. But this only gets us to the start of an enquiry into the process of erasure by which this imagery is re-enacted.

What happens in the ceremonial of death? What happens in the passage between a memory – a remembered individual – and the icon, grave and anonymity into which it is turned? Chinese rituals mark a death by means of a series of identifications abstracting from the multiplicity of names, identities, traces and reputations which the living person left. These memories are turned into a theatre of memory in the rituals by which death and fixation are recognised and the completion of life historicised.

## MEMORY HISTORICISED

Contemporary Chinese rituals at death are in fact two theatres. In one the dead person is identified by a photograph and by the coffin with the corpse inside it. On them are focused a display of eulogy, mourning and procession which represent a household in mourning, set apart from its neighbourhood. Degrees of mourning precedence, signified by mourning dress, rehearse the household as a family in a line of descent and its links of marriage to other lines of households. The quality of the procession from the house out to the burial ground, the presence and number of eulogy readers (honoured guests) and the bond friends of the chief mourner display the social reputation of the household at this fixed point in time. It is a theatre enacted by the household and its public themselves. And it leaves two places and repeated annual occasions in which commemoration continues.

One is the household altar where the name and deathday are entered into a record and honoured at its incense-burner for the veneration of ancestors; the photograph is set aside from this on a side wall. The individuality of the living person, though set apart, can for a period enter into the fixed point and annual rites of identification, for instance by the presentation of foods at the domestic altar remembered as her or his favourites. But this is transitory. The

22

memory is fixed finally by two territorial inscriptions. One is at the centre of the house on a slip of paper or a wooden tablet behind the incense-burner for ancestors. The other is at the grave, outside the place of settlement in which the house is included. The name is inscribed on the gravestone. Even more than the domestic altar, this establishes the position of a place of origin for those who trace ancestry from it. Frequently gravestones bear the place-name from which the ancestors of the new ancestor had migrated. Thus a history is turned into a geography and a past fixed in a present territorial landscape. What is more, the landscape into which these points of settlement are inscribed is itself one of lines of force and positions where they can be concentrated, or gathered, by correct orientation.

The whole of China, the world under heaven, is traced in such a way. There are geomantic maps of the empire tracing all rivers and mountain ranges like lines of descent stemming from their source in the Kunlun range in the northwest. Temples, palaces, government offices, cityscapes, as well as houses and graves are aligned according to such a cartography of earthly energy in genealogical trees. The temple houses gods in imperial imagery, which is enacted in the other theatre of the rituals of death

A much more dramatised theatre than the civil proceedings of eulogy and mourning, it re-enacts the imagery of imperial intercession and command. In this second theatre all the identifications of the individual mourned are transitory. There are no permanent inscriptions and territorial establishments. It is enacted by professionals, priests hired by the family. Instead of being actors the public here is an audience.

The dead between death and fixation by burial and by inclusion in a domestic altar are known as *linghun*. *Hun* is usually translated as ghost or as soul. *Ling* is a volatile and possibly dangerous attribute, a power to respond which in this case is in the other direction from the commerce of spirit-money, a return across the divide between no-longer-alive and the living, in other words across a separation which the rituals themselves establish.

The *linghun*, for the purposes of this theatre, is identified by a number of symbols beside the photograph and corpse. A lamp, an incense-burner and a flag on which its name is inscribed are for it alone, separate from the domestic altar's candles, incense and record. It is also sometimes represented as a puppet. The last ritual act is to burn these representations and to discard their remaining traces including the temporary incense burner in a place on the borders –

roads or river sides of residential localities. But before that these transitory objects are the points of address for a liturgy of salvation and intercession through courts of purgatory and out of their limbos to the Western Paradise and potential re-birth. This is where the spirit-money and petition come in.

In the transition from photograph to puppet, individuality is bleached into the iconography of purgatory, which is the same as that of the gods. Further along this transition the *hun* is rendered nameless, just as its representations are burned. It becomes, anonymously, one of the saved or of the not saved, one in a category of life before or after the living. If it is not saved it is not only in a hell of imperial imagery. It is also trapped in the vicinity like its burned and discarded traces. Trapped and anonymous, the dangerous quality of *ling* is remembered anonymously when harm is suffered at a particular spot between places, the harm attributed to a flare-up of this quality. The spot becomes one where *ling* has to be pacified. But *ling* is also ascribed to the chance of unusual benefit, not only to an ambush of harm, and it is then the object of petition and pledge, not pacification.

The erasure performed at funerals we can now see is a process of territorial fixing, alignment and bounding. The lived identity is turned into names in a landscape, joined in a historicity of lines of descent and places of origin and settlement. Its mood we might say is that of the past present, whereas the process of separation and transition in the dramatised theatre of purgatory has to be in a mood of the past anterior to the present. Separation has to be an enactment of past-ness, whatever is selected and whatever determines what is selected to re-enact that which went before. As for the question of the authority of what is represented as the past, who can say whether the imagery of historical authority is historic or that of an imagery which because of its historicity has been used to gain political authority? What gives the unlikely imagery authority is the ritual which is performed to render a past life doubly into a past present and anterior. Its repetition irregularly, or at annual rites renders a past visible as something uncanny, something beside the present but with the power to transgress the division into past and present.

The tradition with which this book is mainly concerned is that of local festivals and their territorial cults. And it is this *ling*, but as a benign responsiveness, which the annual festival of a territorial guardian god celebrates. It is the power to protect the place marked out by the procession of the god-image against threats, according to the historical mythology surrounding the god, whose fuller title and image denote a military command. It could also be said, more ambivalently, to celebrate the *ling* of protection against the *ling* of danger to the settlement from invasion of its boundaries: the military aspect of the god can be inverted to become the imagery of possession by a military force. But from the inside it is as a protection that the god is celebrated.

The god can also be celebrated as a reminder of a larger, or of a former place of origin from which settlers not only here but in neighbouring localities trace their ancestry. By this reference neighbouring localities are linked in a string of procession days by which a figure of the same god from an older temple visits and is joined by the figure of each locality.

## THE PAST PRESENT

The gap of dissimilarity and of discontinuity which makes the historic into a symbol, is filled with the flame and smoke of incense. The circulation, distribution and exchange of incense, accompanied by the burning of spirit money and the explosion of firecrackers, traces the boundaries and the thresholds of the territory. Its burners mark the central points of households and the temple of that territory. Incense-burner, incense sticks and incense ash are peculiar to the address of ghosts, gods, ancestors and demons. Incense is similar to nothing else.

In Fujian and Taiwan, the procession of a territorial guardian recurs every year, and on its day each year it produces its chief participants for the next annual recurrence. The medium for this production and the main responsibility for the leader is incense. His office is that of master of the incense-burner (*lu zhu*).

The master of the incense-burner is so called because it is he who bears a portable burner through the key parts of the liturgy in the temple. But before that he carries the burner behind a sedan chair bearing the visiting and the home gods in procession, and this is a movement of social compulsion. For the procession passes every threshold in the temple's locality and at each door burning incense sticks, held in honour of the passing figures, are exchanged for incense sticks held by the master. The householder then places the sticks he has received in the incense-burner devoted to gods on the domestic altar. The master thereby conducts a recycling of incense across the threshold of every household which has established a domestic altar. The establishment of a domestic altar is itself the simple act of installing two incense-burners, one for ancestors and one for gods. And it is consecrated by the taking of a little from the ashes in the temple's incense-burner and mixing it with the ash in the new burner.

Advancing incense thus carries with it the two tenses of traditionality which I have mentioned. It carries the past-ness of the god whose being beside historical record is his virtue known as *ling* and his responsiveness in and on behalf of the inhabitants of a place of whose security he is guardian. The burning tips and smoke of incense each year inscribe that territory and its thresholds, taken in from outside, re-consecrating each domestic altar as an installation of that territory, a place in a geography of places of origin.

Before making a final observation upon what this traditionality conveys, I ought to point out that it co-exists with others. To describe them would require descriptions of other objects of representation or of mediation than gold, petition and incense. One such would be writing whose surfaces of inscription and transmission are textual not territorial, and whose imagery is not military. Written authority, and the orthodoxies of a textual tradition describe another historicity than the tracery of territorial guardians and the division of incense. How the two interact will be a long story in the chapters to come. I must also indicate that the traditionality of local festivals celebrated a huge variety of cults, differing according to different places of origin – cults of famous reliefs from drought, or from crop pestilence, or a more medicinal response of relief from plagues – response and content changing in accordance with political and other circumstances, and to surrounding cults; a changing fashion of cults as well as of what is lively (*renao*) and good to see (*haokan*). But when posed in the traditionality I have described, they convey the past-ness and territoriality of places of origin.

What this traditionality conveys is the virtue (*ling*) of security against the dangers menacing the boundaries of places and the thresholds within them. It conveys lines of force and networks of places where they concentrate, where responsiveness has flared. It traces community as an enclosure of domestic altars and the honoured god whose incense they carry across their thresholds.

# Chapter Two

# The annual apocalypse

The most common ritual occasion in which a Chinese is likely to be involved is that of the Spring Festival. It is a season of festivity surrounding the turn of a year of lunar months. The eve is a return home and a completion of the family household. At the very least a member of a Chinese family would feel absence from it. Many would regret their absence poignantly. Most would be home, celebrating the continuing narrative of a complete household, renewed by their homecoming.

The season is also called New Year, or the 'turn of the year' (*guo nian*). This difference of names indicates a political history of calendars. The 'new' year in question is that of a lunar cycle, kept by the imperial bureaucracy which governed China until 1910. There is another longstanding Chinese calendar. It marks out periods of the agrarian year according to a solar cycle. An agrarian people, the Chinese kept both this farming calendar and the lunar calendar, upon which the ceremonial occasions of their year were marked. Both were standard throughout the Chinese empire, whatever variations of climate, geography and crop pattern meant for local farming tasks and the signs for their commencement. But the dominant calendar since the end of that government has been the solar calendar of the modern era.

The lunar turn of the year is now, under republican government, called the Spring Festival. This is because the lunar year turns after the solar turn of the year and comes just before the period in the farmer's calendar called Li Chun – establishing spring. New Year, as it is officially called, names the turn of the solar year in a calendar which is not the old farming calendar. The republican solar year is that of the gregorian calendar which has become the universal global standard. It has no imperial traditional importance in China. The Jesuit scientists who in the seventeenth century advised the emperors on astronomical observation and the making of calendars did not convert the dynasty to the gregorian calendar. Its adoption three centuries later in China was part of the establishment of a new tradition, upon which civil anniversaries of the republic are marked, as the occasions of a nation-state among others, using the same, now world-wide, calendar.

But this change in the nature of the Chinese government, and therefore also of its calendar and authoritatively approved ritual occasions, is not the only reason for thinking the calendar and the turn of the year a politically significant event. It already was one in the imperial, dynastic state.

## THE IMPERIAL YEAR

For centuries the register of the years was prepared in China by a [Bureau of Astronomy] whose chief ranked as a Minister of State, and annually submitted his work to the Emperor for approval. When the Sovereign pronounced it good, copies of the new almanac were distributed to the highest officials of the Empire. The precious documents were conveyed and received with Imperial honours. They were carried to their destinations in sedan chairs, placed on pedestals, and greeted with prostrations and a salute of guns. In the capital, calendars were formally distributed to privileged persons outside the chief gate of the Palace, the *Wu Men*, or 'Meridian Gate', on New Year's day ... [A] present of this important publication to friendly countries, or vassal states like [K]orea and Annam, was considered by the Chinese as one of the highest favours possible to confer. (Bredon and Mitrophanow 1982:5)

Conversely, to issue a counterfeit or rival edition was a capital offence. It was an infringement of the Son of Heaven's authority to regulate the empire. The making of calendars, and the sciences of mathematics and astronomy on which it was based, were part of imperial state power, and therefore closely guarded. To usurp them was to challenge the imperial authority of the incumbent dynasty. To establish a new dynasty was, indeed, to re-make the calendar. 'New dynasties always overhauled the calendar and issued one with a new name, and this might happen even in successive reign-periods under the same emperor' (Needham 1959:193).

The issuing of calendars was by the same token part of the unification of the empire conceived cosmologically as 'all under

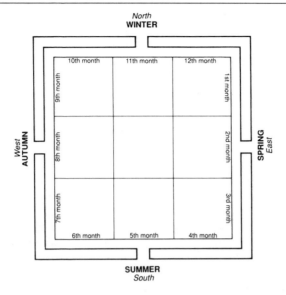

The Luo Shu magic square, which formed the basis for the season-directions of
the universe through which the emperor as guardian of order progressed.

heaven', a terrestrial realm with tributary rulers at its fringes. Since
the third century BC unification into a single named empire (the Qin)
of several states in what is now central, northern and western China, if
not before in several of those states themselves, the making of
calendars was part of the task and the power of cosmic adjustment.

Chinese political philosophy characteristically placed special
emphasis on the interplay between cosmological principles and
human affairs; never was this more true than during the
Warring States and early Han periods [the last 500 years BC]. It
was a nearly universal article of faith in that era that human
actions, and especially the actions of the ruler, could affect the
universe as a whole. Thus, for example, the practice of granting
rewards during the spring and summer and carrying out
punishments during the autumn and winter was not merely
imitative of cosmic cycles of accretion and recision [a concept
explained elsewhere in the article], but rather was an attempt,
by means of sympathetic magic, to insure that those cycles
would remain harmonious. Similarly, a conspicuous deviation

29

from cosmic harmony (such as an earthquake or an eclipse) would be met by a spectacular human act of benevolence, such as a great amnesty, so as to encourage the cosmos to return to an accretion of the life-giving *Yang* force. (Major 1987:287)

One of the first imperial calendars, and therefore a classic to which subsequent calendars referred, was the Monthly Ordnances (Yue Ling). It was preserved and transmitted in three different canonical texts, the Spring and Autumn Annals of Master Lu (Lu Shi Chun Qiu), compiled in the third century BC, the Huai Nan Zi, second century BC, and the Record of Rites (Li Ji) of the first century BC. All of them were copied, printed, studied and edited with extensive commentaries as classics equally of Confucian and Daoist learning. The Ordnances (Ling) prescribed an annual progress through the months and the directions of the cosmos arranged in the form of a magic square of nine halls. The Luo River Writing as shown in the Figure is a magic square in the form of a Hall of Enlightenment (Ming Tang), taken from the eighteenth-century, Qian Long edition of the Li Ji (Record of Rites).

The calendar is a movement through the seasons and the phases of astronomical and astrological bodies disposed about an ideal palace or city, which was also called the Ming Tang. Upon this ideal plan, the capital city and the palace of the emperor were modelled. It was also the notional focus for the siting of graves, residences and important buildings such as temples. So, the imperial calendar itself was issued from the south gate of the palace at new year, the emperor in the north facing south as protector and at the source of *qi* (flows of forces) for those to the south 'under heaven'. In conformity with the Monthly Ordnances, the imperial calendar included a schedule of farming activities. Farmers' practical almanacs were to be constructed on its basis. The emperor, as Son of Heaven, was there to regulate and keep the basic universal harmony. Almanacs on sale even now in China include the same range of practical advice and orientation, based on the same cycles of cosmological symbols as those in the Monthly Ordnances and other classical texts with which the Ordnances were linked.

The ordering effect of the rites performed by the emperor, and his designation as son of the supreme ordering agency, raise the question whether emperors were treated as gods. Jean Levi (1989: 208ff) works out an answer to this question through the texts which I have already mentioned, and through the fourth-century BC Zuo Zhuan commentary on the annals of the kingdom of Lu and a collection of marvels called Soushenji (A Record of Investigations of Gods) compiled eight centuries later. His conclusion is that an emperor and his line were presented as

> crystallisations in the social sphere of a celestial sector [one of a cyclical order of five] which was itself a kind of being and of action. He reached a sacred state even if it was expressed through an abstract language and formal categories. Nevertheless, in becoming part of the cycles [of celestial order], emperors vanished into functions which could only be performed by individuals or at least by imaginary or real rulers (214, my translation).

In this formulation, there is a deliberate and necessary uncertainty between on the one hand the formulation of an abstract and numerological cosmology of cycles of five elemental phases, changing balances of *yin* and *yang*, and the movements and concentrations of material energies (*qi*), and on the other hand the placing of entitled individuals in charge of these processes in a celestial hierarchy and a cosmographic map. Levi (213) notes the tension between the attempts of Confucian scholars to drain the rites of their religiosity and turn them into a cosmological discourse and the rites themselves which included sacrificial offerings that could by their own definition only be made to honour the dead. The tension is all the greater because the individuals in charge of cosmographic positions bear the same titles as the ruling nobility of the empire, and the emperor could honour the dead with the same titles. Unlike a Roman emperor, a Chinese emperor could not receive sacrificial offerings as a deity while alive, neither could his nobility and officials. But after death and as the revered past he could and did, not only as ancestor but also as god. Alive the emperor, his commanders, bureaucrats and nobility addressed their past which was also their transcendental present. Compilations which were indistinguishably both history and myth recorded the appointments of legendary emperors, military commanders, and other imperial functionaries to positions where they were in charge of a mountain, a river, the earth, crops, or a celestial function. They also recorded the demands of the powerful dead to be honoured, and to bring benefits in recompense but harm if they were refused. In the meantime, scholars and scientists attempted to play down these more demonic conceptions of the universe in favour of abstract but equally dynamic processes.

The calendar which emperors enacted by ritual performance was an ordering of the universe, conceived abstractly as a balance of fluctuating, complementary, and resonant forces.

'Resonance' is not only a metaphor. Chinese scientists maintained the high status of music and the establishing of pitches as an activity not only of ceremony but also of cosmology, even when, in their own conceptions of scientific progress, they criticised and improved upon the classics.

This care about a harmony revealed by sages does not of course mean that the calendar and its cosmology remained unchanged from the third century BC to 1910. On the contrary, the frequent dynastic and reign-period changes were occasions for modification. The conception and key symbols of a resonant cosmos did remain, but, for instance, the seventeenth-century scientist Lu Shiyi preferred the Western world conceptions introduced by the Jesuits to China over the older Chinese conceptions because the universe itself was changing and therefore the newer the conception the more accurate it must be. His idea of progressive knowledge and secular change was combined with a conception of an eternal cosmology whose knowledge was already established. Referring to a practice of *hou-qi* (watching for the *qi*) established by the ancients, and one which he sought to preserve, he argued that like the calendar it needed to be adjusted according to new measurements and knowledge. But in this act of preservation, he brought the whole system into doubt. By the eighteenth century, secular changes in an absolute historiography, were straining the whole process of official historical signification. Lu

posited the existence of secular change in the acoustical realm, as well as the astronomical and geographical, arguing that the lengths and tones of the pitchpipes had altered appreciably since antiquity. Lu contended that since the tonic of the pipes ... was theoretically attuned to the pneumas *[qi]* which arose from the earth at the winter solstice, the beginning of the tropical year, then the annual difference between the tropical and sidereal years affected the pitch of this and the other canonical pipes. This implied that the ... 'watching for the pneumas *[qi]*' system which keyed the twelve pitchpipes with the pneumatic emanations that supposedly rose out of the earth, each in a certain season, had to be adjusted with every calendar reform. The recognition of such difficulties undermined confidence in the [watching for pneumas] correlative system and facilitated its ultimate rejection by [many] late-Ming and early Ch'ing commentators [despite attempts to preserve it]. (Henderson 1984:163)

## THE HISTORY OF A TRADITION

A very brief sketch gives some idea of imperial historical signification in cosmological learning. A Buddhist- influenced learning of the Song dynasty, the so-called Neo-Confucian cosmology of the eleventh and twelfth century and its Ming dynasty succession of the fifteenth to seventeenth centuries, is still influential now. But it has been subject to criticism and change, and was itself the product of a similar process. It had drawn directly on the thought of the Han dynasty (206BC-220AD) classics, as an act of reforming commentary.

The Han classics had by means of a complex numerology constructed a unified cosmology out of commentaries on the earliest classic, *The Book of Changes*, and other systems of thought. Song and Ming scholarship and its adoption as orthodoxy transformed the rites for the dead and for the ordering of the universe from the exclusive domain of imperial and noble lines performed for the rest of the social universe to a civilising orthodoxy teaching domestic and social order to the lower orders. In an attempt to maintain a ruling order against the rise in the Ming dynasty of syncretic sects each of which claimed their own originating and divine pedigree, the neo-Confucian orthodoxy was itself corrected by Confucian scholars of the early and mid-Qing, the last imperial dynasty to rule China (1644–1911).

Like the Song and Ming, the Qing scholars

tended to present their scientific studies as a restoration of an ancient intellectual unity, not as a departure from tradition. They maintained that Confucianism and science, particularly mathematical astronomy, were naturally complementary as well as classically connected, though Sung and Ming Neo-Confucians had [in the past seven centuries] severed the link between the two. ... They maintained that astronomical phenomena should not be understood simply as manifestations of Neo-Confucian principles. For there were patterns proper to the heavens that had to be investigated through empirical observation and mathematical calculation before there could be any question of developing a cosmological schema. To the extent that these patterns were found to contravene the fundamentals of ... cosmology, cosmology could be challenged on solid empirical grounds. Moreover, since astronomical patterns were important illustrations of established cosmological principles, the revelation of discord between the two was especially damaging. Astronomy, formerly the handmaiden of Neo-Confucian cosmology, became one of its formidable critics. ... Whereas the Sung rationalists took the classics as only one of a number of sources of ultimate principle (*li*), and Ming idealists even reduced the classics to the position of footnotes to the moral mind, Ch'ing [Qing] classicists were well aware of the heterodoxy and confusion bred by the search for *li* in extraclassical sources. They were therefore more inclined to insist on a relatively objective, authoritative criterion of truth, a condition that could best be met through reliance on the classics. For since the Confucian classics reposited the thought of the wisest men who had ever lived, the sages of antiquity, they might almost be said to have an eternal validity. Thus early Ch'ing scholars hoped that interpretations of *li* based on classical exegesis would be so authoritative as to end forever the kind of sectarian strife that had flourished in the late Ming. (Henderson 1984:153–8)

So, this traditionalism, corrosive of tradition as it was, took place, like the publication of the imperial calendar itself, as a governmental event, to restore and strengthen the imperial hold on claims to authority.

It was a rectification of sectarian differences through a strict interpretation of Confucian classics, to be expurgated of syncretic elements which included commentaries on *The Book of Changes* and various forms of divination based on them. The Ming dynasty sectarianism to which the Qing scholars referred had added to divination using the trigrams of the Book of Changes cults of spirit-writing, preaching, and the transmission of sacred books to a growing urban audience of 'lower' literacy and learning. The cults were syncretic in claiming an even older, original set of principles before and behind those of the standard canons of Confucianism, Daoism and Buddhism. (See Naquin 1985).

In short, higher Qing learning sought to settle any question of authoritative truth by a combination of strict classicism with an exclusive science of astronomy which entailed ever more accurate observation of anomalies and changes. From its perspective, lower, syncretic learning and its truths were deemed to be heterodox and confused, not only by reference to the Confucian canon but by reference to astronomical knowledge established through empirical instruments. Most of these were at the time the exclusive possession of the imperial court.

Eventually 'science' would be what came from the West, a knowledge to be used and if possible made Chinese. But it was introduced into other places in the urban spectrum than the imperial court by nineteenth-century Western commercial, religious, and political imperialism. With these incursions came, of course, a new politics of the unification of China to stand up to imperialist incursions. But now the unification of China was of a people not an empire, Nationalist republican and then People's republican China. By that time, the lower 'unscientific' learning would be classed not as incorrect (*xie*) or confused (*mi*), but by means of a translation of the Western term 'superstition' (*mixin*).

This was also a change of historical signification from absolutist to relativist, from a single fixed centre (the empire and its calendar) to a plurality of centres (the nations of a warring or peaceful international order; the gregorian calendar plus international time zones). It was a change out of one uneasy tension between secular changes and the encompassing eternity of a moral order which is also cosmological, into another. The new tension is between choice and necessity, a political project of popular choice for a future, which is also one of development or modernisation within an order of historical laws and the progress of scientific knowledge. The laws of choice disseminated via popular literacy and through a centralised national system of schooling dismiss other means of choosing and other concepts of a future as backward 'superstition'. Rather than being indifferent to a central state that allows popular choice of religious activity, the religious practices of the common people have thus been further politicised. Since 1980 in most rural areas of the People's Republic of China, domestic and communal religious practices, so long as they are either part of a recognised and registered religious organisation or not part of a large-scale organisation at all, are tolerated. But at the same time they are regulated to prevent the perpetration of fraud and medical harm by religious practitioners. And they are overseen in case they become anti-state representations and these then linked into an organisation. In Taiwan, such political surveillance is less wary, but it is kept there too.

## HIGHER AND LOWER LEARNING

By the end of the imperial system of rule, the organisation and control of knowledge in the Chinese empire had gone through several changes. But there were two issues around which all these changes pivoted, from the first dynasty onwards. One was the distinction between higher and lower learning and the exclusive control of certain kinds of higher learning as a principle of government. On this principle the science of the calendar, and the observations and measurements which supported it, were high and exclusive, the issuing of the calendar a prerogative of the emperor. The application and arts of divination based on this higher learning were lesser, though their practitioners could be employed by the emperor. It was through these arts of divination that the cosmology of higher learning was shared throughout the empire. Of particular importance, because they were a direct reference to a height of literate aspiration, were those methods of divination using the symbols of *The Book of Changes* and the twelve earthly branches and ten heavenly stems out of which almanacs and the geomancers' compass for the siting of buildings and graves were constructed. Other symbols used in these constructions were the more popularly understood horoscopes and principles of *yin* and *yang* and the five phases (*wu xing*) which people themselves as well as diviners used to judge their state of being and the choices they had.

Under different dynasties and in different reign periods, the higher learning could be pursued and its instruments possessed by scholars outside the confines of the imperial bureaucracy, only to be forbidden in other periods. Similarly, the aspirations of practitioners to the heights of higher learning, the readings of the universal condition and its calendar by diviners, sages or savants outside imperial office, could be a threat. They could be decreed as incorrect and heterodox, or else they could be sought out by the emperor's officials and incorporated into imperial orthodoxy, patronage and authority.

The second, and closely related issue around which the political control of knowledge pivoted was the integrity of knowledge itself. Higher learning constituted a moral and physical cosmology. The same seventeenth-century scientist, Lu Shiyi, who wrote about the adjustment of imperial pitch-pipes also insisted that the empirical study of botany was worthy of high learning only so far as it revealed the inner workings of yin and yang and the five phases. For a high status Confucian scholar to study the objects of botany as such and for themselves alone would be, as he decried it, 'trifling with things' and neglecting the great precept that 'the principles of the cosmos are [the same as] the principles of my mind' (Henderson 1984:154–5). Which was also to say that study of things or forms without attention to the inner principles was in danger of straying into other principles of alternative integration: heterodoxy.

The Chinese word translated as 'ultimate principles' and as 'formative laws' (*li*), as distinct from physical forms (*xing*), brooks no distinction between what is mental and what is bodily, nor between the moral and the physical. The source of ultimate principles according to both high status Confucian classics and low status diviners' manuals, such as the handbooks for geomancy, is the upper third of the tripartite division of the universe: *Tian*. The forms are of the lowest third: *Di*. Between is *Ren*: human society with the emperor at its head. So the great precept of higher learning was shared by those who conducted lower learning, including botanists. But lower learning might pay too practical and extensive an attention to the earthly and the immediate for those who aspire to higher learning. And in doing so, they might challenge the higher with another version of the great precepts.

At a position much lower than a court astronomer, and having to deal personally with the practices of common people, where he also had to acknowledge authoritative compromises made with the principles of higher, more abstract learning, the magistrate of the city and district of Wen *xian* in the northern province of Shandong had an inscription carved in 1752. It marked the completion of repairs to the temple of that city, the temple of Walls and Moats (Cheng-huang). His inscription begins to instruct us on the differences between higher and lower conceptions of the world. It indicates a difference, as he found it, between the higher learning and the lower which can barely be bridged by the formal universality of the tripartite cosmology. The abstract, or more purely cosmological symbols, as preferred in the higher learning, where indeed they have been the framework for ever-changing and improved astronomical observations, are already compromised by conceptions of a personalised universe, even according to the very texts the higher learning venerates. Already in those texts, the universe is a personalised, moral harmony written as a history of sages and heroes authenticated by classical records and their commentaries. But the lower learning and the habits of the illiterate below it go too far, in the magistrate's view, with a sensationalisation of the moral cosmology sanctioned by the sages.

> Azure above is *Tian* (Heaven); massive below is *Di* (Earth). Between, with ears, eyes, mouth, nostrils, arms and legs, able to speak and to clothe himself, ceremonious and capable of observing the rites (*li*), is *Ren* (Mankind). But does this imply

that the azure *Tian* is also Ren, with ears, eyes, and nostrils. Since the Duke of Zhou [the most revered sage], it [i.e. *Tian]* has been called Shang Di [supreme ruler] and the vulgar have also called it Yu Huang [Jade Emperor] and have thereupon given it ears, eyes, mouth, nostrils, arms and legs, a crown with pendant ornaments, a jade sceptre, and a personal existence. ... They have given it a retinue of youthful officers and fierce generals as companions; and the people of the Empire following *en masse* the footsteps of their predecessors have also personified it. ... Now as to the deity of Walls and Moats, since it is sacrificed to as though it had a personal existence, why should not such things as songs and dances be employed to give it enjoyment. But let the plays be about ancient times so that they be instructive and prohibit the low, clandestine, vulgar and grosser passions. Fu Hsi, Shen Nung ... [the whole line of legendary sage kings] having been men were later deified. It is proper to sacrifice to them as those who had a personal existence. But Heaven, Earth, Sun, Moon ... Walls and Moats ... although deified, have no personal existence and should not be sacrificed to as if they had. Yet from ancient times even the sages have all sacrificed to them as though they had a personal existence. (McCartee 1869–70, adapted in some details for exposition here)

When we reverse perspective, and view the higher learning from a position on the other side of the line of educated exclusiveness, by those professing superstition even in the knowledge that it is so decried, what is the knowledge and imagery of the new year and the calendar?

The same tripartite cosmos is envisaged in Taiwan and mainland China now just as it was in Shandong in the eighteenth century, with no more distortion than the same sensate and personalised vulgarity regretted by the magistrate of Wen *xian*.

In imperial times, the publication of the calendar was conducted as a benign unification and harmonisation of the universe. That no longer takes place. No longer is government presented as that of a son of heaven who is the agent of a resonant or responsive universe and its science. In its place is another kind of authority, more local and more developmental, according to another conception of historical significance. But it too decries as superstition, the unscientific versions, or sub-versions, of the cosmos which continue to have currency from imperial times. Are those versions simple reflections of the imperial cosmos which the emperor, if he rules properly, keeps in its harmonious order? At first sight, it would appear so.

## NEW YEAR IN MOUNTAINSTREET

The place in which I most closely observed for myself the ritual practices that I shall be describing in this book, is a small town (of 1140 persons in 1965, the year before I arrived), linked in a system of marketing, administration, and education, as well as a system of festivals and feast visits with Taibei city, the commercial, industrial and political capital of Taiwan. I will call this small town Mountainstreet. Mountainstreet is situated at the confluence of two mountain streams which flow into the river basin in which Taibei city is built. At the point where the streams meet they have cut rocky ravines, leaving high above them a narrow, flat area, and at the angle of their confluence a broad triangle. On these areas the town's houses, shops, coal mine, government office, primary school, and temple were built. Further up the valleys of the two streams the slopes are more gentle and have been terraced for paddy, orange groves and tea gardens. The steeper slopes are cultivated for timber and sweet potato, and are bored here and there by small coal shafts. This town and its area was settled by Chinese from Fujian province in the first decade of the nineteenth century. It became a small market town in a few decades, during which the temple was founded (in 1839 according to the republican edition of the local history of Taibei *xian*). The Mountainstreet temple is a branch of a temple in a more central market town, nearer Taibei city, and that temple is itself an off-shoot of a temple in Anxi *xian*, Quanzhou prefecture, Fujian province, on the Chinese mainland.

New Year's day inaugurated for nearly all households in Mountainstreet the performance of a simple act of worship on the first and fifteenth of every lunar month. Its rites display the tripartite division and distinctions of a personalised cosmos. They were also observed in the mainland, for instance in central China in the 1930s by Day (1974:25). At the very least they consisted of the placing of burning incense sticks just outside the main door or window, and another set of sticks in one of the incense burners of the domestic altar shelf. It is important to note how they are spatially distributed, for then a well-kept hierarchy becomes apparent.

Members of two categories were greeted by incense at the main doorway of the house, or the window of the main room when it was on an upper floor. But one of these categories was above the other. This was the category of upright gods (*zheng shen*), which are those of the local temple and the shrines of its territorial sub-divisions. The local temple god is a more identifiable and identifying historical deity, while the god of the smallest territorial division is to most people not a nameable person. He was simply referred to as the Locality God (Tudi Gong), or by a longer honorific title, Meritorious Upright God (Fude Zhengshen). Every neighbourhood has a small shrine, often no more than waste high, for the Locality God, and twice a month incense and offerings are placed in it. Stall-holders, traders, shop-keepers and others in business make the second and sixteenth of the month days specially for the veneration of this god, sometimes adding his wife, as protectors of business fortune. Others include him on the first and fifteenth.

On the same twice-monthly dates, after he has been called and welcomed by households with incense at the doorway, offerings are placed for him inside facing the back wall of the main room, where he is often depicted on a coloured print behind the domestic altar shelf which depicts a hierarchy of deities up from Tudi Gong. There, incense for him is stuck into the burner for the gods. Another burner, in a lesser position to stage right of the gods, is for the ancestors of the household.

This is a steady and universal feature of Chinese religion: the demarcation of territorial guardians and other gods from ancestors. The gods are represented by images, pictures or statues, while ancestors are represented only by name inscribed on a tablet or slip of paper. In Taiwan the ritual demarcation is accomplished in numerous additional ways. The gods have an odd number of incense sticks, the ancestors an even number. The gods have gold spirit money burned for them, the ancestors silver, and so on.

Ancestors are firmly established after mourning rites for them have been completed, within the household. The gods are established in the local shrines at the centre of the temple's or its subdivisional territories. The gods' incense-burners on a domestic altar are established by putting some of the temple's incense dust in them. Just so, they are invited in on these twice-monthly occasions from outside, from within the local territory into one of its constituent residences. But these twice-monthly occasions are mainly for another, lower category of local spiritual beings, according to Mountainstreet residents.

This lower category was called *jun*, soldiers. Their offerings of incense and cheap and skimpy food placed on the threshold of the doorway, was called *kao jun*, rewarding the soldiers with food and drink. The same term is used to describe bonuses handed out to the soldiers of the Republic of China, but these household offerings are to soldiers of the local temple's gods.

As I was instructed, the highest gods, the gods of heaven, whether they be the Jade Emperor or the Goddess of Mercy (Guan Yin), have no soldiers. So here at the centre of the tripartite universe are a closely ordered series of ranks surrounding the household and its ancestors. For all of them, gold spirit-money of appropriate size and elaboration is burned, whereas for ancestors silver spirit-money is burned. But the gods are invited in, whereas their soldiers are not.

There is an even lower category than the gods' soldiers for whom offerings are placed on the threshold and kept outside, as they are for the soldiers. This is a category of spirit propitiated and thereby avoided, rather than invited and honoured for protection as are the gods. Indeed it is the category against which the gods are invited to protect households. In order not to mention them directly, which would be to tempt fate, they were referred to as the good brothers (*hao xiong di*), as if they were the brothers of a secret society or a gang of bullies. They were otherwise called orphan souls (*gu hun*), or simply and most directly, by those that were not superstitious or anxious about tempting fate, as demons (*gui*).

The dead who are not kept in households as ancestors are orphaned and malign. This category is the main object of the monthly offerings in the seventh moon of the year when orphan souls are invited *en masse* to a charitable feast. But they are also included in the New Year offerings. Demons are offered silver spirit money, unlike soldiers but like ancestors. They are the obverse of ancestors, not centred in households. They are invited but only to be returned, beyond the limits of the locality, and kept there by the local gods and their soldiers.

At New Year, an uppermost category is added at the door facing outward on the first day of the first month. And some households in Mountainstreet included this uppermost category at the regular twice-monthly burning of incense outside the door. This is the category of heavenly gods, most simply called Heaven God (Tian Gong) as if they were a single deity. When the occasions for worship of this category were looked up in the almanac they were separated out into the three gods presiding over the three divisions of the cosmos and celebrated at three separate occasions dividing the annual cycle, the upper, middle and lower points (*yuan*). These three were described by many residents of Mountainstreet as a set of brothers or officers appointed by the supreme heaven god, and all three were included in the offerings placed facing outwards at their doors very early after the turn of the new year. Their offerings were raised higher than any others, including those at the domestic altar. But like the local gods' soldiers and the demons they were not invited in. The table of offerings to them was placed inside the doorway, facing outwards.

In order of sequence, the food placed on these high tables must not have been offered before. After they have been offered first to heaven they may be used again for the lower categories. The offerings to the highest category are also distinct in another way from the offerings placed before the lower categories. As the order is descended, first meat is added and then reduced or substituted. It is uncut and without eating utensils, for the retinue of *zheng shen*. Less expensive meat, in small pieces, or substitutes for meat such as eggs, more like the daily human diet and accompanied by chopsticks is placed before gods' soldiers and ancestors. For orphan souls, there is an inversion of the top rank, cheap but uncooked food without chopsticks, or only one chopstick for carrying it away as on a shoulder-pole.

From this account, it would appear that the imperial regime's lasting educational legacy was a replication among the common people after millenia of moral example, education and correction, of its own strict hierarchy of statuses in the form of a personalised and sensate universe. The more abstract cosmos of the imperial calendar and its rites appears to have been replicated among the common people of the empire as the hierarchy of imperial rule itself. The imperial regulation of harmony is repeated in the sentiments of the offerings to the highest category of gods, those of heaven, and of the whole New Year season as a benign new start. As one of the Mountainstreet pharmacists said:

> New year is to have a new heart. If someone wants to borrow money, you lend it without suspicion and without demanding an IOU. Placing offerings before the gods of heaven is not to ask for protection. It is just to purify one's heart.

And good will there certainly is. Children who had a day before shouted 'long-nose' at me, on the new day grinned and shouted congratulations to me. Houses and faces that were closed, on the new day were open and inviting.

But before accepting the strong temptation to interpret popular religious practices as a reflection or a rehearsal of collective political representations, as many have done, we should note some discrepancies. They will take us further toward making out what was the heterodoxy which the magistrate of Wen *xian* and the court intellectuals of the Qing dynasty tried to correct.

## A DEMONIC COSMOS

The most superstitious of the backward popular religious practices, as they are denounced in the republican China of Taiwan and of the mainland, are those which concern demons and which credit local deities with the power to keep them at bay.

This modern denunciation places such practices and beliefs in a different political context and in a different regime of truth than the imperial correction. It places them in an undeveloped past, as a remnant of its insecurities. (See, for instance, Guo Zhichao 1985 and Feuchtwang 1989a and 1989b.)

But I shall ignore this difference or rather postpone taking it into consideration. It is important first to pay particular attention to the category of demons and the corresponding power to control them. What arrests attention here is a conception of authority which is at the centre of the apparent replication of imperial authority, and yet was heterodox in imperial times and was held to be ignorant by aspirants to higher learning, just as it is held to be superstitious now.

Here religious Daoism must be included. Daoist practitioners were employed by emperors, but they were used outside the official state cults. Daoists' rites convert the cosmos endorsed by court astronomers into another universe of esoteric forces. Another kind of imagery of cosmic forces and of alchemy is introduced when the Daoist seeks to concentrate in himself a microcosm of the universal forces in order to re-align and harmonise their imbalance, as the emperor did according to the Monthly Ordnances. For the Daoist adds his own commands, in the form of *fu*, written orders used as talismans.

The practices of popular religion, the imperial state cults and the Daoist rites provide alternative lines of reference through the same cosmology. In Daoism, but not in the system of state rites, the categories of the cosmology are applied as real forces directly upon immediate circumstances. In the imperial rites, the hierarchical and resonant structure of a moral-physical universe was displayed and anthropomorphised in representations of historically exemplary individuals, celebrated in official cults. But the gods in popular temples, though they represent historical persons, are also manifestations of current power to heal and to exorcise. It is true that the powers of these upright spirits, as spirits, were endorsed by imperial commendation and by the incorporation of their cults into the ranks of the state cults, attended exclusively by officials and those they invited. But the initiative for this version of spirits with powers came from below, not from imperial ideology and its education.

While the emperor had his own and delegated powers of cosmic adjustment through the state cults, Daoists conducted rites of cosmic adjustment called *jiao* which the sponsors of local, popular temples hired them to perform. In *jiao*, cosmic powers are represented by Daoist practitioners to themselves and to *cognoscenti* as the transmission of a secret knowledge of forces, their points of concentration, balance and confinement, and of the immortals to whom this knowledge was revealed and from whom it has been transmitted.

To the outside, the Daoist rites are represented in dramas of exorcism. And these outward representations are where the Daoists' performances link up with their clients' apprehensions of the world in rites such as the twice-monthly burning of incense which people practise themselves, without hired professionals.

Doctor G of Mountainstreet thought that the twice-monthly offerings to gods' soldiers was of peculiar importance because when the local temple was re-built and a new hall added, no rite of cosmic adjustment was performed to consecrate it. In other words, the twice-monthly rites are directly related as a popular, simple rite, to the grander communal rites of adjustment (the *jiao*) performed by Daoists in the local temple.

So, what do we find when we ask ordinary people about the gods' soldiers, the main agency of the gods' command and exorcising powers?

Mrs K, wife of a pork-tax collector and mother of a young family of school-children, was someone who frequently prefaced her answers to my persistent questions about religious practices and the meaning of various acts and words with such disclaimers as 'people say' or 'it is a superstition, but . . .'. At the same time, she was anxious about calling demons demons. So, about the soldiers of the God of Walls and Moats – the City God of the region – and the soldiers of the Locality God of the subterritories of the region, she said they are 'good brothers'. The higher deities like Guan Yin (Goddess of Mercy) do not have soldiers. Their retinue is not of soldiers. It is made up of those who have been good.

44

The local doctor said that the soldiers of the City God are *gui* (demons), but that the Locality God had no soldiers. Doctor G considered himself and was considered by others to be better educated, not only in Western medicine but also in popular and traditional customs and culture. He added that *gui* are unworshipped kin. When the dead are worshipped, or cared for, they are in the category of *shen*, not *gui*. *Shen* are ordinary spirits. A person who excels is star-born and is a bright *shen* (*shen ming*). Mrs K called such persons of excellence, immortals (*xian*). They are the gods. Indeed the god of the newer, rear hall of Mountainstreet temple is colloquially known as Immortal God (Xian Gong).

The twice-monthly rites are particularly important for the care of recently dead kin. For the first three years after their death, incense is burned for them by name in the ancestral burner on these occasions. They are, in other words, in the final transition to becoming *shen*.

So, the main objects of twice-monthly incense burning turn out to be dangerously transitional, recently dead ancestors on one hand and gods' soldiers on the other, both between the categories of demon (*gui*) and spirit (*shen*). Holding the line between them stand the Locality God and the gods of the local temple.

Most people I asked said that the gods of the local temple had officers and soldiers. But one person said that the pair of gods who are celebrated in the older of the two halls which make up the temple of Mountainstreet are themselves the generals of the higher god, Xian Gong, who is enshrined in the newer hall.

The picture presented by all their answers is that of a universe personalised into virtuous and illustrious dead who keep malign, forgotten or bad, dead at bay from households where by contrast the living care for their own dead at their altars.

In popular understanding of the *jiao* and the twice-monthly incense burning, it is the drama of ridding the household and its territory of demons which the local temple enshrines. When a more elaborate version of this understanding is compiled from such local and amateur experts as Dr G or his equivalents in previous generations, a version of the imperial cosmology becomes evident.

Seiichiro Suzuki's compilation of old customs and beliefs of Taiwan was published in 1934. It includes a section on spirit soldiers where it reports the belief that some of the soldiers are of heaven where they are disposed into the thirty-six (four times nine) stars of the bowl of the Dipper (Tian Gang). These soldiers are 'malign spirits' (*xie shen*). On earth there are the soldiers of the seventy-two Earth Emanations

45

(Di Sha). These are Evil Influences (Wu Sha). The 108 baleful stars include those of the Great Year, the White Tiger and the Heaven Dog, which are the most frequent objects of Daoist rites of exorcism in Mountainstreet.

In addition to the 108 baleful stars are the soldiers who follow local gods. They are placed in five camps, those of the north, south, east, west and centre, each with its own Marshal (Yuanshuai). The Marshal of the centre is Li Nojia, an adept of fearsome and immensely clever techniques. (The other four Marshals are variously named according to different sources.) This is a disposition of malign or evil forces under the control of military deities in all three parts of the tripartite cosmos. The contrast with the more abstract and harmonised cosmos of imperial regulation is sharp. This one is certainly a cosmos of imperial rule, but one of a military imperium, and one in which malign and defensive forces fill the universe at all levels. This military imperium is repeated in every local temple's area, with the central camp outside the temple (see Schipper 1985:28).

Suzuki goes on to describe what I and many others have since also observed at the procession festivals of local cults, in which the military imperium is performed in ritual practice. On the altar table in front of the main god in local temples there is the god's seal, inscribed with the sign of a conferred rank. To its left is a tub, named the dipper (*dou*), in which are five flags each in the colour of its quarter, including the centre. To the right is a stand for the god's knife or sword. By it is the god's flag or his tablet (*hu*). The seal, the tub, the stand and the tablet accompany the statue of the god when it is taken out in a ceremonial sedan chair for procession to signify his control of spirit soldiers and to dispel plague demons and malevolent spirits. In this procession, a spirit medium may in addition to the statue be possessed and represent the spirit of the god. In the course of special processions at times of plague or other infestation, the flags of the five camps are placed at points in the centre (near the temple) and the four extremities of the territory. This is called 'disposing the soldiers' (*fang jun*). And it is these dispositions which are addressed in the twice-monthly feeding of the troops.

The *hu* tablets of the emperor and imperial officials denoted ranks by the material of which they were made. *Hu* were held before the chest so that the top covered the mouth of an inferior, of the emperor before heaven, and so on down. The seal conferring rank also entails an imperial hierarchy. Its authority stems from the Jade Emperor. Once again, it looks as if the imperial cosmos has been reproduced from below. But what these descriptions, and the simpler, more recent statements of Mountainstreet people convey, is a pronounced ambivalence about the nature of their protectors, the gods' soldiers, and even about the gods who command the spirit soldiers and the demons from whom the people seek protection. True, the gods are illustrious spirits, or immortals. And Daoists are also versed in the art of commanding and of the knowledge by which to cultivate brightness, or immortality. But Daoists are feared, and the protecting gods have fearsome demeanours.

A *hu* tablet is held by Daoist practitioners in their rites, never by ordinary people. And the Daoist rite of cosmic renewal (*jiao*) includes the erection of spectacular altars at the four quarters and centre of the temple area. They are also the points at which huge constructions of lanterns and other means of summoning orphan souls are erected, so that they may be fed and despatched again. A minor and regular version of the same feeding and despatching is then performed by households on the first and fifteenth of the seventh lunar month every year. And the communal organisation of feeding and despatch is in Taiwan and the southeastern provinces of the mainland often the largest annual festival, after New Year. (For Taiwan, see Weller 1987. For an historical account of the emergence of this festival into its more or less final form in the Song dynasty, from texts to be found anywhere in China, see Teiser 1988.)

Those who command demons are close to being demons. The distinctions carefully made in the ordinary rites of domestic worship and the more elaborate accounts of different categories of spirit soldier seem to be rather easily traversed and smudged. Spirit soldiers of local gods are in the same camp with the evil soldiers of stellar and earthly harm.

The euphemism 'good brothers' is not only a verbal avoidance of harm. It has an equivalent in ritual practice which depicts the transition from demonic to worthy spirit. Small roadside shrines looking almost identical to those for the Locality God exist in every rural area of Taiwan. Their equivalents probably also existed in most other parts of China, just as there certainly were equivalents of the small Locality God shrines.

In Taiwan, the only feature distinguishing them from Locality God shrines is the fact that there is no statue or pictorial depiction and no name or title in them. This is because they are shrines for the remains of unidentified dead, found in the area. They are often called Mass Grave Shrines (Da Mu Gong). A defensively ambivalent name for these shrines in many parts of Taiwan is Ten Thousand Joys for Those Gathered Here (Wan Xi Tong Gui). But another description by which they are as frequently known points to their capacity of tuming fear into gratitude. This is their designation as Responsive Shrines (You Ying Gong). Some bear an inscription: 'make a request and it will be answered' (*yu qiu bi ying*). This is more than a defensive euphemism.

Stevan Harrell (1974) describes several examples of these shrines becoming foci of gratitude rather than fear. They are intermediate, with some people despising and fearing and some feeling helped by having placed offerings at them. The former burn silver spirit-money and treat them as orphan souls. The latter burn gold and treat them as gods. Once they are treated as gods – or was it a precondition for their being so treated? – they gain an identity and a biography. The names and lives of those known to have died at the site are told as legends. Frequently that is as a fighter or gang of fighters, for these shrines are typically for those who died a violent death. In many cases they had died in battles between local militia bands or between the forces of larger groupings of fellow-countrymen. In others, men who died as patriots resisting the Japanese colonial forces are remembered. Those for women might be called Saintly Woman (Sheng Ma) shrine, like one near Mountainstreet which was considered particularly responsive. The biography in this case was of a woman who had died childless and therefore alone.

In other just as frequent instances they were shrines to gamblers, robbers, or gangsters killed in action. These too were feared and despised or admired as robbers of the rich and defenders of the poor. Or else they simply became objects of request for success in gambling or seduction, and other favours of a less than upright nature.

In all these instances the mass grave shrines would be a mixture of the enemy and of the male heroes who died expelling the enemy or the female heroines who rescued people from demonic enemy or malign influence. Silver or gold, or both. As feared objects, the act of placing offerings to them is called propitiation (*ji*), the same word that is used for the propitiation or placating of the newly dead. As objects of gratitude, or recompense, for favours given, offerings are made to honour or worship (*bai*), the same word that is used for the offerings placed before the gods, revered elders, guests and historical exemplars.

The responsiveness of the objects of these shrines was reputed to be particularly *xing*, forthcoming and concrete – or just as powerfully and concretely negative to those who neglected them. Similarly, Mrs

K and others used the same word which describes the power of gods to respond (*ling*) when describing 'the good brothers' as being more powerful than other spirits. Locality God and the unknown dead of the area, guardian and guarded against, are as ubiquitous a pairing as ancestral and locality cults. The same pairing occurs at the graves of known and named spirits. On the lefthand side, facing outwards from the tomb, is a small tablet inscribed with the title of the guardian of graves: Hou Tu. And when every year offerings are placed at the graves of ancestors, accompanied by silver spirit-money, Hou Tu receives side offerings accompanied by gold spirit-money. The god of the major local temple also has a side shrine for the Locality God. What this seems to indicate is that historically nameable deities have a similar kind of power to those of the demons against which they are installed as guardians. Their power is different and more like the power of demons than the authority represented by the Locality God.

In other words, what is suggested here is more than the anomalous threat of those who do not fit, or who come in the intervals of a strict and hierarchical system of categories represented at the lower levels by City and Locality Gods. Transitional they may be in the framework of the imperial hierarchy. Transitional and emergent individuals, their border existence seems to make them the most vivid and the most concretely imagined and pictured of spiritual beings. But their powers and the relationships of power in which they are imagined and placed in ritual practice suggest another system of cosmological arrangements altogether: that of command and threat which is demonic and military on both sides of the distinctions and the spatial borders on which those distinctions are drawn and represented by means of the Locality Gods.

In the seventh lunar month, the boundary between the inside and the outside is kept by commanders who are painted on temple doors. They are large versions of the door gods whose colourful prints are bought at the turn of the year and pasted on domestic doors in many parts of China in the Spring Festival renewal. (See Menshikov *et al.* (1988): plates 18–28). One popular door guardian figure, on domestic or on temple gates, is the exorciser Zhong Kui (Weller: plate 3.1 and Menshikov *et al*: plates 27 and 28). Another is the Mountain King, a tiger (Menshikov *et al.*:24). Often a small Locality God shrine contains the figure of this tiger. More usually it contains the figure of a minor official, sometimes accompanied by his wife. This version of the guardian is more like the civil hierarchy, less military and less demonic than the tiger. In Mountainstreet I was told that the Tiger

Marshal (Hu Ye) was an underling of the Locality God. But the closeness of the one to the other is important.

A similar closeness at a much higher level in the categorisation of gods occurs among the guardians of more central and famous temples to the compatriotic dead. For instance, a shrine to the unknown dead after battles between descendants of immigrants from Quanzhou and descendants of immigrants from Zhangzhou, two prefectures in southern Fujian province, was built in Xinzhuang *xiang* of Taibei county. Its responsiveness became famous and the guardian temple next to it enshrined not a lowly Locality God, but the *bodhisattva* Ksitigarbha, known in China as Dizang Wang (King of the Underworld) whose counterpart or other face is the fierce ruler of the underworld, Yama or Yenluo Wang. The Buddhist sutras devoted to Dizang Wang, and first published in China in the seventh century,

> tell the story of Dizang's compassionate actions in previous lives. In several of his previous lives Dizang vowed to end the suffering of any sentient being in need, and in one incarnation as a woman she descended to hell ... to save her mother. These and other sources from Tang times portray Dizang residing in the underworld; they stress his compassionate efforts to free people from the torments of hell, often in contrast to King Yama's stern and impartial administration. (Teiser 1988:187).

This is how Dizang Wang is known in Taibei, where his temple in the old commercial centre of Mengjia is a focus of attention for Buddhist compassion in the seventh-month festivities. Next to his temple is one to the demonic powers of the unknown dead which have become powers of heroic protection, and as such entitled Da Zhong Ye (God of the Masses of dead), a name for controllers of demons. Other shrines to the heroic unknown dead are accompanied by shrines to the best known *bodhisattva* of all, the Goddess of Mercy, Guan Yin.

The important point here is the juxtaposition of compassion, and sweet meatless foods, with stern military guardianship, and meat. Just as guardian deities may have been demons, so their own protective deities' sweet compassion from higher categories in the imperial cosmos can turn into severe military administration and judgement. On the second day of the main ceremonies conducted in the seventh month at the temple observed by Robert Weller in northern Taiwan, the Daoist professionals began proceedings by evoking Guan Yin and Da Shi Ye to care for and to control the mass of ghosts. According to the Daoists, Da Shi Ye is a transformation of Guan Yin, with the fearful features of a controller rather than a saviour of ghosts (Weller 1987:93). Similarly, the highest patron deity of the descendents of emigrants from the county of Anxi, in the prefecture of Quanzhou, is usually known as a compassionate and vegetarian exemplar. But in the annual procession festival in Taiwan celebrating the Honoured Ancestral Master (Zu Shi Gong), as observed by Emily Ahern, the offerings are not only meat, but raw and whole pigs. When she asked why meat was offered to this vegetarian, she was variously told it was for him to feed the hungry ghosts, or that the meat was for his soldiers, the mountain spirits, or to placate a harmful and enormous presence in the mountains, manifested by a bird-shaped rock with a hole in it, against which the otherwise vegetarian exemplar 'acts for us just as Taoist priests do, by helping to manage the ghosts' (Ahern 1981b: 404). Just so, the Jade Emperor, the God of Heaven himself, sweet and meatless at the Spring Festival is offered meat in the Seventh-Month Festival.

The thought begins to occur that even such higher-level deities might be perceived in a version of the cosmos as a system of command over demonic powers, as themselves demonic.

## A COSMIC AND AN IMPERIAL CATASTROPHE

When Chinese people meet each other and go round visiting in the first days of the year they wish each other peace, and speak only lucky words. They deliberately avoid any mention of what might be deemed unlucky, so signifying the closeness of what is to be avoided. They congratulate each other (*gonghe* or *gongxi*), as if upon having avoided the unmentionable.

In Taiwan, when I asked why congratulations were due on the morning of the new year, I was told a number of stories all of which had the narrative structure of a cataclysm barely avoided. On 22 January 1967, New Year's day, I put the question to some members of the family of an old tea trader. The shortest answer, from one of his grand-daughters, was 'because we are not dead'. Her mother's answer, only a little more elaborate, was 'because the world was going to sink into the sea. So people made round cakes and ate their fill. But in the morning the world had not sunk, so they said "congratulations"'. One of her sons added an active mode to the story : the world would have been sunk. But he could not specify the bad influence, hinting at demons on one hand, and at the Supreme Ruler (Shang Di) on the other. His younger brother put a literary gloss on the story, playing an etymological game with the character for 'year', which is like the character for 'ox' with the addition of half a stroke. 'A long time ago' he said, placing the story at the beginning of tradition

> there was a very large animal, bigger than an ox, called a 'year'. It was going to eat all the people. So the people ate up all their food to fill their stomachs, since it was to be their last day. But on the next morning they had not been eaten, so they congratulated each other.

His grandmother, the old tea trader's wife, offered yet another version in which the protagonist was 'Hou Deng Shen (The Lamp Monkey)'. This was probably a version of the immortal monkey from the legend of the bringing of the Buddhist sutras to China, as told in 'The Western Journey' and numerous other tales of monkey's havoc in heaven and strategies on earth ultimately on the side of humans and good.

> Monkey came down to earth to tell humans that the earth would sink (*chen*) on new-year's eve and everyone would be killed. So everyone put on their best clothes and ate delicious food. Next day when they found themselves alive after all, they greeted each other with congratulations. ... Business men still now thank the monkey spirit at New Year.

For a few days in January 1967, in the same small town, I asked the same question whenever I could as I went round visiting. In all I asked twenty-four people, of whom eleven knew no story; just that congratulations were part of wearing new (or clean) clothes, eating sweet things, and being happy. All the others mentioned the minimum core structure: not being dead.

New year at this time, and for these people, certainly evoked images of the whole world, just as it did in the imperial court. But the images are not those of the calendar and its cosmological symbols. Those are available and to hand in the farmer's almanac. Neither are they stories of the origin or discovery of these symbols, as they might have been told by a Daoist recounting the revelation of the map of the world (see Lagerwey 1987:161–3). Nor are they stories of an imperial harmonisation and regulation of the universe, and therefore also the human and earthly empire. Instead, they are of the world being only just saved.

From the perspective of the imperial court, there is also a negative side: of the world in disorder and disharmony if it were not properly regulated, the rites not correctly performed. The cause of disorder is heterodoxy and confusion among humans, the educated and the common people. It is a lack of proper conduct and example among the rulers and the educated, and their inability to exert an ordering influence on the common people.

But from the perspective of the stories I was told among the 'common people', the catastrophe has a hint of a cause which is not incorrect ritual. It is linked to wickedness among the common people, but the crucial point is that the wickedness is perceived by, and angers an agency which is imperial. 'People were wicked (*huai*)', as the daughter of the woman who served the teachers at the local primary school told me,

> so the Jade Emperor ordered that they should all die. The people knew of the order, and so they ate delicious food and put on beautiful clothes. But they did not die. So very early in the morning of new year we thank the Jade Emperor.

Or it is simply the movement of the primordial ox.

> Under the earth is an ox. When he changes position the earth quakes. One day, people knew that the ox was going to take exercise and that therefore the earth would quake so that all people would die on new year's eve. Before that day, everyone ate delicious food and dressed in beautiful clothes. But on the day after, they found themselves still alive, so they congratulated each other. The ox had decided not to take any exercise. (A woman who ran one of the town's two grocery stores.)

The ox may have entered this narrative by means of people hearing or reading about the imperial ceremony which inaugurated the farmer's year a few days after New Year's day. The printed almanacs often include a picture of the spring ox. For instance, the single-sheet almanac, pasted on domestic walls, had at its centre a picture of the ox and its driver, Mang Shen. Above the picture were precise instructions of the colours and sizes of the various parts of the ox and its driver for that year, as if replicas were to be built. These instructions, including the apparel of Mang Shen, are in fact signs predicting farm production and weather in the various seasons of the coming year. In imperial times, the predictions would have been based on the calendar issued by the emperor. On either side of the picture, are named the stellar position of the Great Year, a twelve-year cycle associated with the planet we in the West call Jupiter, and the position of the year's lunar dwelling, a division of the horizon of moon-rise into twenty-eight sections. (See also Palmer 1986:44–5.)

In the imperial capital, the emperor in accordance with the Monthly Ordnances, began the farmer's year by the ritual ploughing of a furrow, probably by an ox-drawn plough. He also performed sacrifices at the Altar of Mountains and Rivers, including the sacrifice of an ox. His representatives in the imperial bureaucracy, the local magistrates, did the same in their counties (*xian*). Later, at the Beginning of Spring (Li Chun), officials performed a ceremony which, exceptionally for official rites, included the common people. They took out to the eastern suburb beyond the city walls specially constructed figures of the spring (or earth) ox and its herdboy, attended by a throng of commoners. On the way back, they left the ox and herd facing west at the central gate of the administrative compound, the *yamen*. Six weeks later, on the spring equinox, they came out and ritually beat the ox to put an end to the cold airs and made offerings to the ox-herd to bless and bring about growth. 'Although this is like play-acting, it is following the way of the ancients', comments the 1721 gazetteer of what was then the county of Taiwan. Plainly, the ceremony was a compromise with a commoners' practice which, though ancient, did not accord with the rest of the imperial rites. The common farmers whipped the spring ox with sticks and tore it to pieces, the pieces taken as talismans and put in pig pens to ward off disease or buried in the fields to ward off pestilence. The figure of Mang Shen, the ox-driver in the farmers' almanac, does not guarantee blessings, it predicts by reverse signs: barefooted, there will be drought; shod, there will be floods. Such predictions of possible disaster occur every year, as well as predictions of good harvests. No year is so well-regulated as to be good for everyone. The agrarian cycle, and the new life of spring submerged in winter is aroused by a violent assault. The avoidance of misfortune is urgent, and precarious. The imperial rites might be performed, but there was still a chance of misfortune.

The Great Year planet, Jupiter, is itself a sign of a dark spirit, the Supreme Ruler of the four directions, whom Daoist priests are contracted to invoke in order to help them exorcise and drive away demons, symbolically represented by a Tiger (see Lagerwey 1987:28). The Great Year planet can itself be in the mood of a demonic attack, along with the influence of the Western Quarter, the White Tiger (see Palmer 1986:58–9). The tiger was, indeed, yet another variant of the agent of destruction in the stories I was told. For instance, a school girl told me:

There was a very remote, wild country place. One night its people heard a loud noise. They were frightened and did not dare to go out. When they looked in the morning there was nothing to be seen. After many nights like this, they decided to worship (bai-bai). They said it was the end of the world, for the noise was not a tiger, nor a lion, nor any other thing. That night everyone ate good food because it was their last day. But next morning no one had died. So they all said 'congratulations'.

Her mother accused her of telling the story wrong, and substituted the fate of the world by drowning for her daughter's world cataclysm heralded by loud noises like those of tigers or lions. But the tiger came much more definitively into the version of the new year cataclysm told me by the mistress of a bus driver, who said she had picked up the story from a book:

In ancient times the tiger was known as *nian* (the character for 'year'). People called out 'the year is coming' when the tiger approached. In the winter the tiger was hungry and would eat people. They were afraid of the tiger. So they lit candles, made delicious food and wore good clothes, and exploded firecrackers. Now the tiger was afraid, and people were not eaten. Before the turn of the year they said 'the year is coming' and after the turn when the tiger had gone, they said 'congratulations' to each other.

In sum, all versions of the world and its rule told from below, in this Taiwanese town, tell of a demonic power or a power over demons. Some of the power is attributed to spirits of human individuals, the rest is attributed to non-human influences, stellar or earthly. In either case it is a power to be warded off and guarded against, as the almanac directs. Whatever it is, Ox, Monkey, Jade Emperor, or Tiger, the potential destroyer is thanked on New Year's day for having desisted. The agency of destruction is thanked, much as one might be 'grateful' in paying 'thanks' to a protection racketeer.

Indeed, one of the attractions of the last day of New Year festivities about which people in the small town told me, was a strange figure who came out on that last night in Mengjia, the oldest part of Taibei city. He represented, I was told, a famous gangster who protected Mengjia. Like others from Mountainstreet, I went to see. It was a magical night, drawing out a lyrical strain in my otherwise more prosaic observations at the time:

On this street one can hear behind several doors the sounds of pipe bands playing good wishes, like the tune of 'Heaven's officials bestow blessings' . The Lantern Festival according to the almanac is the day of heaven's officials. After taking their 'tip', the bands go on to play in the next house. The street itself is dark, unlit. Further down I see and hear orange bursts of firecrackers, and in the orange gloom and gunpowder smoke make out a crowd standing around something. A very thin middle-aged man wearing only shorts and a small shallow conical hat sits nonchalantly on the back of a cane sedan chair, smoking a cigarette and holding a rush broom which he flicks at the firecrackers. They are making a terrific din and a fiery splutter all around him. Not only are the people of the house in front of which he has stopped throwing firecrackers at him, by his invitation, but an enormous string of firecrackers is draped around the sedan chair, exploding. His shorts and chest are covered with black smudges. This is Han Dan Ye or, to give him the title written on his sedan, Tian Xuan Yuanshuai, Heavenly and Mysterious Marshal, the deification of a former gangster (*liumang*) who was also very filial. So a local Daoist upon whom I was calling told me.

The Daoist went out that night to conduct an exorcism in someone's house. On the same day, the fifteenth of the first lunar month, often called the Lantern Festival because the evening is lit up with lanterns, carried or pulled by children, Lions and Dragons are also invited and paid by shops and households to dance outside. They advance, retreat and advance menacingly in ritual steps. They trace the points and the shape marked by the stars of the Dipper, the so-called steps of Yu, legendary sage who tamed the rivers of China and revealed the map of the world to the founders of Daoism. They are steps in the Daoist ceremony of exorcism (Lagerwey 1987:99), in which they seal off demons enacted by a tiger, who is, like Han Dan Ye, surrounded by firecrackers.

Under the sweet talk of a benign imperial cosmos, is another demonic cosmos of great destructive powers and the capacity to withhold or command them.

## THE IMPERIAL VERSION

In his discussion of the actual hierarchy of imperial rule, Gary Hamilton (1989) argues cogently against the Western concepts of bureaucracy by which it has been analysed. These are concepts of a law-making or a command structure and its administration. Imperial administration was quite incapable of such a structure, he points out, both because of its tiny personnel in proportion to the population administered, and also in its administrative ethic and knowledge. It was a machinery of tax revenue collection run according to an ethic of exemplary harmonisation by moral authority and of correction by punishment, in which power 'does not issue from commands, but rather from conformity' (Hamilton 1989:162).

I think we should understand Hamilton to be addressing the Chinese operational concepts involved, or the Chinese ideal, and not the practicalities of administration. He is sketching an ideology of hierarchy to add to Louis Dumont's *homo hierarchicus* drawn from India.

Hamilton concludes that unlike the Indian notion of a hierarchy of purity or the Western notion of a bureaucratic hierarchy, the imperial Chinese administration was a status hierarchy held together by a principle of ritual order. He quotes another study to this effect: '*Lu*, the Chinese term for law, properly denotes the laws of musical harmony – constants of the social order, just as certain proportionalities of pitch are constants of the harmonic order' (Vandermeersch 1985:13).

This type of political system, according to Hamilton, rests on a presumption of clear, well-defined roles in which authority, in principle, is invoked only when role incumbents do not fulfil their duties. In his view, the key relation to this hierarchy is one described by the term *xiao*, usually translated as filial duty. Hamilton justifiably extends it to include the obligation to fulfil duties in a status hierarchy of diadic roles which include those of subject and ruler. It is a recognition of duties, not subjection to a sovereign, nor a domination of subjects. These diadic relations are arranged into a hierarchy of a small number of status groups, each with its own regulations, and no universal system of rules, simply the acceptance of being duty-bound. The officials of state administration are one such status group. The others are the emperor above it, the families of the ruled and their households below it, and another status category beyond all of these which Hamilton calls 'outsiders'. These lack an exact role and serve as status intermediaries. They articulate the hierarchy as foreign advisors, as clerks and runners, as slaves, eunuchs, prostitutes, bandits and beggars, kept out and classified as either non-Chinese or as 'mean people' (*jian-min*).

Disorder (*luan*) is the breakdown of the moral order implied by *xiao*. It is to have forgotten, neglected or discarded ties of obedience to and recognition of duties and roles. In either direction, upward or downward in the status hierarchy, commoner or imperial, neglect of this recognition of duties is, according to the imperial ideology, equally threatening. And the threat is to lose Chinese status and respect, to become alien or to become 'mean'.

Many authors, including me, have been tempted to interpret demons and ghosts as a representation of this threat, of disorder held in abeyance, of those cast out into beggary, banditry, slavery, or prostitution. (For example, Wolf 1974, Feuchtwang 1975 and Weller 1987). More recently the publication by Shahar and Weller (eds) (1996) has shown how close deities can be to the funny and demonic states of ecstasy, drunkenness, gambling, debauchery, and banditry, in a very long tradition of what the orthodox named excessive cults (*yinsi*). (See also Stein 1979). The demonic basis of gods who threaten disorder unless they are honoured is already well established in the stories collected in the fourth-century collection of Investigations of Gods (Soushenji) and cited by Levi (1989: 205–6). Harrell (1974) had already pointed out the transition from demon to god in Taiwan, and ter Haar (1990) then showed that the same genealogy is actually typical of popular temple cults in the province of Fujian. Popular rites addressed demonic power. Confucian scholars sought to curb and denounce it, even though it was already implicit in an imperial cosmology.

The imperial metaphor was not just bureaucratic. There are too many cases of female and unbureaucratic gods to hold to any theory of gods' equivalence to a governmental bureaucracy. In addition they shake an earlier confidence in the correspondence between Chinese religion and the rest of its social life. The classic text for this theory is Wolf (1974). In it he seeks to demonstrate with a great deal of fascinating information that rites and stories of gods, demons and ancestors, though they vary according to the social positions in which they were performed and told, had in common the distinctions between gods, ghosts and ancestors and that these distinctions correspond to lived structural distinctions of family and kinship organisation, locality, strangers and government. I have already objected to such a view, that it is precisely the difference and lack of correspondence of the rites and imagery of gods and demons to the manners and features of the living which give them a metaphoric value. Myths and rites stand in a transcendental and an historicised relation (as an eternal past) to a present and lived reality. Indeed, far from the celestial order corresponding to imperial rule, imperial authority was itself dependent on transcendental authority and its calendar of rites. What I am now proposing is that local temple cults do not repeat the same authority and its imperial ideology, let alone correspond to its bureaucracy. They convey an alternative vision of the same cosmos, a more militaristic one.

Hamilton's article is notable for the absence of any consideration of military force. But the lesser status of the military and its knowledge (*wu*), under civil administration and knowledge (*wen* – the fact that this term monopolises the concept of 'culture' or 'civilisation' is significant) is a justification for this omission. It represents imperial ideology. In contrast to the mix of *wen* amd *wu* in the ideology of maintaining the celestial and civilisational order, an opposite mix, namely a militaristic notion of the cosmos is prominent in popular religion. Moreover, it is no less a version of healing and ameliorative powers than the imperial ideology described by Hamilton. Healing in this version is by exorcism, by written commands in the forms of *fu* talismans, provided by Daoists or by spirit mediums.

It is no less regulative than the imperial harmony. But regulation in this popular version is by command and through a hierarchy of command over demonic (and ghostly) powers, by similar powers. The 'intermediaries' which articulate the boundaries of the official status hierarchy are the central characters in this command hierarchy.

## THE LOCAL VERSION

The full flavour of this version of the imperial hierarchy, seen from below, is provided by the myths of Blood River recorded by James Watson from stories told by villagers in the New Territories of Hong Kong (Watson 1991). In these stories, which can be shown to have a basis in documented events and orders, imperial power is represented as lethal.

The coastal area of this part of Guangdong province was a last stronghold of Ming dynasty loyalists holding out against the new, Qing emperor. To him they were 'pirates' or 'bandits' or hosts of offshore pirates. The villages on which they could subsist or where they could land from offshore islands were to be cleared. All the inhabitants were to be moved inland, away from their homes and sources of subsistence. If they stayed, returned, were accused of, or actually resorted to piracy the emperor would order a bloody and indiscriminate massacre. In some stories, whole villages were slaughtered and the rivers ran with blood. Most significantly, the emperor's is the power to bring ancestral lines to an end, turning the dead into ghosts without care. This version of the emperor's power may be deemed exceptional, because the emperor was the first of a new dynasty, and of a non-Chinese origin (Manchu). But that would be wrong, first because it was not unusual for an imperial dynasty to be 'foreign' when it was established, and second because the same kind of story about a hostile imperial regime and its local garrison or inspectorate was told in periods of 'Chinese'dynasties.

The overture to the Spring Festival season is the winter solstice: Han Zhi. Although this is a point in the solar calendar, it was celebrated in Mountainstreet as 'little new year' (*xiao guo nian*). The main activity of the day was making small, sweet rice balls of red and of white, the colours of the two kinds of ritual, those associated with life (red) and those associated with death (white). Families in mourning only make white rice balls.

The name for rice balls is *yuan-zi (i:-a* in Taiwanese), and many took them to stand for the completing of the family, by coming together at New Year, because *yuan* means complete. They are also eaten at weddings.

Some households who made sweet rice balls still followed the custom, more prevalent in the past, of sticking them to all distinct parts of the house and its furnishings, as well as offering them in the morning after the longest night to the Locality God in his shrine and to gods and ancestors on domestic altars.

As I was discussing the making of sweet rice balls on 21 December 1966 with Dr G in the lobby outside his surgery, a vigorous old man who ran a fruit stall further down the street came in and told this story.

> The sweet rice balls stand for good farming. And they are put on every part of the house and every piece of furniture. Everything has its spirit (*shen*). They are offered to all *shen* except for the Fire *shen*. He is a bad one. He went to see the God of Heaven to report that the common people are wicked and wasteful. The God of Heaven was angry and ordered that the people should die on the last day of the year. But the kitchen Stove God and the Locality God reported to the God of Heaven that the people were not bad. So the God of Heaven sent a *shen* to investigate.

'Which *shen* was sent?' I asked. 'The Immortal God [the god in the newer of Mountainstreet temple's two halls]. He returned to the God of Heaven.' 'When?'

> On the 26th of the last month. He said that the Fire *shen's* report was false. But on the night of the last day, expecting to die, people put on beautiful clothes and ate a lot of food, and families gathered together to die together. They went to sleep. Next morning they woke up and found themselves alive. It was daylight. Others were alive too. So when they met each other they said 'congratulations'.

Dr G commented that this story was well known to anyone over the age of 50.

According to Robert Chard, current observances of the Stove God in southern China are the successors to a Fire God cult, the modern observances being in place by southern Song times (1127–1278). In various texts, most of them with strong Daoist connections, the Stove God is pictured as a recorder of good and evil, overseer of the proper rites of thanks and atonement, compassionate preserver of fire after a cold wind blew out the sun; saviour from inspectors who put signs on houses to be destroyed. But there is also a story, told in Taiwan, where he is known as the Lamp Monkey. The Lamp Monkey was so filthy humans despised him. Enraged by this, he reported to the Emperor that humans were utterly criminal and deserved destruction (Chard 1990).

Intercession to prevent a bad report and the ensuing imperial punishment is the theme of stories told elsewhere in Taiwan for the New Year season. The version recorded by Saso from a temple storyteller and from printed versions, specifies the crime of the people as being lack of filial recognition of duties, not being *xiao*, and adds that the common people knew of the tour of inspection and made sure that all was sweetness and propriety during the period of the tour (Saso 1965:37).

This is reminiscent of stories from other parts of China, in which sweet things are pasted on the mouth of the kitchen Stove God, when he and all the other deities are seen off for their reports to Heaven, on the 24th of the last month. The Stove God in these versions combines the potentially condemning reporter and the investigator who reports good things. The 24th is often named 'small new year', which in Mountainstreet was the name given to the winter solstice.

One version of this story was told to Fei Xiaotong in the late 1930s in Kaixiangong, a village in the Yangze delta. In this version the kitchen Stove God is an agent of a foreign occupation, billetted upon the household as an inspector. In Kaixiangong sticky rice was fed to the Stove God on the last day of the year. It was done in guilty memory of a decision to make this the day when everyone gagged their inspector and killed him, silently. Fearing the revenge of the spirit's soldiers, they now continue to make offerings to the inspector as the Stove God (Fei Hsiao-tung 1939:101–2).

A similar myth is re-told on the occasion of the Lantern Festival, last day of the New Year season, where the foreign power is the Mongol dynasty and the result is the restoration of a Chinese dynasty, the Ming (Eberhard 1958:65). A version of the same myth of simultaneous uprising against a foreign inspector installed by the Mongol dynasty was told in Beijing, though the occasion was the Autumn festival of the fifteenth day of the eighth lunar month (Cormack 1935). But these are, I think, loyalist glosses, heightening what is already there in the ambivalent Stove God stories of imperial power.

These stories tell two tales: 1. restoration of rule in which filial duty is recognised; 2. saved by defensive strategy from a vengeful and potentially destructive, and alien, power. The same cosmos, the same deities and the same symbols used in popular rites bear either version. But the second version is heterodox, and comes only from the common people. This version describes a command hierarchy and the strategy of keeping territorial and household boundaries safe. In Mountainstreet, at New Year, not only is the Locality God honoured with gold, but demons at bridges, paths and crossing points are propitiated with silver.

It should be possible to explore this ambivalence extensively, because the militaristic version is uppermost in local temple cults of military deities and their processions, represented by the pair of generals referred to singularly as The God or The Statue in the older hall of Mountainstreet's temple. Alongside them is the profession of virtue and the restoration of a rule of just recognition and reward, represented by the Immortal God of the newer hall of Mountainstreet's temple.

# Chapter Three

# Official and local cults

First I need to explore the command hierarchy through the institution itself of territorial cults and local procession festivals.

A procession festival, though often focused on a temple, is essentially a territorial tour of boundaries at whose centre an altar is set up. At the altar recompense is offered and petition is made for the peace and security of the area.

The image and incense-burner of a territorial cult may or may not be housed in a permanent shrine. But a territorial cult, celebrated on fixed occasions in a local calendar was, I think, a feature of social life throughout China until civil policies of republican governments began to transform or suppress them. So too was the tour of boundaries by procession.

Territorial cult festivals are often called 'temple fairs' (*miaohui*) – or, more fully, 'competitive procession assemblies for greeting spirits' (*yingshen saihui*). Other temple fairs occurred at centres of pilgrimage, remote from the settlements of normal residence. The festivals with which I am concerned are those which occurred within villages, towns and cities. Evidence of territorial temple fairs of this kind from several provinces in central and coastal China from the twelfth to the twentieth centuries has been collected from local records by Wu Cheng-han (1988). They included not only processions, the display of martial arts and musical bands, but also the holding of feasts and the performances of plays, and they were financed by local contributions collected from households in the locality. The gods they celebrated were guardians of a territory larger than that of the small neighbourhoods marked by the low, shed-like shrines of the lowest level of Locality Gods (Tudi Gong). But the Locality Gods were sometimes themselves, without further name or title but at the next higher levels of territorial inclusion, very often foci of temple fairs or processions, or else they were hosts for the visit to a village in the tour

63

of a plague or rain god or simply a more powerful guardian against ghosts and demons.

Occasions of relative relaxation in the agrarian cycle of work, even coinciding with points in the calendar marked for other kinds of ritual assembly, such as the Spring Festival, may also have been occasions for the celebration of a territorial cult, with or without procession. The Spring Festival may indeed have been the main season for the celebration of local, territorial cults in northern China. Writing of a village music association in the northern Chinese province of Hebei, two musicologists note that 'In the old times, Qujiaying's important occasions for the performance of orthodox-style music were of five kinds'. These were: 1. lunar new year temple tour; 2. going to fairs to pay obeisance at temples; 3. seeking rain in droughts; 4. commemorating the Master of Vastness (a local deity) and entertaining spirits generally (at the Seventh Month festival of Ghosts); 5. funerals. This is what they say about the new year occasion which was a village procession:

> In the past there were seven large and small temples in the village, in which were enshrined deities, most of which came from the *Enfeoffment of the Spirits*, the *Journey to the West*, and other Ming and Qing dynasty stories and records of strange things. They included a Military Spirit Temple, a Three Passes Temple, a Temple to the King of Purgatory, a Dragon God Temple, a Lying-down Goddess of Mercy Temple, and others. The most important use of these temples was for villagers' prayers to avert calamity and bring good fortune; if in any family someone wanted, they could go to the temple, select a deity and pay obeisance, burn incense and make a pledge. Since normally there were no ceremonies of collective offerings, on the first day of the first month each year the Music Association represented the wishes of the whole village by touring and performing for the pleasure of the deities of each temple, praying for good fortune and to redeem pledges, and this was called 'touring the temples'. (Xue Yibing and Wu Ben 1987:2, 89)[1]

A procession festival may have any deity at its centre. The local cult to the deity which becomes the object of its territorial festival will have started in various ways: as a cult favoured by a particular household on its domestic altar, as the inspirer of a spirit medium, as the ghosts or their guardian in a shrine to the forgotten dead, as an off-shoot of a famous temple in the home of a new settler, as the guardian of a trade which has started in the area, as the chosen deity of a local defence association, or the inspiration of a spirit-writing association, either of which may have been part of a larger network of such associations and its deity. But in every place, there would, if I am right, be one or more cults which, starting in any of these ways, had become the focus of an area-bounding festival and acquired a reference which is simply territorial. Such a cult will co-exist with others which remain those of an association, specialist, pietic, or exclusive to a family or surname group. The cult which has become territorial will have become inclusive of all established residences within the territory, even if some households have more exclusive claims to it because of the origins of the cult.

An institution inclusive of all established households within territorial boundaries: does this not smack of the state, or at least of imperial sovereignty? That is certainly one good reason to concentrate on territorial cults for an exploration of the command hierarchy and the political metaphor which Chinese deities, whether they be centres of territorial cults or not, so often present. All the more so if I am right to contend that the whole landscape of the Chinese empire was divided into territorial cults.

## IMPERIAL CONTROL

One evidently empire-wide set of territorial cults were those included in the official rites of the imperial hierarchy itself. The question is: are territorial cults beyond the administrative cities merely replicas of the same imperial hierarchy?

The official, imperial cults were organised as part of the territorial division of the empire, centred on administrative cities down through provinces and prefectures to counties. The objects of the imperial cults were meant to include everything below the level of the county. At each level of the official hierarchy there were, outside the walls of each administrative city, altars to objects which were equivalents of the emperor's own prerogatives: heaven and earth, rivers, mountains, winds, rain, grain. Below the imperial capital, there were the local rivers, mountains, rain and winds, and two altars which had a particular standing in relation to subcounty territorial cults. One was for an impersonal object, the Altar for Local Land and Grain (She Ji Tan). The other was for the ghosts located there, the Altar for Those-who-died-without-future (Li Tan). Tablets of carved and inscribed wood, naming each of these categories were kept in the temple of the administrative city's Wall and Moat (City) God temple. They were taken out of the city to the altars on the prescribed days for their rites.

Histories, which is to say classifications, lists, chronologies, and comments on official and popular cults at the lower levels of official administration are contained in what are called 'area records' (*fang zhi*). These local historical records compiled by the *literati*, the educated elite of the locality, celebrated the worthy and corrected the errant. They recorded official ceremony and, in other sections, local customs which were of interest for their ancient pedigree or for the danger of their heterodoxy. Area records were a means of exerting moral control, as a return to ancient ways, while at the same time they recorded official imperial adaptations to the emergence of newly popular cults of responsive spirits. As we shall see, many of these popular cults concerned ghosts and demons, which area records were concerned to re-define as *li*.

*Li* is the more classical rendering of what in common speech were and are called 'orphan souls' (*gu-hun*). But *li* also means 'severe discipline', and this seems to me to be no coincidence, for the *li* are, according to the local histories and the official cults, under the discipline of the Wall-and-Moat God. He is referred to as the equivalent in the *yin* world of spirits to the imperial magistrate in the visible and living *yang* world. The general term for spirits of the dead and for demons, used both in the records and in common parlance, is *gui*. It can refer either to the ghosts of human souls (*hun*) or to natural malign influences which have no incumbent human spirit The former become spirit-ghosts (*shen-gui*) when honoured by their descendants, and thus have a future, as ancestors. But without such honour, they are closely attached to the locality's natural features, and are potentially malign. Either as ancestors or as remembered *gui*, spirits become spiritually-bright (*shen-ming*) if as honoured ghosts the memory of their life-time virtues was deemed influential and exemplary in the more strictly memorialising official cults.

Officially sanctioned cults might also memorialise and offer rites of paying returns (*bao*) not only to the virtuous deeds of a lifetime, but also to the benign effects of spirits after death. But this was still a ritual of celebration and evocation. The non-official, popular cults, on the other hand look as much to promised as to proven and exemplary effects; their main rites are to gain response to petition, which is to say to the promise of recompense for favours to be granted. In any case, here, at the lowest level of official cults where the God of Walls and Moats was ranked, there was evidently, as recorded in the local histories, some accommodation to the popular belief that the honoured dead have, after death, a manifest power to perform miracles of general blessing, such as saving the life of an emperor or an official.

Inside the walls of the administrative city there were also official commemorative tablets celebrating civil (Wen) and military (Wu) exemplars. These were housed not in a Wall and Moat temple but in a temple often called the Wen Miao (Temple of Cultivated Accomplishment), and the rites of their annual commemoration were exclusively attended by holders of official rank. The official temple to the city's Wall and Moat God in contrast, was shared with the city's populace. Furthermore, it was presumed in the histories written by those educated to the point of ranked literate accomplishment (*wen*), that beyond the administrative capitals each locality would have its own two shrines for the locality as the county capital had: one for land (*she*) where its soil and grain spirit (*tu-gu shen*) would be worshipped and another for its unworshipped dead (*li*), both overseen by the local City God.

This at the very least indicates the imperial universality of a pairing of local guardian and care for ghosts, which in the imperial interpretation was a celebration of order and filial charity. But recall that this was a disciplinary interpretation, that the City God was itself a disciplinary institution within which the tensions between popular and official interpretations were contained.

We may assume that what the *literati* described as *she* or *tu-gu shen* and as *li* were, respectively, the small shrines to the Locality God and similar small shrines to lost, uncared-for souls. The Locality God shrines in the Pearl River region, Guangdong province, were in many cases called land – *she* - shrines, and villages centred on these shrines were themselves referred to as *she*. But they may also have been meant to cover larger local temples, if only to control their cults by counterposing to them the official rites to land and grain. The Pearl River *she* were the base territorial units for township procession festivals (Siu 1989:78). So, for instance, the area record for Foshan township, in Guangdong province, prescribed the performance of spring and autumn rites for land and grain in every neighbourhood of a hundred households in which those with official authority read the imperial edict and encouraged villagers to help the poor and respect age and rank. The passage ends with a recommendation to officials that they 'use the gods to assemble the people, and to demonstrate the rules. This may be a good way to improve the customs and traditions' (Yang 1961:98–9, quoting the 1923 edition of the area record).

Evidently this was part of the system of imperial surveillance and registration best known as *baojia*, which one Qing dynasty scholar called 'the use of the art of war to control the people' (see Dutton 1988:198). 'Using the gods' suggests not only control, but also a counteridentification of what both the controllers and the controlled call gods. But in this case, counteridentification was by means of establishing corrective institutions alongside the institutions to be controlled, whereas in other instances, to be considered later, the control was by adoption and counteridentification of the same institution, a popular cult. In both, the official task was to control popular cults with their centres in villages, towns and cities which were not administrative capitals.

## THE VILLAGE PACT AND TEMPLES OF THE LOCAL ELITE

Control (*ge*) by means of a juxtaposed example was a correction of meanings by the celebration of spring and autumn rites which cultivated moral example and were backed by such powers of punishment as the imperial regime could assert. Moral example was set by the performance of rites in which good conduct was not only preached and honoured, but in which distribution of food in crises, establishment of schools, building of bridges and maintenance of paths, and care for orphaned children, destitute old, and crippled people were encouraged by a call for alms from the households in each unit of registration. Non-registration was punishable by the erasing of unregistered households, the catastrophic act of imperial wrath against conspiracy (Dutton 1988:209), causing an increase in the population of local ghosts without a future.

The *baojia* was a system of household registration, which qualified the registered for emergency relief from state granaries. It worked by means of the appointment of local elders as heads of artificially defined sets of households for registration. Registration was the instrument for tax collection and labour requisitioning by the county magistrate's agents, so-called *yamen* runners. It was also an organisation of mutual surveillance and for the reporting of unregistered and unpermitted travellers.

Dutton has argued convincingly that what lay beyond the frequent historian's assessment of the failure of this system and the as-frequent acknowledgement of its persistence in every dynasty of the Chinese empire, was a strategy of moral control and surveillance. Regrets of its failure by imperial historians were exhortations to revive or strengthen it. Modern historians are wrong to take these records at face value, and to concur that *baojia* was a failure. They point to the units of registration being artificial, never becoming rooted in a continuous establishment of residential organisation. But Dutton observes that *baojia* deliberately cut across natural settlements, for its operation was that of moral control and occasional, terrible, correction. In any case, the *baojia* units did in places merge with units of local settlement and political organisation (Duara 1988:101ff). Perhaps this merging was a truer measure of their failure.

The hundreds of households were, as Dutton points out, never meant to become rooted in everyday social life. On the contrary, they were units which could not, as the natural ones of family and local settlement could, become units of threat to imperial rule. They were to prevent the unities of ancestral line or of locality from erupting into the violent disorder which would disgrace the county magistrate of the emperor's peace.

One of the corrective rites prescribed as part of the system of *baojia* was a reading of what was called the village pact (*xiang yue*). The unit (*xiang*) although usually translated 'village' was usually a great deal larger than a a single natural settlement. It was an administrative division of the imperial magistrate's 'county' (*xian*), possibly larger even than the area covered by a standard market town.

According to a Ming dynasty diagram reproduced in Dutton (1988:2 13), the setting of the rite was a closely prescribed arrangement of positions before a narrow platform upon which stood a tablet inscribed with a short edict of rules of proper conduct. In order of precedence, they were filial duty to parents, honouring elders and superiors, harmony in relations with neighbours, instilling discipline in sons and grandsons, peaceful conduct of work for livelihood, and being without error and evil. Beside this inscription, in the superior position to its east, was another tablet on which was inscribed 'The cardinal guides and laws of the spiritual lights of heaven and earth' (*tiandi shenming ji gen fadu*). Perhaps that was where the Spirit of Land and Grain would be placed, according to the writer of the Foshan gazetteer some centuries later. On the table in front of these tablets were placed registers of virtue and of error, and behind them knelt praiseworthy and blameworthy people, flanked by groups of the mass of ordinary members of the pact unit.

This Ming dynasty prescription was re-published in 1892, to show the proper form of corrective ceremonies of mutual surveillance. It was a guide to the local leaders who were recruited below the paid imperial administration and placed alongside and obliquely across the territorial boundaries of popular local cults.

The pact united the households of a rural territory made of a number of overlapping units of five households with the central household being the object of surveillance of the surrounding four. As Dutton describes it

> From this surveillance, neighbourhood reports would be written up and on the fifteenth of every [lunar] month a meeting would be called which had, as one of its functions, the discussion of reports. These meetings would be led by an elected 'pact head', the *yuezheng*, and he would be aided in his duties by two deputies called *fuyue*, and by a pact historian and an official called the *zhiyue*. ... [The organisational details and the titles varied according to place and dynasty in the life of this institution.] It was the task of the *zhiyue* to read aloud the pact at each monthly meeting. This reading would be followed by speeches from the head and his deputies. Following this the good and bad deeds of a family as reported by neighbours would then be commented upon, and the information, following verification, would then be passed on. (Dutton 1988:212)

A village register, after verification at the monthly reading of the pact, was evidently an extension and a source of an area's records (*fang zhi*) and of the celebration of local worthies centred on the administrative capital's Temple of Civil Accomplishment (Wen Miao).

This model was interpreted variously. It was probably implemented only at periods of administrative zeal. But it was a very long-standing framework of implementable moral surveillance.

The village pact (*xiangyue*) was not simply an institution of ritual and moral education. By late imperial times it had also become an inter-village council which served as a police court, functioning under the shadow of the magistrate's county seat, a means of settling inter-village disputes, and for the organisation of local defence militia (*tuanlian*). In this court suspects were arraigned, not by the county's runners but by locally hired constables and militia raised by local patrons. These patrons were the local gentry and the local wealthy who acted as intermediaries between the common people and the officials in the county capital.

The places in which the *xiangyue* meetings were held may either have been organised strictly along the lines of the Ming dynasty prescription in buildings called halls (*tang*), or they may more loosely have been held in gentry-sponsored temples (*ci* or *miao*) as they were in the part of Xin'an county studied by Michael Palmer. Here the temple was dedicated to the two governors of Guangdong province who had served the people. In the seventeenth century when the imperial garrisons forcibly removed coastal villagers inland to clear the coast and remove sustenance for pirate brigands and opponents of the new dynasty, the two governors successfully petitioned the emperor to allow the villagers to return to their villages on the coast. In gratitude for this return and to commemorate the intercession for imperial clemency, the temple was built by a subscription raised by local gentry with the encouragement, if not the order, of imperial officials. It served not only as a place for the meetings of the *xiangyue*, including ceremonies for the honouring of the two governors, but also as a place open to common people for their forms of worship. Thus it contained both the exclusive ceremonies and literary competitions appropriate to officialdom, and the organisation of militia which could accompany the festival processions of the common people, centred on the same cult of the two governors. A similar temple in another part of the Pearl River region honoured with official inscriptions, which also had a shrine to one of these two governors and was similarly sponsored by local merchants and gentry, was the focus of an annual procession festival (Siu 1989:79ff).

The Temple of the Two Governors in Stone Lake Market is typical of a range of sub-official temples sponsored by local elites for their exclusive rites, banquets, and meetings, as well as for occasions when their rites were attended by the common people, for instructive veneration of the virtuous.

The official rites and those conducted at these local temples of the elite, were ordered and led quite differently from those of popular territorial festivals even when focused on the same temple. The popular festivals were minor versions of the great purification ceremony conducted by Daoists, and called a *jiao*. The official and elite rites were those described in local gazetteers and in the imperial codes of ritual for honouring the virtuous. These were the rites of *shidian*, which could be translated as 'instructive veneration'.

In both kinds of rite there were experts who guided the rest of the participants. And in both there were among the participants some who took leading parts and others who were generally passive. In the *shidian*, the ritual experts were members of the local directorate of education and teachers at the school. Their role was to stand on either side of the chief celebrants and guide them from their appointed places to wherever the rites demanded they be, there handing them the proper offerings and announcing the proper number of kneels and kowtows they were to perform. In the *jiao*, the ritual experts were Daoist religious practitioners. They performed all the rites themselves, the leading participants delegating to them even the presentation of offerings and merely standing behind them, holding incense and bowing and kneeling when signalled by the priests to do so.

The knowledge that the experts in the official religion had was qualitatively no different from that of the rest of the participants. They were set apart from the other participants only to the extent that specialists in one branch of government were different from specialists in another. Neither did the ceremony itself remove the leading from the other participants. The leading participants led by virtue of their rank, which had been established outside the ceremony. The knowledge of the Daoists, on the other hand, was gained only after a rite of passage that initiated them to a more sacred status than that of the rest of the population. Their knowledge was esoteric, and at points in the ceremony they addressed those patron deities through whom their knowledge was revealed, deities whose worship was not shared by the other participants. And the ceremony itself gave the leading participants a more protected and more sanctified status than it gave the rest.

On the other hand, for the *jiao* everyone in the temple's region had to be ritually clean, whereas for the *shidian* only the leading participants needed to be. In the *jiao* everyone made offerings outside the temple and in their homes, while the leading participants witnessed the presentation of offerings in the temple itself.

The precautions for the *shidian* fast were read out in ceremony to the leading participants and guides three days before the main ritual:

> There will be one communal fast when they [the leading participants] will lodge together in the fasting house thinking of the *shen* [in this case Confucius]. They will think of the *shen's* eating and drinking, the *shen's* residence, the *shen's* laughter and talk, the *shen's* will, whatever the *shen* enjoyed, the *shen's* occupations and tastes. Each will purify his own mind and be the more reverent and discreet and care for the precautions.

The climax to this meditation came on the main day of the ceremony when the great gate of the temple was opened and the *shen* welcomed to the august rites and the munificent offerings.

There is a core ceremony of showing respect that was common to both *shidian* and *jiao*, just as the kowtow and other gestures of deference are common to all Chinese culture. This core is the *sanjue li* – the triple offering of wine. But the *shidian* and the *jiao* differed in their elaborations of this rite, in the contexts in which they set it, in the beings respected, and in the wordings of the eulogies and texts read, and the music played.

Within the official religion itself, elaboration of the *sanjue li* differed according to the being addressed. There were minutely specified differences in the amount of offerings, music and obeisance required and in who constituted the proper worshippers. The official pantheon was divided largely into three levels of ritual importance. Within these levels the gods were again kept distinct by finer ritual prescriptions, such as those for the measurements of their altars, the positions of their tablets on the altars and the number of steps up to the altar. When there was more than one god in a single temple or ceremony, the gods were ritually ranked by whether they were housed in the back or front shrines, or by whether they received as animal offerings *shao lao* (which was without an ox) or *tai lao* (with an ox). Ceremonial statutes (*sidian*) defined which gods were to be worshipped by whom and at what time and place.

The *jiao*, in contrast, meant setting at the centre of a region a ritual area that was movable and the same wherever the priests took it. It consisted of the Daoist pantheon of cosmic forces and deities superimposed on whatever the *shenming* and *gui* of the local temples happened to be. In other words, it was the whole structure every time and not an exclusive part of it. The *jiao* was a purification of the region: the gods were called upon to protect it and to act as mediators to greater powers, and the ghosts were fed to keep them away from it. *Shidian* was rank-specific, whereas *jiao* was place-specific. Both evoked a universe, but in the *jiao* the Daoist becomes a sage and each *jiao* represents the macrocosm. *Shidian* was of rank in a hierarchy so that only when it reached the emperor himself was there a full vision of the cosmic order of heaven and earth, linked by the emperor-sage.

The emperor's birthday was itself celebrated with grand *shidian* rites very similar to those for Confucius, rehearsed, as were Confucius's rites, within the Wen Miao complex in the Ming Lun Tang and performed in a Longevity Hall that was in all respects like a temple. On New Year's day (lunar) and at the winter solstice the emperor himself in the imperial capital worshipped heaven and his own ancestors, while simultaneously in the provinces the same rites as those for the emperor's birthday were performed in the local city's Ming Lun Tang. Receiving the orders of the emperor in the provinces involved going out into the eastern suburb to welcome them, as spring was welcomed in the same suburb at the vernal equinox.

> We must welcome the spring in the eastern suburb because the people rely on it, and present the military banners in the west drillyard so that confusion and evil can be suppressed before it rises. It cannot be said that the rites (*li*) were invented today. We are following ancient practices

says the introduction to the record of ceremonial (*jisi*) in the area record for Taiwan *xian* of 1721.

A lesser form of *shidian*, called *shicai* was performed on the first and fifteenth of the month at the school-temple, the Wen Miao. According to a handbook, it was also performed in weddings at the visit to the bride's family, and in funerals at the viewing of the dressed corpse. Worship in ancestral temples was also, as I have observed it, a lesser form of *shidian*.

There appear, then, to be two sets of ritual. The one is kin ritual, memorialism, officials, and tablets. The other is god ritual, magic, priests, and images. To ignore these differences, or to note only the similarities between official and popular territorial cults and rituals (as does, for instance, Duara 1988:136), is to miss out the drama of their juxtaposition in Chinese religious and political life. The two could occur at the same ritual occasion or be separated by performance at different occasions or in different temples. Festivals of processions and *jiao* could include more exclusive performances of *shidian* or *shicai* for those with patron status. In the areas of southeastern China dominated by local lineage corporations, the dominant local lineage sponsored the township temples' procession festivals which were inclusive of all residents whatever their surname (Siu 1989:47–8, 53). Their exclusive ceremonies were held at their own ancestral halls. But the properties and fees commanded by both kinds of temples, ancestral halls and locality temples, were controlled by local merchants and gentry or the strong-men who managed their estates for them, and they would have more exclusive aspirations to official status marked by *shidian* or *shicai* ceremonies.

## THE CITY GOD, CONTROLLER OF DEMONS

The tablets (*pai*) for the administrative capital's Land and Grain Altar and the local Unworshipped Dead were stored in the city's Wall and

The City God in procession, republican Taiwan, October 1966. Even after the demise of the imperial cults, the City God continues as a popular cult in Taibei city. This is the City God at the level of the province of Taiwan, with Taibei as its capital. The figure is robed, bearded and solemn in a sedan chair decked with wreaths of honour for his annual procession of the centre of the city.

Moat (City) God temple. In the cult of the City God itself, instead of being counterposed, the corrective rites coincided in the same temple with popular rites to the same deity. The use of the gods here was direct, a reflection back on to the common people of the harsh disciplinary control of ghosts implied by the name of the altar for the unworshipped dead outside the walls.

As Wall and Moat, the object was impersonal, or as the ultra-cultivated magistrate of Wei county in Shandong wrote in 1752, to commemorate the completion of his refurbishment of the City God temple there:

> although titled, [Wall and Moat, along with Heaven, Earth, Sun, Moon, Wind, Mountains, Rivers, Thunder, Land and Grain, Well, and Stove] have no personal existence and should not be offered sacrifices as though they had.

But the people do, so, as I have already noted, he sought to avoid sensate and immediate address to these personalised forces, and advised that the performance of theatre put on for the City God be 'about ancient times, instructive, and prohibiting the low, clandestine, vulgar and grosser passions' (McCartee 1869–70).

As part of the state cults, Wall and Moat was represented by a tablet, not a statue. Yet as a popular deity used by the local official, an image (*xiang*) may often have been officially donated, as it was in 1445 by the prefect of Ningbo, in Zhejiang province (*Ningbo Eu Zhi* 1733 (Tanmiao section)). There is no point in guessing whether such a magistrate was making a concession to others' beliefs, whether he was using those beliefs cynically, whether the others' beliefs were themselves sincere, or not. The City God was a point of symbolic negotiation between popular and official cults. For the official, the attitude often described in relation to the popular spirits was one of *ge:* influence, investigation and limit or correction. For the commoner, the attitude was one of fear of the ghosts which the City God controlled, and of petition for favourable responses to the Wall and Moat God's fellows in a personalised universe.

The City God as a personalised deity was not only popularly believed to be a magistrate of the ghost world. This belief was acted upon and ritualised by imperial magistrates themselves to strike fear into miscreants and even to discover them. As the 1788 edition of the gazetteer for the county of Yin, capital of Ningbo prefecture in Zhejiang province, noted:

All the old regulations order officials when they [first] come to attend the people [i.e. take up the office of magistrate], to fast and lodge [in the City God temple], and offer meats to the spirit, swearing: 'If I govern disrespectfully, am crafty or avaricious, get my colleagues into trouble, or oppress the people, may the spirit send down misfortune [upon me] for three years.'

A similar oath was sworn when going to report to the emperor and when leaving office. In commemoration of this City God, the gazetteer continues with the following account of the other rites in which the City God was the host or master.

For the annual offerings to the local unworshipped dead (*li*) the spirit is again welcomed to be host. The offerings are not as abundant as they are for the spring and autumn rites for Land and Grain, Mountains and Rivers. But the ceremonials (*sidian*) are [always] abundant and the spiritual power (*shenling*) magnificently manifest. Pray and he responds (*yinggan*) throughout the year. When rain is inclement, people have to grieve [as in mourning] to the spirit and the spirit will bring luck to the people munificently. ('Tanmiao', *Yin xianzhi* 1788, Ch. 7 p. 5 *verso*, column 9)

Of all the natural or impersonal spirits in the official rites, the Wall and Moat spirit straddled the living world of land and grain, mountains and rivers addressed at their altars, and the world of ghosts. Other official cults celebrated the exemplary, bright spirits, historicising and commemorating their illustration of ancient virtues. But the City God cult was the point where the hierarchy of regulation, the status group of officials and those who aspired to it, joined the hierarchy of demonic command and response usually considered a popular, customary aberration. The oath quoted in an inscription of 1810 in the Taiwanese county of Zhanghua begs the spirit to help control what is beyond the ears and eyes of the magistrate. This was not unusual (see Hsiao 1960, Ch. 6, notes 193 and 197).

In the rain ceremony, the image of the City God was taken on parade. Where there was such a cult, a figure of the Dragon King accompanied the City God. Like the parade of the spring ox at its annual whipping and dismemberment, officials went in procession with the City God, and used what they otherwise condemned as part of their official duties of control and supervision. The City

God had to be exposed to the parching heat until Heaven (Tian) was moved to provide seasonal rain. In the same way Dragon King figures were neglected, their paint faded and peeling, if they lacked the power to respond or gain response to end a drought (Duara 1988:283, note 55).

Officials relied on the City God and Dragon King cults for their official duties to prevent calamity and keep order. The area record for Yin county gives this text for a memorial to be addressed to the spirit of Wall and Moat in official ceremonies. It was composed in 1447.

> You have your officers, Wall and Moat,
> On whom the people depend, for protection and defence.
> The Court commands, the officials administer:
> The oath to you, Yang mirroring Yin;
> If we are pure and bright, you bestow good luck;
> If we are covetous and dark, you administer misfortune.
> The ceremonials are lustrous, boundless as the empire;
> Offerings of meats, libations of wine;
> Come and taste, come and drink.
> Seasonal rain, seasonal shine; the year's crops flourish and abound.
> Chase off disease; people live long.
> Officials administer, rank and position gleam;
> The military stand guard, martial awe prevails;
> Throughout the years, the happiness you bring never ends.
> (*Yin xianzhi*)

Zito quotes the account by an imperial magistrate, Wang Huizu (1731–1807), of how he successfully prosecuted a case. Wang transferred his hearing of a murder trial to the City God temple. There he burned incense. Immediately, the culprit burst in and confessed, saying he had been lured there by a black demon. The magistrate records how he then offered thanks to the City God, not so much for his obvious efficacy but for the speed with which he had acted (Zito 1987: 335; see also Balazs 1965).

Another magistrate's handbook advises his fellows thus:

> The district magistrate governs the visible, the City God the invisible. Generating benefit and warding off harm for the people are duties of the magistrate. Bringing down blessings and warding off natural disaster are the duties of the City God.

According to this handbook,

Spirits are efficacious because of their connection with people. Sacrifice, through integrity leads to knowledge. The invisible is made apparent [by means of effort in] the manifest world. Therefore those who govern people of the cities must pay their respects to the spirits, and the spirits will respond. (Zito's 1987 translations: 341–2)

The City God cult was one of the oldest and most widespread of popular cults. It may have been a model for incorporating others into the official rites.[2] It might also have been a model for territorial cults. But moving on to consider these, in particular their processions, we approach the local version and will see what was joined and controlled from above through the City God cult.

## THE TERRITORIAL PROCESSION

If a full calendar of the City God were kept, it would have been taken in procession four times a year, every time followed by penitents wearing instruments of punishment and accompanied by demon masqueradors (Zito 1987: 355, 357). One of the hall-marks of commoner territorial cults is a procession described as a tour of the boundaries (you jing). These occur at annual occasions (nian li), and in Taiwan used frequently also to be organised for the seventh-month propitiation of orphan souls and at the first month's Lantern Festival.

Every procession is headed by a figure who acts as the local territorial guardian or his underling, who warns or actually sweeps away the ghosts which may be loitering on the route. A broom is a frequent prop of a procession herald. He may be outlandishly dressed, a clown with pans and other clanking utensils hanging from his waistband, in which case he represents a jester and drummer colloquially known as The Old Boy (lao tong) or the Young Gentleman (lang jun ye) drawing demons to him and despatching them like Han Dan Ye does at the Lantern Festival in the old part of Taibei city. (See Schipper 1966.)

One of the other features of the tour of boundaries is a retinue, a band, playing instruments, demonstrating martial art, performing in masks or inside grotesque figures representing the Old Boy Jester or another figure of demon control. The martial arts are sponsored by patrons and displayed in the same way as are theatrical performances on these festivals. They are done for fun; they are also, as one member of a lion troupe said to me, 'putting ourselves at the service of the

Master Xie, demon and demon catcher, court runner of the spirit world – the oversize man-puppet in the retinue of the territorial guardian of Mengjia, one of the three main commercial centres of the city of Taibei. He is striding in martial honour of the deities in the biggest temple of Mengjia in front of the covered market, the main point in the procession from the territorial guardian god's own temple, on the 22nd of the tenth lunar month, 1967. Following Xie, his squat partner puppet, Fan performed the same strut of honour.

god'; and this act is one of command over demons – their capture or their dispersal – to cleanse the territory of their presence. Not surprisingly, the figures thus impersonated are often those which are also paraded in the processions of the City God.

There are two outsize puppet figures which are a stock-in-trade of the procession artistes and which accompany City God and other territorial gods' processions in Taiwan. They are a pair of loyal, martial friends called Fan and Xie. One of them is very tall and thin, with his tongue lolling out of a fierce but mournful face. He is coloured white. The other is round, short, and black. They are sometimes accompanied by militia bands wielding instruments of torture. As inquiry will elicit from the bandsmen or from onlookers, and indeed as a comic strip featuring Fan and Xie relates, these two were runners of a local magistrate's office. Their story is one of faithful friendship. They had made an appointment to meet by a stream. Xie got there first and waited. But there was a tremendous downpour. Xie waited faithfully in the arranged spot as the waters rose. Still his friend did not arrive. Loyal to the end, Xie waited until he was overwhelmed. Fan arrived to find him, black, swollen and drowned. In his guilt, Fan hanged himself, and so is white, stretched and with his tongue hanging long and red from his mouth. The drowned and suicides are two of the commonest figures of demonic haunting of waters and trees. But these two are also illustrations of the virtue of loyalty between friends. So they are portrayed, not as the guarded-against, but as guards, or rather as soldiers and servants of the guardian, shades of magistrate's runners, threatening detectives, with extraordinarily penetrating sight and hearing, reporting the deeds of the living for the records of the City God or other territorial guardians and capable of capturing and putting into irons the souls of miscreants after death. Other figures, variants of these qualities of martial strength, detection, and extraction of true records, are features of any procession of the boundaries, making it a patrol like the watch against thieves mounted in many villages by militia bands who in ritual perform for the guardian god.

As the regulatory harmony of virtuous conduct centred on the emperor, who stands for the unity and order of the terrestrial portion of the universe, reaches the lowest levels of imperial administration and goes beyond its personnel, it is transformed into an organisation of violence.

An obvious conclusion is that these portrayals are an extension of the functions of imperial control and surveillance into a popular

Reed-pipe (*suo-na*) players of the Mountainstreet band in the temple yard announcing the emergence of the figure of Ang Gong the township guardian god, 1966.

imagery of territorial definition and identification. Yet the actual imperial surveillance and control beyond the administrative City God was juxtaposed to, and designed to survey and control, among other things, precisely these popular territorial cults. Even in imperial times, these portrayals were not approved replicas of imperial power and official rites. This acute ambivalence comes out, forcefully, in an illustration from post-imperial times. In a North China county administrative capital, in 1937, rebels led by Communist activists used the capital's City God temple as a gathering point to rescue some villagers held in the Fire God temple. The Fire God temple, which had probably also been an official temple, was used by the police of the local Guomindang government as an interrogation and torture chamber. The assault by the City God rebels was the first step in establishing Communist government of this county (Thaxton 1983:153–4).

The rites of petition and command performed in procession festivals were quite separate and distinct from those of the officially favoured instructive veneration and recompense. If they replicated imperial power, it was the martial and the terrible aspect which they portrayed. But in this very replication they marked the boundaries and set the framework for local organisations of violence and defence which could become threats to imperial power.

Territoriality in the popular religion is the marking of the borders which distinguish inside from outside, protection from invasion, identified by locality guardians and orphan souls.

Old men sitting in the City God temple of Xinzhu in Taiwan would say to Michael Saso when he was inquiring about temple gods, that when there was no official government, the gods were our officials (personal communication from Saso). This may have been especially true of border regions and newly settled regions – and Taiwan was both. But remoteness from central control was to a great extent cultivated. Avoidance of officials on the part of the common people, and officials' valuing of a state of harmony which meant not being brought into the trouble which demanded their attentions, was true throughout China. Furthermore, new settlement could occur anywhere in China which had been devastated by flood, drought, the exaction of rents and taxes to the point of bondage and starvation, or the putting down of the resulting disorder.

On ordinary days temple grounds were places for exchanging information on the weather and prices, and where the old could spend the day telling stories and swapping gossip. In the Taihang region of

North China, as elsewhere, temple grounds were assembly points for work on common lands, including the temple lands (Thaxton 1983:8). But temples and their grounds were also places of muster for emergency action. In the Taihang region such emergency action included the quartering of militia bands of the Heavengate Association (Tianmen Hui) in Guan Di (God of War and Commerce) temples to resist tax collectors and protest against the hoarding of relief grains. Temples and festivals were themselves targetted for tax. Even more than those dedicated to Guan Di, who had officially been promoted to the highest level of the imperial cults, the temples and festivals to the saviour deity, Guanyin (Goddess of Mercy), whose cult had not been officially adopted, then became objects of contention between residents and local government.

In 1920 the tenants of one village in Shanxi province, called Qilipu, boycotted a Guanyin feast. Traditionally all had contributed to this feast. But the local landlord-and-tax-collector had taken over and provided the food from the exorbitant rents, fees and interest in kind which he had exacted. In 1927, the Guomindang government of the region rased several Guanyin temples in its suppression of the Heavengate Association. In 1941 the temple in Qilipu was used as the headquarters of its first peasant association and elected village government (Thaxton 1983:89, 141, 155–6).

## BEYOND CENTRAL ADMINISTRATION: *LING*

An incense-burner or, later, a festival and a temple, represented a form of self-organisation and defence. Incense is burned to communicate with an object into which *ling* (efficacy) has been imputed, or ritually injected as into a statue by the magic (*fa*) of dotting eyes and ears. Accuracy of response to the burning of incense confirms it. The circularity of a response that is already found is surely a quality of its already being imagined. In any case the metaphor is acted upon, it is performed: and performance of this communication is itself the organisation of an association.

Only when the object and image are conceived as a person are they *ling*. The White Tiger was dreaded even more than ghosts. But in Mountaintsreet it was never said to be *ling*. Neither were the gods of heaven. Only ghosts and the middle level of gods were *ling*. *Ling* seems, therefore, necessarily to include the conception of a past life. Invariably the account of that life records an extraordinary quality in the circumstances of her or his death – the achievement of immortality, self-sacrifice, being cut off before the span of life was spent, dying without having children. Beyond that, the same subject, being at the same time an historical person and a general force, can be identified at several points and named several times and in different eventualities. Each naming and location becomes a subject in its own right, its own *ling*.

Many, possibly most local temples' cults started in the confines of a domestic space. An incense sacklet or an incense-burner and an image on its owner's altar next to the space for the honouring of his ancestors can be the focus of a new reputation for efficacy (*ling*). The fortunes of the householder and the deference to the deity by which he registers those fortunes gain repute together. The relationship of deference is respect for the quality reputed. In Mountainstreet that quality was frequently called responsiveness (*gan* or *ying-gan*) or simply the extraordinary effectiveness (*ling*) manifested in response to correct deference.

*Ling* is also translated as extraordinary intelligence passed on through a transmission of experience. In such instances it describes the virtuosity of a master of some skill or knowledge being demonstrated and thus taught (Farquhar 1991). In the case of a deity, *ling* is not necessarily taught, but its effectiveness is transmitted in some manifestation of extraordinary or unexpected success or simply the avoidance of danger, actual or expected. *Ling* of a deity is also the power to cause that danger and inflict harm or extraordinary failures. The *ling* used to describe mastery of a skill acquired by art and discipline and passed on by demonstration and apprenticeship applies to many of the skills associated with temples: Daoist magical, liturgical, bodily and meditational knowledge; traditional medical knowledge; martial, theatrical and musical arts. It is not the same as *ling* describing the power of divine protection and intervention. But that both kinds of transmission are given the same name is I think instructive. The relationship of learning by apprenticeship, in which the bond of fellow-students is like that of siblings – whether or not segregated into brotherhoods and sisterhoods – describes the martial arts and the musical bands which make up a god's procession. It also describes the relationship among the initiates of a spirit-writing cult learning by direct scriptural revelation from one or more deities. On the other hand, they are bound in a deference to a master or a superior which can be so elaborate it requires an expert to perform it correctly. Just so, deference to a deity is performed by a ritual expert (usually a Daoist) in a territorial cult long after the deity's local *ling* was first celebrated.

There are several famous old temples in Taiwan dedicated to a female most commonly identified as Ma Zu. They are stops on organised tours and pilgrimages of the island. A number of Mountainstreet residents had been on these tours. They recounted going to the 'First, Second, Third Ma Zu', each a separate entity of the same name and associated with one past life. Either the temples or the figures in a single temple were counted and distinguished as separate points of *ling* in this way, much as a saint's cult is multiplied.

The past life of Ma Zu, transmitted verbally as a commonplace as well as in countless printed texts published by folklore organisations, historians, and the temples themselves, is that of a young woman, a seafarer's daughter located in Meizhou, Putian *xian*, Fujian province, who lived a virtuous and self-sacrificing life, but refused to marry, dying young and childless. Before she had died, so the myth goes, she had already demonstrated powers to guide seafarers through storms to safety by appearing as a beacon vision. Because of her nun-like purity the attributes of her images are often similar to those of Buddhist saviour deities, particularly the *bodhisattva* (male in India, feminised in China) called Guanyin, Goddess of Mercy. Other icons and versions of the myth give her fierce, war-like attributes capable of powerful defence of territories. These are male attributes. Yet other icons and versions of her death as a suicide and refusal to marry, identify her as a protector of women.

Since her cult was also adopted by the imperial state, another of her identities is that of high virtue in saving officials. In this version she is the child of gentry, not of an ordinary fisherman or boatman (Watson 1985).

Emigrants from Fujian consider her to be, as one person put it to me, an ancestral god (*zufu*) of Fujian people, even though she had no children. A god is in any case never known by personal and family name. But people identified with Fujian are more likely to know the deity which can be traced to this past life as Ma Zu (Great Mother). Others, such as the equally numerous followers in Guangdong of cults traced to the same past life, are more likely to know her by her imperial title, Tian Hou (Heavenly Concubine), but interpreted not as the virtuous daughter of gentry, nor as an unfilial daughter who refused to marry, but as a fierce defender of the territories of lineage villages.

References to the past life allow folkorists and historians to follow any of these manifestations down to an origin in an historical person, and to refer to the rest as legend. The practices of division of *ling* certainly make this a possibility, divesting the legend of all but a curious or an exemplary life and its myths. But this approach does not recognise the specificity which the temples and their festivals, the incense burners and their altars, have.

There are other grounds than scholarship or professional history for an attitude of condemnation of *ling*. For instance, a woman who had received some instruction as a lay Buddhist said:

> whether a god has power (*ling*) depends on our own sincerity. The two are mutual. When some people pay their respects (*bai*), it doesn't work. For others it does. When it works, well and good. One does not worship (*bai*) gods because of their power but because formerly they loved people and walked a straight road. The gods make unruly people behave.

Nevertheless she lived in the context of already established chains of the multiplication of *ling*.

The myths of *ling* complement local organisations around an incense burner. Conversely, what these organisations surround is the image of local power and its communication through incense.

In Taiwan, a procession, theatre, the sacrifice of pigs, their public display, and the ritual of petition and purification at the centre of this display, performed in front and on behalf of the representatives of the locality is the greatest occasion in the calendar. Its chief is the appointee to a post called Master of the Incense Burner (Lu Zhu). He is in charge of financing the festival and of managing its collective events. This management is in principle and usually also in fact separated from the building, or refurbishing, of temples and their properties. It may be focused on the same cults as are housed in temples, but it does not depend on the existence of a temple. All it requires is a local incense burner, which can be kept at other times on a domestic altar, its possession between each festival rotated through the households of the area.

In most small towns and large villages where such events are organised, a musical or a martial arts or a theatre troupe will have been formed particularly to perform at the local festival, but also in the hope of being invited to perform in the processions of neighbouring festivals. The same men would in the past have formed the local militia for crop-watching, for fire and night watches, or for acts of banditry in other territories, and in cities the martial arts performers frequently are now what are called *liu-mang*, organised brigands. In Mountainstreet, many of the band members were volunteer firefighters.

87

The procession often brings to a local incense burner the figure of a protector god from a temple in a more central place. This is the temple from whose incense burner ash was taken to inaugurate the new local temple in a ceremony called 'division of incense' (*fen xiang*). The very act of bringing a figure from a more central place defines the place to which it is brought, for it is met as it arrives at the boundary of the local temple's area and is paraded in a sedan chair on a tour of its boundaries and residences accompanying the figure taken from the local temple. After it has passed every household within the boundaries it is placed centrally and an altar is established before it for the ceremony of bringing peace and paying recompense. The visiting figure may not be that of the main local deity. It may be a rain-making or plague-exorcising deity, sharing the local temple's incense-burner.

The visiting figure enacts at the same time a link not only with a more central place and its territorial cult, but also a rivalrous identification with other localities who also invite a figure from the same temple. By celebrating the same cult, the residents of each are identifying themselves with each other and, by inviting each other to take part in feasts and the entertainment of the procession, displays of offerings and the theatrical performances in the afternoon and evening, they are also engaged in a competition to show the liveliness and prosperity, the reputation of their own territory.

Division of incense involves return for renewal of the link to the root incense burner. The fetching of an image from the root temple is a regular occasion for such a renewal, but there may be visits to an even more central incense burner, the root from which the immediate root incense was taken. Every such trip may be described as a pilgrimage. Sangren (1987) shows clearly that these hierarchies of pilgrimage constitute an organisation which cannot be reduced either to the structure of marketing and its central places or to the hierarchy of administrative capitals. Even though the central places of territorial cults are usually the central places of the marketing structure, and division of incense and visits of figures follow the routes of marketing, the largest, most famous centres are often primarily religious, such as the biggest centre in Taiwan of the Ma Zu cult in Beigang.

The principle of magical power (*ling*) whose intensity and historical authenticity is traced in the routes of pilgrimage to their high points does not concur with imperial state cults. *Ling* imagery and rituals appear to mimic imperial government, but its centres are not an extension of the state cults to places below the lowest level of imperial state administration.

Pilgrimage centres do not coincide with either the imperial or the republican administrative centres any more than they do with marketing centres. And the *ling* which protects the peace of a territory within the bounds of its festival defines itself directly in relation to its neighbours, not as a unit in a nested hierarchy.

Internally, within each procession territory, the rotation of the office of master of the incense-burner each year and for each procession festival is in effect a circulation of heads of households through a practical involvement in the knowledge conveyed by the performance of petition and purification through which a professional ritual expert takes him. The professional acts as a guide and as an intermediary with the invisible subjects of *ling*. To be master of the incense-burner is to be committed before the eyes of the community. In Mountainstreet some people believed the master to be in danger of his life, if he did not perform his duty of recompense adequately. Certainly there was a social pressure on him to provide, if necessary out of his household's purse, enough of a display of offerings to meet the dignity of the festival, god and place.

One of Mountainstreet's pharmacists told me that he did not make offerings on the day of the greatest of all procession festivals in Mountainstreet, the one which is organised every four years for the visit of a figure of Ma Zu from one of the centres of Ma Zu pilgrimage. The festival was a commemoration of the first visit when an image of her was brought to a nearby hamlet to rid its crops of a pestilence, and because a number of its inhabitants had been stone-masons in the construction of the root-temple from which she is taken, in Guandu. The pharmacist said it was nonsense to believe she could keep the land clear of pestilence. But he organised a feast on the festival, as did every other household because otherwise people would think he was strange or miserly. Similarly the appointed master of the incense-burner cannot refuse selection without breaking with the community, which would be either to leave it, or to become a Christian.

## FEASTING

A festival is an occasion for eating meat and drinking wine, to have a feast, not just a meal. It is the time when people plan to afford or go into debt to provide enough to be able to present their homes as host to guests, to eat with people beyond their most intimate social circle. Feasts are meals taken in the main room, not haphazardly in and out of the kitchen.

Just as it is difficult not to go to someone's feast when invited – and the more ostentatious hosts tour the town waylaying guests and almost forcing them physically to their tables – so it would be embarrassing not to be holding a feast to which they can be invited in return.

At no other times was the population of Mountainstreet so mobilised as on a procession festival day. The nearest equivalent was the quarterly meeting of household representatives called to discuss local government issues and projects. But they were perfunctorily and poorly attended.

Feasting is a recognised occasion for reinforcing commercial associations. A young man born in a hamlet above Mountainstreet but now working and living in his sister's husband's general store in Taibei said, with a generally sceptical attitude towards people's belief in the efficacy of ritual, that worship is only a formality. The important thing is that a festival is a day for inviting business associates and eating more than usual.

The feast, and the drinking of alcohol which marks a feast, are a formal means of association. Toasting formality completely governs the drinking of alcohol at feasts. No-one may drink unless he can induce another to drink with him. And he cannot induce another to drink with him until some disclosure or reminder about their social lives has been made and, best of all, a bond of identity has been established between them. The discovery of a mutual friend or a new bond of identity is the occasion for a new toast. Most common and basic among such bonds, each being the ground for seeking more specific bonds, are the sharing of a family name, the sharing of a place of birth or of ancestral origin, having attended the same school or college or military unit, or being in the same line of business, office or work. The very invitation to the feast assumes some such bond. Not to respond to an invitation is, as I was told by the mother of the school principal and someone who is perhaps more careful of formality than others, to deny relations of reciprocity with the host.

In festival feasting, the bond of the festival itself, between the people simultaneously feasting, is the base bond. The unit feasts, in each household, are an opportunity to enact additional bonds of other kinds above it. The integrity of the festival, of territorial, residential identity, is not expressed in the voluntary action of a host household inviting guests. It is represented, on the contrary, by the involuntary, from the individual household's point of view, social fact of all households in the area feasting at the same time. Over this unity are bound voluntary ties between household members within and, more so, beyond the festival area. The territorial unit, apart from being a mere aggregate of unit households feasting simultaneously, is manifest through their voluntary invitations by the fact that many guests are shared, and sought out by members of one household to be coaxed away from the tables of others, finally to attend as many as a dozen feasts in one evening.

The guests I noticed as having the largest numbers of feasts to attend were the wholesalers of goods that were retailed or accumulated in Mountainstreet, for instance the wholesaler of soft drinks or of rice or the buyers of tea and edible fungi, all from Taibei city. All of them were welcome in several households and could use the opportunity of paying a social visit to their many actual and potential Mountainstreet clients very conveniently on the same occasion. Others who benefited from the same kind of opportunity were political patrons seeking office near election time, to revive associations and arrange local campaigns, including the dispersal of vote-buying funds. Thirdly, emigrants from Mountainstreet often chose festivals to pay a return visit and were invited to several households if they had lived in the area for any length of time and if the members of their native household and those of other kin had not also emigrated.

But a feast is not only the recreation of otherwise established relations. New ones are made and drunk since guests often do not know each other. Even their host may well not know all his guests since some bring their own family, or friends, quite possibly from a feast attended earlier in the evening. Clearly the central area of simultaneous feasting, where there are the largest number of households within easy walking distance, is a centre for social brokerage and it is an obvious site for the temple itself and of the central place of marketing.

A festival is a feast rota taking one of the principles of association I have mentioned, that of common place of residence, to its most literal and extensive extreme. At this extreme it is, like an ancestral feast, ascriptive. It is subject to the use of other principles of association and forms of organisation by which strata are made within it. A feast table is a table of equals, but when there is more than one table, differentiation between them becomes possible.

Those who can only afford to invite a few or just one table (guests are reckoned in tables) entertain only close family and friends and close work associates. Those who can afford many tables of guests from as wide a geographic range as they have trade or political dealings, entertain them as well as locals, collateral and affinal kin. But they entertain them at separate tables, or at different sittings. There is not enough space for all the guests to eat at one time, and at a festival people attend more than one feast, in the course of the afternoon and evening, forging and renewing links. The separate sittings are separate kinds of association. The festival and its feasts combine in their performance an association of equals and a differentiation according to wealth, patronage and connections.

## PEACE

Feasts are prime occasions of peace and security. This is a peace kept by the rules of reciprocity, obligation, patronage and respect which produce not only feasts themselves, but also the temples and territorial cults whose calendars mark the occasions for feasting. Into this festive mood, it is possible to read a political economy of commodity production, peaceful competition and local charity, rising beside the imperial rites, from the twelfth century onwards. Even if the hierarchies of pilgrimage did not coincide at their peaks with either imperial administrative capitals or marketing centres, the peace of each was congruent with that of the others.

I am eliding the meaning of 'peace' in European political economy with the meaning of *ping'an*, the most frequent summary of what householders petition gods for themselves and for their residential territory in China. What are the contents of this plausible peace? Maintenance of person and property against violence and theft is one part. Upholding the trustworthiness which regulates the pursuit of livelihood by productive activity and commerce is the other. In short, peace is the state of accumulation of wealth through exploitation of natural and human resources without the use of force, plus the regrettable necessity of an authority to maintain the peace by an administration and its courts. These seem to have formed the ideology not only of the empires of late medieval Europe but also of China from the southern Song dynasty onward. In both, the unit of the husbanding of resources was ideally a patriarchal household. In both, small units of production (agriculture and manufacture or craft) were in fact linked through a barter and cash economy of private property in a great commercial network of rising scales of accumulation.

Peace like paradise seems to induce a vision of harmonious sameness. Somehow Chinese imperial ceremony, the cults of the common people of China, their histories, and the universal history (moral, political, and economic) of petty commodity production and civilisation in the Europe of the Enlightenment harmonise. But does this happen when we look at the obverse of peace? Is there a similarity of discord? I think not.

William Rowe (1990) reviews a consensus among historians of modern China that from the sixteenth century, commercialisation and local gentry between them began to create a public sphere between domestic and governmental relations. The Chinese middle level was equivalent to the public sphere identified by Habermas and others for the Europe of the same centuries. But this comparison does not include the critical issue of control of military force. In Europe it had by the eighteenth century become, ideologically and in deed, a monopoly of the monarch and the sovereign state, whereas in China, the sphere of 'public', which is to say local, control was a sphere of patronage which included the organisation of military force in militia bands. The imperial Chinese control of military force in the eighteenth and nineteenth centuries was increasingly delegated to regional commanders in the course of suppressing the risings of peasants and their patrons, risings based on these same local militia.

In China, village landlords could still, in the twentieth century, decide to have recalcitrant debtors killed by their own gangs of bullies (Potter and Potter 1990:49). If similar licence was allowed work-house and other guardians of the incarcerated in Europe and the USA, in this century too, the licence did not extend into the sphere of right and freedom. Both the local public control of force and the use of imperial garrisons in China was much more openly terrorist, I think, than would be compatible with the European public sphere of rights and freedoms, even though these rights and freedoms were never fully won by the European working classes.

The disorder of sixteenth- to eighteenth-century Europe was religious strife over conscience and calling before a single god. The individual person, or each household, was (and still is in common-place social thinking) set in relation to a single, sovereign master: be it God or Society. European disorder was also strife of mercantile empires, making and unmaking balances of power through marriage, treaty, and war. Seventeenth- and eighteenth-century history gave it the mythical and philosophical status either of a degeneration from original innocence or, on the contrary, of an original state of war of each against all. In either case, its avoidance was by a social contract between each household and a single, sovereign authority of, and over, all. Chinese ideologues wrote a history of sages, not of a creator's laws of moral and natural history. China's like Europe's disorders were peasant uprisings. But Chinese sectarian violence was not that of conscience and redemption. It was over the restoration of ancient and original order and the re-creation of the balance of cosmic forces, not the creation on earth of a new Jerusalem.

*Ping'an* assumes no single authority, nor any contract. It is celebrated by a giving of thanks for a local protection. Imperial authority was sanctioned by a cosmic mandate, the rules of heaven empowering their post-holder – deity or emperor. This was no external and supreme master like the creator god of the religions of the book, or its secular equivalent the monarch or sovereign (even if constituted) dictator. Chinese authority could be divined or revealed as an original source, but not as an originator. European ideologues imagined the sovereign as a leviathan, a monster, perhaps a demiurge of the ultimate Creator. But the sovereign was also the means of keeping the peace, whereas in the Chinese political drama the emperor is simply the punisher for not keeping the peace, or else the final object of petition against lower-level plunderers.

Local protection intercedes with this Chinese behemoth (tiger, ox) and guards against incursions by strangers from uncontrolled localities. European villagers and townspeople would also have needed protection, from plague, pestilence, marauding troops and predatory tax-farmers, and from the attentions of the nobility. But the imagined threat was Satanic, or of witches and strangers (Jews, gypsies) acting for Evil. Protection and deliverance were sought from a saintly intercession with a redeeming Christ. In China, threat and protection were not thus concentrated, no Christ and Antichrist, no Good and Evil. Demons were located – malign stars, trapped and orphaned spirits. Protection against them was a ritual of exorcism by means of a local patron deity, by an act of petition and covenant with an office-holding or responsive demonic power (*ling*) which could bring about changes in the forces of partly-anthropomorphised cosmological categories of wind, rain, thunder, mountains and rivers. The official ideology decried this petitioning and protection as heterodox. It was a danger to the negative peace – the quiet – of imperial rule kept by the cultural accomplishments of students, scribes and ceremonial leaders of a harmonised universe revealed by sages. In the maintenance of *its* peace imperial force was terrible, a cosmic upheaval, a massive expulsion or annihilation. In the maintenance of *local* peace, avoidance of that fate and protection against more local depradation was in the power of exorcism and local bands of gods' soldiers. The two, the imperial and the local organisations of military force, the orthodoxy of peace and the heterodoxy of protection and exorcism, existed uneasily together.

Peace by social contract is not after all the same as peace by cosmological mandate. And peace by demonic protection is not the same as either of these. So let me now turn to a more detailed description of the peace of festivals and local temple cults, to explore further the differences between the imperial and the local versions.

# Chapter Four

# Local festivals and their cults

To a resident the calendar of festivals presents four different possibilities of identification. There are days which local people assume are observed everywhere in China. Among these in Mountainstreet were the three principal points (*yuan*), on the fifteenth day of the first, seventh and tenth lunar months, when the three cosmological divisions were addressed as a set of offices to which the supreme god of heaven had appointed what were also called 'gods of heaven'. That they are pan-Chinese does not, of course, mean that all Chinese do observe them, just that the local people think every other Chinese does. In Mountainstreet itself observance of some of the pan-Chinese days was effectively voluntary. There was little social pressure to burn incense either at home or in the temple.

Then there are days observed locally or by a cultural subgroup only, such as the birthdays of local temple deities, with which we shall be most concerned.

Third are the days of honouring tutelary deities of professional or other associations to which the resident belongs. Among these may be sectarian versions of cults to the same deities which are otherwise those of local or pan-Chinese festivals. Spirit-writing groups, spirit-possession or martial arts groups, centred on their master's or medium's revelations and traditions stemming from them are often called 'sectarian' or 'secret' societies in the Western literature to convey their exclusive claim to a discipline and the rituals of initiation to it.

Fourth are the days observed only in his or her household. These are the death-days of the household's ancestors.

A local temple is for the celebration and reverence of pan-Chinese dates as well as for local gods. On the first two of the three *yuan* the Mountainstreet temple was used only when some residents brought their domestic offerings to its altar tables and burned incense. On the third *yuan* the temple was the centre of Mountaintsreet's greatest annual festival, that of its territorial protector, and its local and cultural subgroup identification.

In Mountainstreet three other pan-Chinese dates were observed. Two of them were for the Locality God (Tudi Gong), on the second day of the second month and the fifteenth day of the eighth month. The third, on the ninth of the ninth month, was for prolonging life and for the remembrance of ancestors whose deathdays had been forgotten. The latter was done in the temple. The two Locality God days involved Tudi Gong shrines and not the main local temple.

Places are differentiated in the organisation of even the pan-Chinese rituals. For instance, around *zhong yuan* (the middle *yuan*) during the seventh month, the three main compatriot temples in Taibei in imperial days used to have processions on different days. In the same way, Mountainstreet town was divided into two halves, eastern and western, for rival processions on different days in the seventh month. On the fifteenth of the first month, the first of the three *yuan*, the same two halves put on rival lantern processions. Each of the two halves also had its Tudi Gong shrine, and in 1966–8 there were still two separate celebrations of the Locality God's twice-yearly days.

Tudi Gong in Taiwan is paid particular attention by shop-keepers and others engaged in commerce. The Tudi Gong association of the eastern part of Mountainstreet was a feasting association whose costs excluded all but the wealthier shop-keepers. But in addition there was the duty of burning incense in the Tudi Gong shrine every day. This duty was inclusive, passed on in the form of a wooden tablet from house to neighbouring house in this part of the town.

The western Tudi Gong feasting association contrasted with the eastern one of shop-keepers. The feasters, or rather drinkers, I saw on the second of the second month in 1967 were mainly labourers, miners and drivers. Of the residents of the western half of town, the relatively status-conscious – which were the doctor, one of the mine's owners, the winch operator at the mine, the fish and prawn trapper, two tea merchants, the keeper of the only grocery store in the western half– were all absent. The feast was held in the house of that year's host, not in one of the eating houses as was the eastern association's wont. It was a much smaller, more convivial, looser celebration. Members of the association contributed to the feast a few coins of cash and red long-life buns called *hong-gu* (red turtle) if their or their sons' wives had given birth to sons during the year – a ritual at once of thanks, registration and protection. In addition the feast always included the little red and white sweet dough balls which are given the bride and groom to eat at their wedding, and are also eaten by households with young children after they are presented to the Bed Mother on her day, the first of the sixth.

Every hamlet had a similar feast association, including representatives of all the households in it. On the morning of the feast they cleared the paths in the hamlet's area.

Tudi Gong feast associations are the basic units of a religion of territorial co-residence and local differentiation.

## THE SMALLEST TERRITORY: A HOUSEHOLD AND ITS LOCALE

A household is ritually defined as a unit in several ways: as a house, as a family, as part of a Tudi Gong and of a local festival area, as part of a family, and as a site or place. These several definitions are not at all times distinguished from one another, but distinctions can be made between them within the competence of the ritual language at the disposal of Mountainstreet households. Let us take them in turn.

The construction of a *house* was beset with ritual moments which were timed according to the almanac. The relation of the builder with the householder was fraught with tension that could result in accidents and misplacements and turn the finished construction into an unlucky or haunted home. The raising of the roof-beam intact was one of two important ritual moments. In the finished construction the centre of the roof-beam in the main room of the house was often marked with the design of the Eight Trigrams in one of the circular Heavenly Orders. At commencement and completion of building, the patron god of builders was worshipped. And the builder's square and line, used in the construction of the house, were sometimes kept on the domestic altar shelf after completion.

The second important ritual moment came after completion. This was the ceremony of 'entering the house' and could be performed long after completion because, unlike the raising of the roof beam, it was a celebration of the household not just as a house but also as a *family*. It celebrated the installation of the domestic altar itself, and was the occasion for the first worship of ancestors at it.

No 'entering' had been performed in the new Mountainstreet town house of the younger of two mine-owning brothers, three years after construction, yet it was a household for the purpose of temple festivals. He and his wife and children lived there, but they worshipped his ancestors in the *ancestral home* where his father and brother continued to live. Offerings were presented in the *new house* when just the Locality God (Tudi Gong) was to be worshipped, such as the Autumn festival on the fifteenth of the eighth month, and on the twenty-eighth day of the twelfth month during the New Year season when the God of the Foundations (Diji Zu) was worshipped. The Locality God was worshipped at an altar that had been established in rudimentary form at the back wall of the main room where the fully established altar would be. This was also sufficient for the worship of other gods, to establish *the household as a separate unit of the temple area* and for the worship twice a month of the temple gods' soldiers.

Sometimes the incense-burner to gods was, unlike the incense-burner to ancestors, a fixture of the house as such. I came upon two instances of the new owner of a house maintaining at its incense-burner his respect for deities whose dates and figures had been left behind by the former owner. It was in this same vessel that incense was burned to gods of the local temple. The gods of the local temple are in one sense a fixture like the Locality God, to be contrasted with other gods which were peculiar to *the one household*. Were the householders to move, they would probably not keep the days to their former local temple gods.

The Locality God and the God of the Foundations are fixtures, for they are the gods of the house as *a site or a place*. The first breaking of earth on a new site was often marked by the presentation of offerings on the ground to both the god of the particular site and that of the locality in which it was situated. For a public building an important person was usually asked to break the earth, and similarly for a house's site, a bringer of luck might be asked. Worship of the Ancestors of the Foundation and of the territory was then repeated after completion of the building. Even the plastic-covered frame sheds for cultivating edible fungi in Mountainstreet were inaugurated in this way.

## THE HOUSEHOLD IN A SYSTEM OF TERRITORIAL UNITS

In short, the household, as a territorial unit, had its own territorial guardian, the Ancestor of the Foundation (Diji Zu). He was variously described to me as the building's own Tudi Gong and as a kind of *gui*. His worship at New Year, on the twenty-eighth day of the twelfth month, was accompanied by the burning of silver, as for ancestors and *gui*, not gold as for gods and for Tudi Gong. The offerings were presented to him at the entrance to the kitchen or in the kitchen itself, on a low bench, not at the altar in the main room where offerings to ancestors, gods and to Tudi Gong were presented, nor outside the house where offerings to *gui* were made. He was, it was said, like a landlord and the Newyear offerings were like rent. One person said that before the Chinese came to Taiwan the land was supposed to have belonged to the Foundation God so that when Chinese came to use it they had to make offerings to him. This identifies him with non-Chinese. But this does not mean he was a religious borrowing from the indigenous religion, for the same Diji Zu is described in households in Fujian province, settled by Chinese for many centuries longer than is Taiwan. Rather he is the ancestor or founder of the household as a site.

In Mountainstreet, the Stove God was an unremarked member of a set of Merciful Lords (Enzhu Gong). But in other parts of China the Stove God occupied the same point in the ritual of the twenty-eighth day of the twelfth month as does the Ancestor of the Foundations in Mountainstreet. He is an outsider but inside, and so he can be conceptualised as the classic case of the orphan soul whose whitening bones have not been properly buried, namely the soldier killed abroad or at the frontiers. Alternatively he can be thought to be like the inspector billeted on the household.

I have already noted that the Ancestor of the Foundations was thought to be the Tudi Gong of the house. But unlike the Ancestor of the Foundations, Tudi Gong, the god of the neighbourhood, field or village, that is to say of the larger territorial unit, was unambiguously a god to be honoured. He was juxtaposed with orphan souls, not ambivalently identified with them. In fact he was known generally as 'the king of *gui*, the locality's official'.

The graves of the properly buried and remembered are counterparts in the *yin* world of the living, *yang* world, dwellings of households. They too have each their own tutelary deity. He is also said to be a kind of Tudi Gong but is formally known according to the title inscribed on the stone beside every grave as Hou Tu.

One of the stories of Tudi Gong current in Mountainstreet linked him with Hou Tu thus. A man, only three days after marrying, was called to do military service and was killed on duty at the Great Wall of China. His soul visited his wife in a dream, begging her to come and find his bones to bury them properly. But when she came to the Wall there were so many bones she did not know how to identify her husband's. An old man with a white beard, Tudi Gong, advised her that if she cut her finger and let blood drip from it the bones at which it would stop dripping would be those of her husband. (Another version of this story has it that the bones which would absorb her tears of mourning would be her husband's.) In this way she found and collected her husband's bones together in her skirts and carried them home weeping. She wept so profusely on to the bones that they began to come to life again. But Tudi Gong considered it unjust that her husband should be singled out from the other soldiers to be brought back to life. When the wife had to go and find food to eat he offered to guard the reviving bones for her. On her return she found that they had lost their life again. She was very angry. But that is why there is a stone for Tudi Gong beside every grave. To keep the dead dead.[1]

The graveside stone comes out of this story as a representation of anger and resentment, resulting from the clash of two upright exemplars, the widow and the Tudi Gong.

In any case, as one man put it: 'Each place has a Tudi Gong. There are several kinds of Tudi Gong. There are so many kinds of Tudi Gong. He protects the area (*te hng*). He is the area's god.'

## THE LOCALITY GOD (TUDI GONG)

'Whether out of doors or indoors, one depends on Tudi Gong', explained an old woman. The guardian of a large area and the guardian of a smaller area, the guardian of a neighbourhood and the guardian of the house were not neatly conceived as superior and inferior in a nested hierachy of ever smaller territorial units. The one may be guardian of a larger area than the other so that it encompasses it, but this relative size of command was conceived as relative strength of protective power rather than as a relation between two levels in the administrative hierarchy to which they are likened. As at New Year, the immediate reference was to heaven, to the apex of the hierarchy. The household is under heaven and so is the area. 'I have heard that Tudi Gong is both the greatest and the smallest', one woman explained. 'At a grave he guards just that grave. But he is also close to the God of Heaven reporting to him every three days.' And as a young miner said, more flippantly, and in rhyme: 'God of heaven, god of earth; And under the bed, king of the pot.' (*Thi: Kong, Te Kong, Bin-cng kha, Sai-thang-a Ong.*)

Out of doors, under heaven, there are on the one hand *gui* and on the other hand the territorial guardians which protect one by controlling the *gui;* at named graves they guard the remembered dead from rejoining the living; at mass graves they prevent the abandoned dead from afflicting the living. But indoors, that is to say within the doors of the dwellings of the living themselves, the tutelary deity is both guardian and *gui.*

Tudi Gong is consulted for regulating the time in the annual calendar when an agricultural task must be started and is celebrated when it is completed. There is a commercial equivalent of these Tudi Gong occasions in the towns. Tudi Gong is a notion which covers the regulation of making a livelihood, in farming or commerce. It also represents the security or peace necessary for safe travel and outdoor activity, as well as neighbourhood co-operation of all kinds. It is part of the notion of regulation through a hierarchy of imperial administration and the keeping of *gui* in their place.

Everyone whom I asked about the nature of Tudi Gong either referred to the republican and colonial or to the imperial administrations saying he was like the local official. The story told by one person illustrated well the conception of Tudi Gong as an underling in an imperial administration of gods. The miner who told it to me had, he said, originally read it in a magazine and had since recounted it to many work-mates who had applauded it. He tried hard to remember all the details, saying that 'this kind of story is serious'. In his reading and his recreation, as a member of the band and in the past as one of the small theatrical troupe which Mountainstreet sported, he was closely involved with the culture associated with local temple religion.

Since the story is about the way the present incumbent of the Locality God shrine came to that position from his mortal life it also illustrates the way in which the religious imperial administration was conceived as an effective force in the world of the living. We may note that as soon as an incumbent is conceived, the plurality of territorial positions and the notion of an imperial administration implicit in the name Locality God are confused by the singularity of the identified person. The place of his posting is not made clear. He may be the incumbent of one or of many shrines, but he is in this story a man from Anxi and therefore appropriate to settlements like Mountainstreet formed by immigrants from that county.

The present Locality God [Thote Kong, in Taiwanese] is not the same as the old one. The present one has no beard. He is called Ng Leto, and comes from Ankhue [Anxi]. He was employed as a cashier. On the fifteenth day of the eighth month,

Thote Kong's birthday, as he was going home to his wife, a long walk, the cashier stopped because it was hot and went for a swim. He put his clothes on a Thote Kong shrine's table and swam in the stream nearby. There is, or should always be, a stream near every Thote Kong shrine. This [dumping of the clothes on the shrine table] offended Thote Kong, and when the cashier got home he had a stomach ache. His wife asked him whether he had done anything wrong on the way home. He said no, but told her about his swim and putting his clothes on the Thote Kong shrine table. She guessed that this might have been the cause of the trouble and took offerings to the shrine, asking for forgiveness. Her husband then got well.

The cashier was indignant that Thote Kong had made him ill in order to receive offerings and he saw that the gods of the Earth Court [one of the three major regions of celestial administration] were capable of extorting money (*tham ci:*). He wanted to take Thote Kong to court and he asked his boss whether this was possible. The boss said it was very difficult to take a god to court. But he did write for the cashier a yellow despatch containing the accusation against Thote Kong, appealing to the judgement of Sengong Ia [the City God], and the cashier burnt it at an incense burner. Then the cashier went to sleep so that his soul could depart and go to court with Thote Kong to appear before Sengong Ia. Thote Kong said in court that it was not he who had given the cashier a stomach ache and that the offerings were made at the cashier's wife's own wish. But the cashier said that it was Thote Kong who had agreed [through divination blocks] to acquiesce to his wife's request that after she had presented the offerings he, Thote Kong, would make her husband's stomach ache better. It was now up to Sengong Ia's judgement. But Sengong Ia being boss of the Thote Kong was on Thote Kong's side and also thought that someone in the world of the living who accused a god would be a great trouble-maker once he entered the Yin world. So he punished the cashier with forty strokes across his behind.

When the cashier awoke he told his boss that he had an aching behind and that he would appeal to Yok Hong Siong Te [Yu Huang Shang Ti, the Jade Emperor of Heaven]. But the boss said it was not possible for a human being to do so. Instead the cashier appealed to Thai Pe Kim Sien [the Great White and

Golden Immortal] who is a kind of secret agent who reports to Yok Hong Siong Te on both the Yang and the Yin worlds. But Thai Pe Kim Sien did not dare take charge of this case, the first in which a human accused a god. Instead he reported it to Yok Hong Siong Te, who got a headache with it. He called for the cashier and asked him to report all that had happened. He then praised the virtue of the cashier and said he would forgive him for accusing a god. Yok Hong Siong Te summoned two gods, Ia Iu Sin [the Night Wandering Spirit] and Zit Iu Sin [the Day Wandering Spirit]. People say that the Day Wandering Spirit is the same as Cao Kun [the Stove God, in every household], but he is not. Every time you raise your head three inches, the Day Wandering Spirit is there – he wanders everywhere. These two were sent down to the Yang world with the cashier and Yok Hong Siong Te also gave him a pearl.

Back in the Yang world whenever the cashier shook the pearl a heap of money came out of it and he became very rich and the Day Wandering Spirit protected him. He spent money on helping the poor in his county, and was so influential that even the county magistrate who also extorted money, as was so common with human officials, was afraid of him.

Meanwhile the Night Wandering Spirit changed form into a Wilderness Demon [Ia Kui, whose control is one of the special provinces of Thote Kong] and thus met Thote Kong. He offered Thote Kong gold taels in exchange for food. Thote Kong accepted the gold but did not give him any food, saying that he should not ask a god for food. For food he should go to humans. At this, the Night Wandering Spirit turned back into his true shape and told Thote Kong that he now had evidence that he, Thote Kong, did extort money, and went to report to Thai Pe Kim Sien.

In the Yang world the county magistrate sent his bodyguards to demand the pearl from the cashier. But someone had notified the cashier in advance, so he ran off, taking the pearl with him. When the guards came to his house they questioned the cashier's wife and she was forced to tell them that her husband had run off. They gave chase and the cashier's wife followed them. They caught up with the cashier at a great rock, and he leaped from it, killing himself. This is why people often call Thote Kong the God of the Rock (Ciouq-thau Kong). The cashier's wife leapt off too, and she became Thote Ma, the wife of Thote Kong.

104

In the imperial administration there was no hard and fast definition of the punishable acceptance of gifts or extraction of extra taxes and the proper approach expected by the officials of imperial rule. This story of a Locality God as a virtuous mortal who successfully accuses the incumbent Locality God of corruption dramatises this ambiguity for the god was at once functioning well as a protector, demanding respect and at the same time cash for protection against the harm he himself had done.

To understand the system of religious territorial units, the relation of protection between territorial guardian gods and *gui* is crucial. For this, an investigation of the way territorial cults organise the meaning of *gui*, apparently a negative and residual category, is in fact essential.

## DEMONS (*GUI*) AND THEIR GUARDIANS

Now, as in all likelihood they would have done in imperial times as well, the common people of Mountainstreet do not observe an exclusive distinction between past lives and present effects. The system of territorial administrative units is a system of control of demons and ghosts (*gui*).

Ghosts were often described in Mountainstreet as 'wanderers', the equivalent of the vagabonds of all kinds (*youmin*) which were the constant objects of imperial surveillance and proscription, being agents of banditry and rebellion. They are not only orphan souls to be pitied and given care. They are also subjects cut off in life whose potential force is outside the hierarchy of gods and can be used for good or ill. The same man who told the story of Tudi Gong thought that the spirits with most efficacious power (*lieng sia:*) were spirits without descendants. He also called them hungry ghosts. They will, he said, support anyone who feeds them, without principle.

Ghosts and Tudi Gong between them mark social territorial boundaries which have ancestors and local kin or compatriot groups and their gods as centres. Locality Gods mark these boundaries from the inside, ghosts from the outside. Tudi Gong is supposed to protect one when travelling or working out of doors. Local temple gods are supposed to give the same protection over a larger area. It is a matter of common courtesy now, if no longer common prudence, to burn incense in the temple of the local god of any place to which one has travelled.

Ghosts are supposed particularly to haunt paths, streams and bridges. *Gui*, in short, connotes the dangers of the road, of bandits and strangers and accidents beyond the reach of familiar people, thus incurring the danger of one's self becoming a *gui*. *Gui* also mark the edge of the home locality. One euphemism for *gui* in Mountainstreet was 'outsider spirit' (*wai shen*).

A few hundred yards from Mountainstreet, the main road, which links it to the more central places in its marketing system, passes through a tunnel. The tunnel marks the edge of Mountainstreet's local marketing area and that area is centred on Mountainstreet town and its temple. 'Within the tunnel' (*dongnei*) as the area is widely known, people use Mountainstreet's shops, send their children to its primary school, and share its temple's festivals. The people 'beyond the tunnel' (*dongwai*) usually go elsewhere for these things. A great many stories of the haunting of the tunnel were told. One of the *gui* supposed to haunt it was a former gangster who came from the nearest market town 'beyond the tunnel'. He had a secret liaison with a married woman of Mountainstreet and wanted to visit her on the Lantern Festival. Despite warnings from a diviner that he was doomed if he went out that day, and from the Japanese police that someone in Mountainstreet was after his life, he came after dark. On his way back in the middle of the night, three people hired by the cuckolded husband killed him at the entrance to the tunnel.

Another haunting of the tunnel resulted from what amounted to a fatal ritual accident. In a ritual now no longer performed in Mountainstreet, the Daoist exorcised 'outsider spirits' with a straw figure which was then discarded, in this case at the tunnel. It would have been the 'replacement body' (*tishen*) of someone attacked by demons (Schipper 1985:31). The straw figure was found there by a boy. He kicked it and urinated on it. Soon after he got back home he died, urinating blood.

These were stories of malicious strangers, to be propitiated and easily taking malign offense. At the outermost boundary of culture and society, *gui* are the equivalent of foreigners and aborigines, and the Mountainstreet local temple god, Ang Gong, is said to have defended that boundary. The border with non-Chinese had within it equivalent compatriot borders, making subcultural breaks between regions, each in their turn defended in the names of their local gods. After communal battles, which frequently took place between such subregions, mass shrines were built for the bones of those killed, either because individually they were unidentifiable and could not be returned to their ancestral homes or because they were too young to have descendants or because they had died violently and before their span was run, all these eventualities leading to trapped, cut-off and uncontrolled activity on the part of the soul and all classified as *gui*. But they were honoured *gui*. Their shrines were sometimes (if they had supported imperial troops in suppression of their enemies) sponsored by an official inscription, and there are cases of these shrines becoming new ritual foci for the respective compatriot groupings.

Whether loyalist or bandit in the eyes of imperial administration, the spirits were to their compatriots beneficent rather than malevolent, honoured rather than propitiated. By special ritual care, possibly instituted by the building for the dead of a temple to a saviour or guardian god, they were considered saved. The assistants of these saviour gods, and some controllers of *gui* were themselves known to be saved *gui*.

The ritual of general salvation (*pu du*) is devoted to the feeding of orphan souls which come into the category of *gui* in common usage. Its greatest regular occasion is in the seventh month every year. But it is also a major feature of the great rite of cosmic adjustment which inaugurates a new local temple or its refurbishment.

After arranging their own offerings to *gui* in front of the temple, people face the priests making the charitable distribution to orphan souls. From amongst the people massed in front of the priests, women, children, the sick, and the destitute scramble for the coins, sweets and cakes which the priests throw out. And it is the right of beggars at large festivals to take what they will from the people's own offerings to *gui* in front of the temple. Wu Cheng-han (1988:142–3) gives instances of processions of City Gods and of the God of the Eastern Peak, in charge of purgatory, in which beggers and children were paid to dress up as *gui* in shackles. Beggars and orphan souls are dependent on the charity of strangers. They are called 'orphan' (*gu*) because they are not able to rely on membership of a unit of kinship, because it has come to an end or lacks the means or will to conduct rituals to lead them out of purgatory.

In the 1967 seventh month *pu du* ceremonies at the temple in Taibei city to one of the best known saviour gods, the Di Zang Wang Miao, women of a Buddhist charitable association, the Association of the Six Paths, prepared special paper tokens of scriptures read on behalf of orphan souls. After the rituals were over they continued their charity by taking some of the food offerings to an orphanage and a hospital for old people.

That women and children, rather than men should be more concerned with *pu du*, and be prominent in the scramble for coins and cakes, is significant and appropriate. In the orthodox Chinese system of reckoning descent patrilineally and of residing in the home of the husband (unless she is the only source of continuity of descent and a husband marries in to her) a woman is isolated. An unmarried woman in terms of descent and ancestor worship is an outsider in her natal home. Her parents already have or hope to have a son who will remain and carry on the line. She on the contrary will marry into another line of descent, and that is the line in which eventually she will be an ancestor. A married woman is the womb from which a new branch of the family into which she has married will spring. She also brings with her a dowry which is the beginning of a new budgetary sub-unit. A separate bedroom is created, if only temporarily, for her and her husband in his parents' house on the day of the wedding, whereas until then he may have slept with his father or brothers. In short, even if she is not a newcomer, a woman on marriage is the agency of separation and a new household and, if she does not have children she will either have to marry out again or suffer the fate when she dies of being at best the most marginal ancestor and the most easily forgotten. Hence, the most popular deity on Mountainstreet household altars after Tudi Gong was the goddess, Guan Yin, to whom mainly women's prayers were addressed, both for fertility and easy birth and for the saving of orphan souls from purgatory.

In the imagery of an imperial judiciary of purgatory, gui are the subject masses. They are by definition outside the structure of the gods and the ancestors, at the same time as being subjects of the control exerted through the structure of the gods. Yet people likened gui to gangs of bandits or to the young men who swore brotherhood and ran rackets, gangs which also formed the militia who acted as the gods' retinue in procession. Gui were, therefore, also gods' troops.

The common identification of bandits and gangs of wandering people with gui was not usually the chosen identification of militia bands. Their identification was more likely to be with gods' soldiers. But at certain times of great hardship and disorder militia organisations' identification with hungry ghosts could come very close.

Village protection militia bands could be predators and bullies, the sons of the richer peasants and landlords or landless men hired by them to protect their property and to collect rents, fees and taxes. They would protect the crops of all the farmers in a village, including those of poor tenants, for a fee. Their identification with the local temple and its festivals would be a predatory form of patronage by the wealthier residents and landlords.

108

The Eight Infernal Generals wielding their instruments for the capture of demons. This exorcising dance was performed for a house of a Daoist in Mengjia in 1967 in the evening of the procession festival of Qing Shan Wang. The young men, skilled in martial arts, are made up as ferocious demons acting righteously to redeem themselves.

For instance, in the 1930s, the festival militia of one Guangdong township temple were under the control of merchant-strongmen working in collaboration with the police who were themselves under the command of warlords who had joined the republican government of the Pearl River region (Siu 1989: 84–5).

In the North China region above the Huai River and around the Taihang range of mountains, hard landlords were called Kings of Hell for condemning their tenants to hunger, and local temples to the saviour goddess Guan Yin became centres for rallying against them. The militia organised to oppose the landlords' injustices formed a sect called Heavengate. Militia turning against local landlords and the government which backed them were separated from their normal patrons, and the egalitarian sentiments of feast and mutual protection in sworn brotherhoods which all militia could and usually did profess then became programmatic. On the other hand, landlords and local governors organised militia to protect their property. The landlords' militia bands were taught by masters of a tradition of martial arts practising disciplines partly of possession by invoked deities and partly of breath control as well as a series of initiation hardships ending with bearing the master's sword cuts and even the firing of bullets without flinching. They met in local temples to Guan Di (God of War and Commerce), or set up their own altars, which were not for general participation. In their activities of protection against bandits and other similar groups, these bands became known as the Red Spears and they could turn against local governors and landlords. It should be noted that the militia of both sects protected their own locality while raiding and plundering others'. The last decades of the dynasty and the first of the republic were times of desperate shortage which had swelled the ranks of landless vagabonds and so of bandit organisations.

Some years later, in the late 1930s, the Seventh Month Festival of the General Release of Hungry Ghosts (*pu du*) became a regular occasion for guerilla attacks on Japanese invaders' garrisons (Thaxton 1983: 90, 192; and Perry 1980: 186–205).

Even in normal times village militia joined with other bands trained by the same masters or linked by festival and cult, clashing with the bands of other sects, cults and localities. The dead of their own side were identified as loyal. But the dead of the other side were identified as predatory ghosts. This is a projection of the activities of their own militia's plundering the areas of others.

What identifies both as *gui* is not their isolation in the sense of not being organised. It is their existence on borders between local loyalties and between self-defence and bullying extortion.

## THE HOUSEHOLD'S CONTINUITY IN SYSTEMS OF KINSHIP AND SALVATION

Considered as a unit of territorial administration, the household is a place to be guarded and controlled. But as soon as we consider it as a unit in the process of reproduction over time, we have to take the kinship system into account and at the same time the household's identification as a subject of saviour gods.

The identity of a household over time is the identity of an ancestral home from which several households will descend. It is also the career and prosperity of units of shared income. The gods chosen for special attention on the domestic altar are chosen in the hopes of enhancing the household's prosperity. The ancestors, beside them, are remembered as its past career and as those to which its present existence is due.

There are a number of occasions in the domestic religious calendar when the retrospective continuity of the household receives special attention. New Year's eve and morning, and the fifth of the fifth month[2] are two of them. A pair of solar dates make two more. They are either the spring day when graves are spruced up – Qing Ming – and the winter solstice, which I have already described as a festival for marking out the household as a place in itself. Alternatively they are the dates of the spring and autumn equinoxes.[3] At these times, ancestors and a unified household are celebrated. Sons who spend most of the year working and living elsewhere and may even have established their own units of residence but have not yet inaugurated domestic altars complete with ancestral shrine, are expected to come home at these times. Qing Ming is devoted at the same time to the dwellings of the ancestors themselves. They are offered at their graves special spirit paper to make repairs in the spirit house which had been despatched by burning at the time of the mortuary rites for the deceased. Qing Ming is also the time for making special glutinous rice cakes to be distributed to children.

Other occasions in the domestic religious calendar when the prospective continuity of the household receives special attention are at times of the year when marriage and birth are subjects of special hope and attention. Both the weeks of the New Year season and the weeks around the Autumn Festival are thought to be good times for weddings. They are times for making arrangements, divining the prospects of the household, or completing arrangements for new households, a wedding and the installation of a domestic altar. Furthermore, both the New Year season and the Autumn Festival are times of increased licence. Gambling is sanctioned by custom if not law. And the evenings of the Lantern Festival and the Autumn Festival are spent by both women and men out of doors, the autumn moon-viewing in particular being a time for courting. They are not times for returning to ancestral homes.

A third occasion, the seventh day of the seventh month, is in effect the complementary opposite of Qing Ming. It is yet another evening occasion, and is in the lunar calendar, whereas Qing Ming is in the solar calendar and its ceremonies take place by day. On the seventh day of the seventh month the hardship of young and newly married women and the seeking of brides for men are recognised when offerings of the special food for the occasion are presented at the door facing outwards to the Seventh Woman (Qi Nu). She is the young woman immortal who, according to two alternative sets of myths, is either the weaving girl who meets with her cow-herd husband once a year at this time across the Milky Way, or one of seven girl immortals who married a mortal and was made to do impossibly hard tasks. The rain is said to be her tears, falling while she washes dishes endlessly.

If an infant has been born, then the Bed Mother, or alternatively Guan Yin the Saviour Goddess, are also presented with offerings on the seventh of the seventh.[4] In other words, on that day the process of forming a new household in its early stages are recognised, whereas at Qing Ming the fullest extension, the extremities of household continuity, are recognised in the Yin dwellings of the ancestors and in their youngest descendants.

As a line extended in time and as a territorial unit within a locality which includes the graves of its ancestors, a household is included in the festivals of its locality. As an extension over time, its focus is more on saviour deities and its own, individuated career. As a territorial unit it is much more caught up in the local procession festivals of territorial guardians.

## THE LOCAL TEMPLE

The ritual identification of a household in a subsystem of territories is distinct not only from its identification as a unit in a system of kinship, as I have shown it to be. It is also, distinct from either of these, a ritual unit in a subsystem of local cults and local temples.

The names Ang Gong, Xian Gong, and Ma Zu are honorific titles of gods celebrated in Mountainstreet but whose cults have many centres and branches but are at the same time identifiable as cults of deities with legendary biographies. Each cult centre and branch is a particular manifestation of the deity's reputation for efficacious response. Each can be characterised as a manifestation of the god's intelligence, brilliance, and power to respond (ling). In contradistinction to these identified immortals or spirits known by their titles or their personal mortal names, are other gods known by their positions and the titles which go with the position and not by any personal identification. Examples of this kind of god, as known in Mountainstreet, are The Supreme Rulers of the Three Offices (San Guan Da Di) celebrated at the three yuan, and the Locality God (Tudi Gong). They were always known as positions in a territorial administration. But sometimes people would tell stories about the god who held one of these positions, such as the story of the Locality God who had been a cashier. For another instance, I was told that Guan Di Gong, the God of War and Commerce and the god whose cult was probably the most widespread in late imperial China, had replaced Heavenly Master Zhang in the position of the Supreme God of Heaven, the title of which is the Jade Emperor.

Either as the image in which power is manifest, or else as the particular place of the position held, such as a stone, or a tree, or the corner of a field, the deity may be reputed to have some particular powers and be identified with a title and a legend. If the reputation grows sufficiently there may even be branches of the cult of that deity. So, for instance, the City God of the old city of Da Dao Cheng, now a part of Taibei, was known as the Xiahai City God because he was also identified with the place Xiahai from which immigrants brought his image as protection before his cult became that of the territorial guardian of a city. As an identified god his cult had a branch temple in another part of greater Taibei. But as a position in a religious territorial administration, the City God, like the Locality God, had no roots or branches. His shrines do not spread like the cult of an identified god. Instead they are automatically established in every settlement.

This could be interpreted as the posting of territorial guardians at all levels between the City God of administrative headquarters and the shrines of neighbourhood, ward, field and village. Indeed, unless the cults included gentry and officials among their adherents, the only way in which town and village temples were recognised by the imperial administration itself was as territorial shrines. The obligations on every household within a defined territory to contribute to festivals of a local territorial cult upholds the interpretation of its god as a territorial guardian. But the special remedial powers of such a cult are known too, and deference is paid to its deity by households seeking attention to change their condition. Moreover, as the institution of an identified spirit or immortal, a local cult is the centre of the division of the incense of that god. A local temple is thus a combination of two systems of religious institution: territorial unit and cult of a deified person.

The main god of the earlier of the two shrines which made up Mountainstreet temple was Ang Gong. Since he was very much a local god, I will continue to use the Taiwanese pronunciation of the name. Ang Gong was no longer renowned for effect, but he was said to have been very effective once, in a fundamental past defending Mountainstreet from aborigine attacks. As a resident of present-day Mountainstreet conceived it, 'You cannot just come and farm on your own, you need a god to trust in'. This was Mountainstreet's, a new settlement's, god and its incense-burner. But it was and is also a division of the incense of a more central and older burner in a larger temple, that of the town on the plains which I will call Palisades.

Every year a figure of Ang Gong was brought from that more central temple to Mountainstreet and accompanied Mountainstreet's incense burner in procession past each household. Representatives from contributing households too far in the mountains to be passed in procession came and burned incense in the temple or shared in the worship at a kinsman's household in the town. A second, smaller figure from Palisades' temple was taken on from Mountainstreet's temple in procession to a settlement of hamlets even further in the mountains which had no temple of its own, and formed the third subregion of Mountainstreet's temple area.

Once built as a local amenity, the Mountainstreet temple came to house many other incense burners and be a meeting place for the groups which took part in or had their own festival celebrations focused on the deities to which these burners and, later, commissioned statues, were devoted. One of them, a spirit-writing association for communication with Xian Gong was attached to the temple and eventually became a shrine to Xian Gong in a hall added to Ang Gong's.

A local temple is the focus and point of assembly for a number of activities. The most usual and ordinary of these is divination by drawing lots. This is done by the shaking of sixty sticks, each marked with a pair of characters. They are shaken until one falls out of the container. For each of the sixty pairs a couplet of classical verse is to be found on a slip of paper. There are sixty pads of these couplets on a board. The person seeking divination tears off a sheet of the appropriate couplet and consults an expert or a book of standard interpretations kept in the temple. In the Xian Gong shrine of the Mountainstreet temple there was in addition to a container of general divination lots of this type, a special set of sticks for the divination of sickness. The prescription for each of the sixty was in a book kept not in the temple but in the pharmacy owned by the head of the temple management committee.

The temple cleaner, paid a small fee by the committee, was often at hand to advise on the proper ritual of divination and offering but she was illiterate and so could not help in its interpretation. Regular users of the temple who were literate would often be at hand for interpretation and for reading the couplet and book if the person seeking divination were illiterate. In more central temples and formerly when Mountainstreet performed more central place functions than it now does, a full-time keeper who is also a ritual expert would be available to interpret. He would also perform rituals of remedy and exorcism if necessary, for more recompense (not exactly a fee because it is handed over as a gift, in a red envelope).

The local temple is also a centre for entertainment, its festival theatre and procession. For these and for the upkeep and refurbishing of its fabric, it is in addition both the object and the headquarters for the collection of funds. When the yard in front of the temple was still the main marketing area, the temple keeper kept the scales and collected fees for their use in the temple fund. In 1966–8 the yard was no longer used for market fairs. There were in any case other ways of raising funds, by voluntary donations for the temple and by a head tax for procession festivals. But the yard was still used for theatrical performances. The planks and poles and canvas for the stage were kept in the temple building.

Mountainstreet town had sustained a small theatrical troupe. Now it sustained just a band of traditional instruments. The band performed on Mountainstreet's festivals for no fee but when invited to the festivals of other places it was paid a recompense and entertained by whoever hired it to perform. The band rehearsed in the temple but its instruments were kept in the houses of its present and former sponsors.

Ang Gong was undoubtedly a territorial guardian in Mountainstreet. But he also had a compatriotic definition, referring to Anxi county, Fujian province, from which came the ancestors of the majority of the residents of Mountainstreet and its surrounding region, via Palisades. Ang Gong was a collective title for a pair of gods whose separate titles were written Zun Wang (Venerated King) and Da Fu (Great Minister). Da Fu is the lesser of the two, but he had a festival and an older temple of origin separate from those of Zun Wang. The Palisades temple, usually thought to be the main temple from whose incense Mountainstreet's was founded, was specifiable as a temple dedicated to Zun Wang. It was, indeed, identifiable even more exclusively. For the Zun Wang temple in Palisades was not only a local, territorial temple. It was associated with those bearing the family name Gao. Every five years the Zun Wang god was taken out in a gigantic procession through Palisades. It took six hours to pass in 1966. It was made up of delegations from a large region of the Taibei basin, including Mountainstreet, in which Anxi compatriots of that name were numerous enough to form a local surname group for the purpose of sponsoring a contingent of the procession. Mountainstreet's contingent carried the Mountainstreet Zun Wang figure.

The size and magnificence of the procession and the accompanying feasts in the households of the families of that surname was a challenge to, and a response to the challenge from, the procession and feasts held every nine years by families of another surname, Zhang, from the same region centred on the Zun Wang of another, nearby, local temple.

These rival festivals continue the more exclusive, descent principle in the identification of a cult which has become that of local, territorial temples. Indeed, the property of both temples, which was extensive before land reform, had been contributed (and what remained of it was still managed) by a committee of the respective surname associations. The revenue from it was used not only for town festivals but also for surname festivals and the annual commemoration of ancestors of local families with that surname.

In Mountainstreet no surname group was prominent, either numerically or as an organisation. But two surname associations existed in rudimentary form. One of them was the five-yearly organisation of a contingent to the surname festival of Palisades' Zun Wang. But it combined for no other function to my knowledge. The other surname association was not linked with the local god. It manifested itself only at funerals of families of that, and of no other name in Mountainstreet, to contribute gifts and eulogies in the name of the association.

So, in Mountainstreet at least, descent reckoning does not affect the social definition of the temple area through dominance of any surname grouping, and neither does any grouping of descendants from a place of mainland origin. Once a household had an incense burner for gods, that household was included in the Ang Gong procession festival whether or not its ancestors came from Anxi.

Zun Wang is not the only god of Anxi compatriots in the Taibei basin. Two of the major popular temples of Taibei city originated as Anxi immigrants' foundations, the Qing Shui Zu Shi Gong temple and the Fa Zhu Gong temple. But the latter functioned as a territorial guardian's temple and had no exclusively compatriotic festivals, or subdivisions. The former grew from the domestic altar of its founder into an extensive compatriots' organisation, maintained into the present day. The organisation was made up of five major regions of Anxi compatriots' settlement, three of which rotated the responsibility for providing the master of the incense-burner for the Seventh Month Festival at the Taibei city root temple. The other two were organised around the festivals of its two largest branch temples in Taibei county. The regions of branching and surname organisation of the Palisades and the other surname's Zun Wang temples together coincided roughly with two of the Taibei city Qing Shui Zu Shi Gong temple's regions. A figure of Zu Shi Gong was carried from the Taibei temple in their processions as a matter of course. And just as subfigures from the root temples toured the areas of the branch temples of Zun Wang and Da Fu every year, so every four years a large subfigure of Zu Shi Gong from the Taibei city temple toured the Palisades region with Ma Zu in the series of processions which started near Mountainstreet.

In short, surname associations in this system are divisions of place-of-origin organisation and conversely, place-of-origin organisations can become inclusive territorial organisations as local territorial cults.

This was not a neat structure of subregions fitting well into larger regional units. Nor was it expected of every household which could trace its ancestry to Anxi that it pay respect to either god. All that is demonstrated here is that the Taibei basin is defined into networks of compatriot communities by the division of incense, subfigures and regional organisations of root temples and their festivals. Their gods are referred to as 'ancestral gods'. Kenneth Dean (1988:218ff) describes a similar subdivision of the Penglai plain in Anxi.

Processions of the root Zu Shi Gong figure in 1987, stopped at ancestral halls in three carefully demarcated regions called 'altars'.

When a person is buried, his ancestral county of origin is very often inscribed on the gravestone, and less often the district (*xiang*) is also noted. But this is a smaller differentiation than that marked by compatriots' temples. What mattered was the growth of centres focused on temples of settlers in Taiwan. Zu Shi Gong's temple is in what used to be known as Mengjia. With the rise of Mengjia to a central city, it became a larger temple with a wider network than Zun Wang's, which is in a less central place.

On the other hand, Zu Shi Gong's temple in Taibei city is only a compatriots' and a devotional temple. It is not a territorial guardian. It has no territorial procession. Indeed, this is apparently the reason for its very small attendance by residents of Mountainstreet, whose festival visits to Taibei city are much more frequent on the days of the processions of the city's territorial guardians.

One of the main territorial procession festivals in Taibei tours the old city of Da Dao Cheng, the river port to which Mountainstreet's tea traders went to sell what they had collected in the Mountainstreet hinterland. It is also the place from which most of Mountainstreet's groceries came. Its territorial festival was therefore attended by Mountainstreet's bigger shop-keepers and traders. They were entertained by their suppliers and buyers who were in turn entertained in Mountainstreet at its main festivals. The other Taibei festivals to which Mountainstreet residents went regularly and in numbers of more than one family were those held in parts of Taibei to which kin or ex- neighbours had moved.

Apart from attendance at other places' festivals, there were pilgrimages, especially in the days following New Year. Temples which have become famous and large, also become centres of tourism. One of the five temples regularly visited by Mountainstreet residents was the Ma Zu temple in Guandu, Taibei county, from which the figure for the four-yearly procession came to Mountainstreet. Another, for the better off, was the most toured Ma Zu temple in Taiwan, to the south in Beigang on the coastal plain. Closer was the Zhi Nan Gong, the temple from which the figure for the annual Xian Gong procession came to Mountainstreet. The remaining two were centres in Taibei city of the syncretic cults which originated in the sub-official religious culture of local gentry and merchants and then thrived with the colonial removal of the imperial state religion. (See Feuchtwang 1974.)

118

A hierarchical network of territorial cults and pilgrimages has been described for another part of the Taibei basin by Sangren (1987: Part II). He pays close attention to its compatibility with administrative and marketing hierarchies, and is able to show in systematic detail that it coincides with the marketing hierarchy up to its first three levels of centrality. But rather than assuming an historical priority of the commercial function, he successfully demonstrates that the pattern of settlement and mutual protection according to a tracing of place-of-origin commonality and trust was *at the same time* a ritual identification and a system of trading relations. Division of incense pioneered the paths of settlement and it retraces them once they have become routes of commerce. Above the third level of centrality, routes of pilgrimage to the most famous temples and their incense-burners bind territorial cults without obeying the centralities of commerce. Cult centres at this level attract their own, ritual commerce, but are not commercial or industrial centres of equivalent scale.

Territories described by procession festivals at these different levels of encompassment have been surveyed elsewhere in Taiwan as 'liturgical' or 'ritual' spheres by Lin Meirong (Lin Meirong 1986 and 1988). A similar spatial system of ritual territories had been established far longer, and been revived again in the region of Putian, Fujian province. Kenneth Dean (2000) demonstrates that local temple areas in Putian are an appropriation of the Ming dynasty establish-ment of altars of *she* :

> within fifty years of the founding of the Ming and the establishment of official altars of the soil in the subcantons of Putian, most of these altars had already merged with temples dedicated to local gods. What is more [their] statues were carried on procession ..around the boundaries of the cult. (pp. 6–7)

Temples became corporate landlords using the rents to pay for ritual performances, and centres for the organisation of local defence militia and such public works as repairs of irrigation channels, roads and bridges. Temple land-holdings have since then been redistributed, both in the mainland and in Taiwan. But investigations by Dean and Lin Meirong confirm the continuing vitality of these systems of territorial ritual.

## PROCESSION AND BIRTHDAY FESTIVALS

The greatest ritual means of differentiating a locality is a procession festival. The day of a procession festival is not the listed birthday of the god as it appears in printed almanacs. It is not a birthday (*sheng dan*) but a 'welcome with incense' or an 'offering of incense' (*ying xiang* or *jin xiang*) on the anniversary of the first time the god was invited to the place. Mountainstreet town had three such days every year. Two were for the two gods named together in the single title of Ang Gong in Mountainstreet and the third was for Xian Gong.

In addition, every four years there was a fourth procession festival for the much more widely known Ma Zu. But she had a special and peculiar effectiveness in this region. More usually she is known as a protectress of sea-travellers. For this reason and because her biography places her birth in Fujian so that her cult is particularly popular in that province, she was often invoked and carried, in incense dust and images, across the straits to Taiwan by early Fujianese settlers. But in the Mountainstreet region her power (*ling*) had been invoked to get rid of a crop pestilence, and it is for her responsiveness on that score that the great four-yearly procession festivals are held.

The two procession festivals for the Ang Gong gods framed the year. At the beginning, a figure of Da Fu, the civil half of Ang Gong, was fetched from a root temple in a village on the plain on the sixth day of the second month and joined with Mountainsireet town's Ang Gong in a procession around the town. At the end, the figure of Zun Wang, the military half of Ang Gong, was similarly brought to Mountainstreet on the third *yuan*, the fifteenth day of the tenth month. Every local temple in this part of Taiwan had two such dates called the 'beginning of the year' and the 'end of the year' (*nian tou* and *nian wei*). The many local temples dedicated to Ang Gong in this region had one or other or both dates, the first at the end of the first month or beginning of the second, the last in the tenth month, to entertain visiting figures from one or other of the root temples. Although in the same season, their actual days of procession were different. So the season was one of exchange feasting, friends or relatives visiting each others' places to eat and watch theatre on their respective festive days. Government pressures to reduce feasting and in effect reduce the representation of communities to each other had, however, resulted in the amalgamation of the end-of-year processions into the one day.

Ma Zu's four-yearly tour summed up the others in Mountainstreet. Of the annual procession days, only one merited the ritual slaughter and offering of whole pigs in Mountainstreet, the end-of-the-year festival when two pigs were offered, one by the master and one by the vice-master of the incense-burner. But to welcome Ma Zu every household tried to have a pig to slaughter, those with less ready money bringing up a piglet in the preceding years and fattening it with their waste. In addition, the head tax for festival expenses was twice as much for Ma Zu as for the least of the annual procession days, the one for Xian Gong.

She was the only one to be accompanied by a figure of Qing Shui Zu Shi Gong, taken from the root temple in Taibei city. And in addition she was escorted by figures from the root temples of the three annual processions themselves. In other words, her procession marked from the broadest to the narrowest definition the levels of compatriotic territorial identification, down from Fujian (Ma Zu herself), Quan-zhou prefecture and Anxi county (Qing Shui Zu Shi Gong), the local settlements of descendants from Anxi (Ang Gong), and the cult of a saviour deity particularly cultivated in Mountainstreet with reference to its nearby cult centre (Xian Gong). What is more, within the district of Mountainstreet, she toured places on different days which on the annual processions were subregions of the same one procession.

Territorial ritual organisation of this kind exists all over Taiwan, with considerable variation. For instance a larger territory in Tainan county, studied by Fiorella Allio (2000), is described by processions of all the gods in the area touring every street and path of its sub-regions. There is simply a sharing of incense between the sub-regions of the area and the same rivalry between the bands and deities of the sub-regions as there is in Mountainstreet, but not a division of incense from a root temple. In Mountainstreet there is a less clear distinction between sharing and division of incense, between local territorial processions and the invitation of incense from a mother temple. But in both cases, the festival of processions marks out temple territories.

The organisation of procession days is, with the procession itself, a territorial definition. Mountainstreet's temple area was made up of three subregions whose boundaries coincided more or less with administrative boundaries. One temple subregion was made up of the town itself and the surrounding hamlets. In government administration they were two *cun*, the base units of local government and representation on the district council. This temple subregion was one place on Ma Zu's tour, and was the only one of the subregions involved in Xian Gong's procession. A second temple subregion was that of a nearby village which made one administrative *cun*, and it was another place which Ma Zu visited separately on her tour.

A third temple subregion was the most mountainous and the furthest from the town. On both the annual Ang Gong procession days, this remoter subregion took its own figure from the root temple via Mountainstreet town's temple. In local government, this subregion was three *cun*. It was also three separate places on Ma Zu's tour. One of them, having been the first to invite Ma Zu, thus inaugurating the local tradition of four-yearly Ma Zu processions, maintained the privilege of being the first stop on her tour. Men from that place had worked as stonemasons for a late Qing dynasty refurbishment of the Guandu temple and so had what was referred to as a share in the temple from which the mother figure was brought.

Each of the three subregions of Mountainstreet's temple area had its own young men's band which accompanied the gods in procession. The first was a band of musicians, the second a band of lion dancers, and the third a band of dragon dancers. Since the third took its own figure in procession, it also had its own organisation of the incense-burner master and his assistants. The remaining two subregions had a single consolidated incense-burner organisation of seventeen representatives or assistants (called *toujia*).

The assistants were chosen by means of incense and divination blocks from lists of heads of household in each of the seventeen neighbourhoods. Again, although their boundaries coincided with those of administrative *lin* (neighbourhoods) whose elected heads were supposed to meet in a *cun* assembly, the festival neigbourhoods in some cases included more than one administrative *lin*.

Festival neighbourhood heads had the function of collecting festival tax from the households on their list. Single-member households were excluded, and thus the festival organisation excluded most recent immigrants, and those too poor to have married and made a household. These single-member households were included in the official *lin*, but it had no administrative function other than being a level of registration.

Zun Wang, Da Fu and Xian Gong were also celebrated annually in the other kind of festival in Mountainstreet, a more voluntary festival without procession. Zun Wang's was the greatest procession festival of the three, while Xian Gong's birthday was again the least communal, in having no theatre performed, but, on the evidence of the two years I saw them, of the three birthday festivals it was the most actively celebrated in the temple.

## A PROCESSION FESTIVAL: ZUN WANG

The annual festival for Zun Wang was linked with its predecessor as a new coil in a spiral. The coil begins in the afternoon of the ceremonial of the previous year's festival, in the temple itself. Here, while the Daoist priest continues to conduct the religious ceremony, the god is divined to select who should be the seventeen heads of household (*toujia*) representing the territory for next year's end-of-the-year festival. Each of the seventeen represents between 50 and 250 individuals living in his neighbourhood. He brings with him to the temple written on red paper (the colour of good luck) the names of all the heads of the households in his neighbourhood and under each name is the number of males and of females living in the household at the time. The chances of a household head being *toujia* for one procession festival in a Mountainstreet town neighbourhood is about once in six years (the average number of households in a neighbourhood being twenty and the number of annual procession festivals three, plus one more every four years). The chances of being *lu zhu* (master of the incense-burner) are of course much less, between seventeen and twelve times less (seventeen being the number of *toujia* from which he is selected at the beginning and the end of the year, twelve being the number of *toujia* at Ma Zu's and at Xian Gong's processions). Although the experience itself is shared by him with his sons and brothers, or even collateral kin, to whom he can delegate some of his duties, nevertheless a number of people besides children have never had the experience of being *toujia*, and an even greater number have never experienced being *lu zhu*. The longer the period of residence in Mountainstreet, the higher the chance of having been *toujia* and therefore of having had the kind of information and experienced the social pressures and commitments that involves.

The selection continues throughout the afternoon in the temple's front shrine hall. For that day, the hall is hung with the images of the mediators of the Daoist sacred area: the Three Pure Ones. The altar table is laden with offerings and with the ritual implements of the Daoist. The air is jammed with the sound of pipes, gongs, drums and the bell the Daoist shakes as he incants scriptures and steps through the rites. It is lit by great shafts of sunlight that come under the porch, fall just inside the hall and reflect off the stone floor, and it is filled with the smoke of spirit-money, incense and cigarettes. Standing to the side of the altar table in order not to bump into the Daoist, but using the divination blocks from the altar, the *toujia* with their lists go through the selection of next year's representatives.

The rite brings out more interest and attention in a larger number of people, participants and non-participants, than any other rite that takes place in the temple during a festival. The divination blocks are two pieces of wood shaped like cupped hands, and held in them with their flat sides placed together, curved sides outwards. After communication has been initiated by burning incense, the blocks are taken and held in the hands with precisely the same gesture as that of offering incense and polite acknowledgement, thanks or greeting. While they are held and shaken, and, by the more flamboyant, passed through the smoke of incense burning on the altar, a question is formulated, either in a whispered voice or spoken out clearly, and then they are dropped to the ground. If one falls with the curved side up and the other with the flat side up, the answer is in the affirmative. This is the most common form of religious communication. Children of three are already imitating it. Each *toujia*, watched by the others who have not yet done it and by an audience of those who are interested, goes through each head of household on his list other than his own, asking if he is to be next year's *toujia* and then throwing the blocks. If the answer is in the affirmative he burns a hole above the name with a stick of burning incense, and then throws the blocks for the same name again. In the end the name on his list with the most incense marks, that is to say the greatest number of consecutive affirmations, will be the next year's *toujia* for his neighbourhood.

From the resulting list of the seventeen *toujia*, the *lu zhu* (master of the incense-burner) and the *fu lu zhu* (vice-master of the incense-burner) are selected by the same means. Once this is done the man who has been asked to be treasurer and secretary for this day's festival, and who has been sitting working at a table at the front of the shrine hall all day and will go on all night, writes out on red paper eighteen times the names of the *lu zhu*, *fu lu zhu* and the fifteen other *toujia*. Each of them has one copy, and another is posted on the wall of the front hall of the temple.

The first action of the seventeen is to meet on the fifteenth day of the first month in the house of the *lu zhu*. There they each contribute a fee, and partake of a feast prepared by the *lu zhu* who keeps their donations. They leave with two red turtle buns each. Once they have been offered, eating them brings peace and luck (red for luck, turtle for longevity). In this case they had been offered to the God of Heaven (Tian Gong) in the house of the *lu zhu* when just he, his family, and the temple treasurer, whom he had already appointed, presented them with the help of the Daoist priest of Mountainstreet.

Within the next few weeks the *toujia* go round to each household in their neighbourhood to collect a head tax (*ding qian*), which in 1966 was three Taiwanese dollars for every member of the household. The tax varies with each procession festival: it was two and a half for Xian Gong and four and a half for Ma Zu in 1967. The money collected is handed to the treasurer on the day of the festival. The amount of money collected by each *toujia*, and the expenditures, are recorded by the treasurer and publicly displayed after each festival on red paper which joins the list of *toujia* pasted on the walls of the temple.

A *toujia's* next action is the negative one of avoiding funerals for the few days before the day of the festival itself. If at any time during the year there has been a funeral in his own household and close family, which he would have been obliged to attend in one of the severest mourning grades, he has to abdicate as *toujia* and another one is chosen or else neighbours and friends join to stand in for him.

He might as a further act of preparation go to the barber on the eve of the festival. On the day of the festival, dressed well, he and his household prepare a table of offerings on the covered terrace outside the temple. Because it is on public display, it is more lavish than it would be were it in the home, as all the rest of the tables in his section are. After the Daoist has, at a certain point in the rites, gone around the *toujia's* offerings, lustrating them, they are cleared and the offerings taken home again for the evening feast. At around the same time, *toujia* bring their lists for the selection of next year's representatives. And this year's coil in the spiral has been completed, next year's starts.

The extra interest in the selection of *toujia* rests in the fact that someone is going to be committed to spending his resources on a relatively large amount of meat and other offerings at next year's festival. There is even more interest in the selection of the *lu zhu* and *fu lu zhu*. They are each expected to hire a band or a lion troupe for the procession. Besides, they must each, early in the festival morning slaughter a pig in offering (it should be a boar, castrated before it has mated) and then present it shorn and decorated, accompanied by their tables of other offerings immediately outside the temple doors.

The method of selection is in itself egalitarian, but gendered by the convention of Chinese kinship that household heads are male. All names of household heads are brought equally before the god. Further bias is introduced. It is extrinsic. Although the festival tax is collected from every household, except single member households and households of Christians (not included in the lists of names put before the god for selection), the names of the poorest, who would be seriously embarrassed by the extra cost of being *toujia* and much more so by the cost of being *lu zhu*, are passed over. There is, therefore, a bias toward the wealthy and the established in Mountainstreet becoming *toujia*, and a stronger bias towards their becoming *lu zhu*. But it is only a slight bias compared with that effective in the selection of *toujia* for the larger procession festivals in big towns and cities. There no lists of households are used. The few who put their names forward to be *toujia* are automatically chosen, and the blocks are used only to select *lu zhu* from them. Since the expenses expected of *toujia* are so high in these city festivals only the wealthiest volunteer, for their own prestige as local patrons.

The method of selection itself is the embodiment of an egalitarian ideal of representation, but the representative must also be a patron, just as the god before whom he is selected is treated as a patron. Selection in egalitarian principle and in the presence of last year's *toujia* constitutes a social sanction on the *toujia*, whatever the strength of his belief and feelings of obligation to the god by whom he was, ostensibly, selected. The meeting and feast on the fifteenth day of the first month in the *lu zhu's* house, and the contribution he makes to it, places him in a group of fellow *toujia*. He is present in that role before the households of his neighbourhood when he levies the head tax. He is further committed before the day of the festival by the investment he has made in the table-full of offerings and on the day itself by its display at the centre of the day's attractions.

The *lu zhu* has all the pressures and makes all the investments of a *toujia* and more. He is in charge of all the arrangements for the festival: the choice (though usually it repeats those of his predecessor) and hiring of the priest and his musicians, the treasurer, the procession band, his own band or lion troupe, the theatrical troupe, the temple cooks and transport to fetch the visiting figure. He is responsible for the choice of the two plays to be performed and he must supervise the accounts of the food and ritual goods bought by the Daoist, the cooks and their assistants, accounts kept by the treasurer on the day of the festival.

The visiting figures were brought by taxi, and placed on the altar tables in the front hall of the temple. Mid-way through the morning the smaller one was collected and strapped into a small uncovered sedan chair and carried off, accompanied by firecrackers, a banner,

126

drum and cymbals. The larger figure was strapped in the place of honour at the centre of the back of a larger, covered sedan chair which had been brought out from the front hall of the temple where it was kept. To its sides and in front of this figure were strapped the figures of the Mountainstreet Zun Wang, and its resident figures of Tudi Gong, Ma Zu and Xian Gong. The sedan chair was draped with red cloth and carried away, preceded by two bands, one a band of musicians playing *suona* (pipes with reed mouth-pieces and horns), gongs, drums and cymbals and one with a lion, both heralded by firecrackers and banners. Behind the sedan chair, the Zun Wang incense-burner is carried by the *lu zhu* or a member of his household or close family. Another member helps him hand out incense in exchange for incense sticks which each household offers at its door as the procession passes. The route of the procession was past every door in Mountainstreet town and then to the village subregion and back, taking over two hours. It went first to the edge of town on the road to Palisades and Taibei. That was the official starting point. There it was joined by the head of the temple committee and the elected head of the *xiang* office, a position which was filled at the time by a Mountainstreet town man. They followed the sedan for only a little way before dropping out and going home. Others joined the procession. Supplicants and givers of thanks to the god for favours brought up the rear, behind the sedan, holding sticks of burning incense.

Meanwhile the cooks and the Daoist priest, on most procession festivals helped by a second Daoist priest from a town further into the mountains to the east, made their preparations. They hung the scrolls of the Daoist imperial cosmology around the altar and placed offerings to them. When the procession returned, the religious ceremonials began.

Apart from being general manager of the festival arrangements and distributing incense in the procession, the master of the incense-burner, whatever his personal religious habits have been, is brought as representative of the community on to the religious plane of activities much more than anyone else except the religious practitioners themselves. The other *toujia* need only participate in the temple rituals once, in the selection of their successors. The *lu zhu* takes home the incense-burner that hangs at the temple door to the God of Heaven during the festival. The *fu lu zhu* takes to his home the Zun Wang incense-burner. On the day of the festival the *lu zhu* must represent the community at certain crucial rites while the Daoist priest performs them for him. In fact they extend beyond the day, for the first such rite is to report to the God of Heaven on *shang yuan*, the fifteenth day of the first month.

On the procession day he is witness to a sequence of rituals that distinguish rites and deities commonly confused, and if he chooses to hear the Daoist's use of the formal literary names of the gods, he can follow up the multiple identities behind the colloquial blanket terms. He is not required to be present at all times. But he is required, and it is the Daoist who, if necessary, reminds him of the requirement, definitely to attend the following rites: once the Daoist has called on the Supreme Emperor of Heaven to open communication between Heaven and Earth there is the initial rite of announcing the place, date and occasion to the gods and inviting them to attend; (the Daoist then establishes his sacred area in the temple as a microcosm, through standard Daoist mediators to the Great Unity (Tai Yi) according to the tradition of Daoism to which his master belonged): then the rite of lighting the oil-lamp in the tub of rice called the *dou* lantern, which embodies the astrological fortune of the whole area represented at the festival. It is marked 'Peace for the Whole Region', in common with other notices and banners, and with the names of the *lu zhu* and *fu lu zhu;* (at the other side of the altar stands another tub of rice which, however, is there only for the Daoist. He places in it, when he is not using them, his own ritual implements, not those kept in the temple, and he addresses it during the course of the rites as the embodiment of his master and the tradition of Daoism passed to him through his master); then the invitation to the gods to partake of the offerings in this order: The Three Heaven Offices (San Tian Gong), Bao Yi Zun Wang and Bao Yi Da Fu (the formal titles of Ang Gong) and Lie Shen (Eminent Gods, a formula which is meant on this occasion specifically to include the other gods worshipped in this temple); finally a separate offering in the temple kitchen, where the food on the altar has been cooked, to Zao Jun, the God of the Stove.

The food offered is not only that on the altar within the temple, but also that on the *toujia's* tables outside the temple on its porch and around the yard. Beyond them, and within houses in the seventeen sections which the *toujia* represent, more offerings are or have been made to the same gods. The *lu zhu* follows the Daoist priest, as he lustrates the offerings of the *toujia*.

The presentation of offerings culminates in the reading by the Daoist of a petition and memorial to the gods, thanking them, asking them for their protection and telling them who the offerers and

128

petitioners are by reading out all the names of the household heads in the seventeen sections. The *lu zhu* must stand behind him as he reads it. The memorial is then burnt with a great deal of spirit-money. A final offering is made to the troops and officers of the gods and another to orphan souls. Then the Daoist priest sees off the gods. The offerings are cleared away, the *toujia* tables taken home, and feasts begin in every household. The collective rituals are over.

## BIRTHDAY FESTIVALS: XIAN GONG AND ZUN WANG

A Buddhist priest, not a Daoist, conducts the ritual in the temple on the fourteenth day of the fourth month, Xian Gong's birthday. And the woman who used to live in the temple as a celibate Buddhist vegetarian until she left to marry, and was not replaced, comes to help with the preparations and cooking. Only eight *toujia* are selected, and with less propriety. On the occasion I saw the selection the names of the households were not read out from prepared lists but from memory, and the name which was first to get three, four or five consecutive positive responses – the number varying according to the disposition of the *toujia* casting the blocks and writing down the names – was selected. A certain bias towards the most easily remembered was thus introduced. For this festival it was not the *toujia* who took the initiative of planning and starting the day and providing the continuity from one year to the next. It was the temple committee or rather those members of it who felt some extra commitment to Xian Gong. As we shall see, at this festival, but not at procession festivals, or at Zun Wang's birthday festival, the temple committee is *formally* represented in full.

On neither of Mountainstreet's two birthday festivals (Da Fu did not have one) do the *toujia* collect money or display tables of offerings outside the temple. They merely present *shengli*, the three or five meats, wine and sweets, tea and fruit in the temple on the altar tables. There is little or no pressure on others to make offerings at home, such as is exerted by a procession. And although the birthday festivals may be the occasion for those who have involved themselves to eat special food, meat and red buns on Zun Wang's day, vegetarian food on Xian Gong's day, cooked and eaten in the temple, they are not feast days. The meat offered on Xian Gong's day is for 'the eminent gods', automatically included in temple offerings as a matter of courtesy. As on other feast days, these are the gods of the area other than the principal god of the day. Following them, the meat is offered to

129

orphan souls in a much longer session than on Zun Wang days. Xian Gong in Mountainstreet, as one of the set of Sage or Beneficent Gods, receives no meat and has no troops. Zun Wang and Ma Zu, on the other hand, have both meat and troops.

Expenses, chiefly theatre and red buns on Zun Wang's birthday and the vegetarian food and priest on Xian Gong's, are met with voluntary contributions. A brief description of the mode of offering in the temple on Zun Wang's birthday will illustrate further differences between Xian Gong's and Zun Wang's days even within the birthday mode of festival. The *lu zhu* of the eight *toujia* of Zun Wang's birthday was responsible for buying the red buns and hiring the theatre troupe, but the money came from contributions made by people who came to the temple and took one of the buns displayed on an altar table, having thrown blocks to see if it was divinely permitted to do so. The buns taken in this way were then eaten for protection and luck. The contribution was calculated by treating one bun as one share of next year's expenses. This kind of bun is called *da gu*, great turtle, and one of them was in fact turtle-shaped. Another kind of red bun offering was also made on this day, not ordered from the baker by the *lu zhu* but brought in individually by those who last year had petitioned the god for protection. Once placed on the altar table, other worshippers marked and reserved them until the end of the day, when they each took their claimed bun home. Claims take the form of a burning incense stick stuck into the bun. To take one is to seek protection and promise to bring a bun double its weight next year if the year has been a prosperous one.

This kind of bun offering is called an 'incense disk' (*xiang pian*). Separate accounts of such offerings were kept in a book whose entries are often filled by the donors themselves, and casually checked by whomever the woman who cleaned the temple asked, she herself being unable to read. On the occasion I saw, the accountant for most of the time was one of the young pipers in Mountainstreet's band. The temple management committee chairman did not come and check them.

By contrast, on Xian Gong's birthday, as on all procession days, the temple chairman did check the accounts. On Xian Gong's birthday, contributions came to 3449 Taiwanese dollars at the end of the day, of which only 1560 was needed for its expenses. The remainder was written down as *shen e* (the spirit's sum) and he took it, presumably as a reserve for temple repairs.

When I saw the Xian Gong birthday festival, affairs were started by three other committee members, none of whom was *toujia*. Two were brothers of a relatively wealthy tea-farming and trading family and the third a rice and tea farmer who sold his own tea in Taibei. They discussed the arrangements of extra altar tables, moved them around, swept the temple and consulted as to the time and order of ceremonies for Xian Gong and Tian Gong (the God of Heaven). After a time the temple cleaner came in and helped. Then the first contributors began to arrive with offerings. One of the first was another, now poor and tubercular, tea merchant who was both a committee member and a *toujia*. He then stayed and kept the account book for the rest of the day.

Contributors gave between 20 and 100 dollars in cash. In return they received a wafer wrapped in pink paper and called a longevity biscuit. Many of them had in the past sought Xian Gong's protection for their young children by presenting them to him, to be a child to him, as it was called, in exactly the same manner as a nominal foster parent was sought, by giving a present which was spirit-money and offerings in Xian Gong's case. Xian Gong in return 'gave' the child rice gruel, actually given by the real parents after having presented their child. Nominal foster parents are always people who have been lucky, that is to say have prospered and had many supportive and accomplished children themselves. They may, if the relationship continues, act as their nominal children's sponsor for school, wedding, job, or commercial venture. The real parents in return must invite the nominal parents to their feasts and the children go to the birthday and funeral feasts of their nominal parents. With Xian Gong as nominal parent, so the wife of a Mountainstreet mineowner and member of the temple committee told me, you do not have all the trouble with feast invitations, you just have to pay respects on his birthday. Among the parents of his nominal children I counted that day were one third of the membership of the temple committee, themselves likely targets for nominal parenthood. Another third of the membership made ordinary contributions. In addition to exchanging a cash contribution for the pink wafer, each year every parent of Xian Gong's children renewed an incense sachet to be hung around the neck of each nominated child.

The mother of the head of the temple committee, wife of the main sponsor of the temple's last rebuilding, was on hand to give advice to the many contributors where and how to make their offerings. For much of the morning she and the brother of the aforementioned rice and tea farmer handled the renewal of incense amulets.

The head of the committee himself, who was also principal of Mountainstreet school, came and burned incense and for a while stood behind the Buddhist priest with three other members of the committee. When the priest bowed, they bowed, kneeling when he knelt. This and the ninth day of the ninth month when the same Buddhist priest came again for the establishment of a *dou* for subscribing households, were the only times I saw the school principal take part in temple ritual, even to the extent of burning incense.

The important junctures for members of the committee to be present behind the priest were whenever he read the memorial of the names of the full committee as paying Tian Gong, Xian Gong, the Buddhas and the Bodhisattvas their respects (*zun jing*). By the time this was done for Tian Gong the account book of contributors was necessarily closed, for all the names in it had then to be read out, petitioning the protection of the God of Heaven through Xian Gong.

In 1967, there was an extra memorial, on a separate sheet of paper, from the tea-farming family. In the past few weeks the old head of the family had suffered from a gall-stone, which the local doctor, Dr G, was able successfully to treat. The old man soon afterwards had sprained his foot in a fall. The memorial was a petition for his health, and was the only ritual remedy his wife and sons sought for him. His wife flicked dust from the incense burning to Tian Gong into a cup while the priest was intoning the Golden Light Penance for Heaven scripture (Jin Guang Ming Chang Zhai Tian *ke yi*). The third son of the old man was rather embarrassed but helped her. The memorials were then burned with spirit-money. Later in the afternoon new copies of the memorials were read outside the temple, facing outwards in an offering of charity to orphan souls. Between the ceremonies two vegetarian meals were eaten by the petitioners present, and anyone else they had persuaded to come. These meals were called 'eating [by courtesy of] Xian Gong'.

The vegetarian meal cooked and served in the temple on the ninth day of the ninth month was called the same, even though it was not Xian Gong's day. It was on his altar that the *dou* was set up and the Diamond Sutra was read by the Buddhist priest in support of a similar memorial. The festival on this day was a so-called 'meeting for the ritual of *dou*' (*li dou fa hui*).

A *dou* is a set of symbols which stands for the fortune, fate or cosmological condition of a household or a larger collective unit. At procession festivals there is a *dou* for the whole community of the temple's area. But on the ninth-month occasion, the memorial listed only the households, members of which had come to be registered on it and to pay their contributions and, without their having specially to attend, or pay, the households of all members of the temple committee. On this day there was even less involvement of the rest of Mountainstreet than on Xian Gong's birthday, many people not even knowing that there was this ceremony in the temple every year. But exactly the same families as participated actively on Xian Gong's birthday were the only ones active in the ninth day of the ninth month ceremony five months later, in October: the school principal and his mother, the consumptive tea merchant and his rather moralistic wife, the other tea farmer and his wife and sons, their tea trader friend, and the rice and tea farmer.

Xian Gong's birthday and the *dou* ceremony were the only two Buddhist ceremonies conducted in Mountainstreet's temple. Xian Gong was identified with both, and the temple committee with him, particularly the school principal, a direct descendant of the head of the spirit-writing association that brought Xian Gong to Mountainstreet. As head of the temple committee he had, albeit perfunctorily, for a few yards of the procession, also to be associated with Zun Wang's Daoist ceremonies.

The terms 'Buddhist' and 'Daoist' are used here to indicate definite tendencies, not any orthodox purity of tradition. The *dou* as a set of symbols, and Xian Gong's legend, are both Daoist in origin. Possibly, as a member of the ruling party and administrator of the official culture in school, with its view of popular religion as superstition and its admonitions against feasting, the head teacher felt more able to support and participate in the Xian Gong kind of birthday ceremony.

## COLLECTIVE PROTECTION AND INDIVIDUAL ADVANCEMENT

There were, then, two temple festival modes of ritual in Mountainstreet. There was that of Zun Wang and procession festivals with its greater emphasis on communal and territorial definition. And there was that of birthday festivals and Xian Gong with its greater emphasis on the self-selection of individual households.

There was a separation of festivals and their *toujia* from corporate temple management, and the temple management committee was definitely aligned with Xian Gong. But it was also the committee of patrons of the whole temple, with its complete calendar of festivals, including those of Ang Gong. So the identification with Xian Gong was an internal process within the locality's religious formation.

The local territorial guardian was a cult patronised by the most status-conscious and esteemed of locals, but his festivals, identified so closely with the control and use of the power of *gui*, was avoided precisely by these patrons in their status-consciousness. The newer cult of Xian Gong, and in particular the birthday, not the procession festival of that cult, because it focused more particularly on the individual household and its career, suited them better. Within the repertoire of popular rituals, they chose the saviour deity and the household as a temporal extension, with ancestors and expectations of social esteem, to set themselves apart.

Whether through a territorial guardian known only as a position, like Tudi Gong, or a more identified guardian such as those celebrated in festivals of local territorial cults, direct access to the top of the hierarchy of gods, even adoption of a top deity as the object of a local cult, brings the system of popular territorial guardians into an odd relationship with the imperial cults and with the imperial and republican officaldoms themselves. As expounded by storytellers and answers to the questioning stranger, they are obviously modelled on the imperial hierarchy. But according to the authority of the officials of that hierarchy, and those of its state cults, adoption of high deities by the common people for their local worship was an aberration. On the other hand, to get round the rules of officialdom and gain access to higher reaches without passing through the lower was and still is possible by bribery, or by personal contacts, or by petition. The first two means are incorrect, while the latter is an appeal to an upright and just authority at the same time as it is a supplication to a more powerful patron. The popular versions of political protection enacted in territorial cults thus enact every practice. Yet they are considered aberrant by all regimes, because they are models and organisations which could be substitutes for the actual political channels.

The civil, upright surveillance and register of birth, marriage and death enacted by the Locality God standing guardian over *gui* is the closest to the orthodoxy of policing and of the state cults themselves. The syncretist and saviour gods of pan-Chinese appeal such as Xian Gong are exemplars of spirit-writing morality books, favoured by the patrons of local cults aspiring to official political status. The procession festivals of territorial and place-of-origin cults with their military command over and by *gui*, are obviously the most aberrant.

# Chapter Five

# The incense-burner: communication and deference

'Where did people go to make offerings before the temple was built?'
I asked the keeper of a Mountainstreet general store and his assistant.
Both were sources of advice about ritual matters to their neighbours
and customers. They answered, 'It is not necessary to go to a temple.
Everyone makes offerings in their own house.'

The simplest domestic altar has just two permanent installations,
an incense-burner and a pair of divination blocks. Most commonly an
incense burner is a glazed earthenware or porcelain bowl filled with
sand or chaff as a base and with incense ashes at the top. Incense is
burned on sticks, held in the common gesture of formal greeting,
hands folded over each other with the thumbs next to each other
resting against the side of a forefinger. In worship, the incense sticks
are inserted between thumbs and forefinger. Then the incense stick is
stuck into the chaff and allowed to smoulder down, adding to the
ashes in the pot.

The similarity of burning incense to formal greetings was given
most commonly as its meaning: 'burning incense is an invitation (to
the god)' or 'a polite formality', 'a signal of respect', 'to open
communication', 'like handing out an invitation card' or 'like offering
a cigarette', or tea. It is of the highest formality because it is addressed
to someone who was outstandingly able and is now like an important
person who must be treated attentively, it was explained. Burning
incense was likened to the lowest form of deference: incense, one
person said, is to separate men from a god like going behind a
partition to speak (to the god). Burning incense, then, is an act of
opening communication by formal deference, at least as a host to a
guest, at most as subject to emperor.

Burning incense goes with greeting and commensality among the
participants themselves. At first it seems paradoxical that among them
the feast table celebrates collectivity and equality, especially if it is also

an organisation around an incense-burner, such as a sworn brotherhood, a secret society, a group of classmates, or of compatriots, or a guild.[1] As a person at a feast table at the festival of one of Taibei city's territorial guardian gods said: 'You may be an official tomorrow and I just a common person, but at table we are all equal.' Since the burning of incense is a form of deference and gives prominence to a dyadic and hierarchical relationship, the paradox of equality is resolved: the feasters are only equal before a god.

The singling out of a pair of subjects along a line of communication is apparent in the image of the incense stick and its smoke. By means of the smoke curling up, it was explained to me, the god is notified of the intention to communicate. The smell of the incense catches the god's attention and the smoke directs him to the person and the matter at hand. Referring to the god and his image on the altar one person said 'the god sits in meditation. When you burn incense, the eyes light up and take notice'. While holding the burning incense the person starts his communication by naming the god and the day. The person's own name and address are also given. An invitation to take the offerings presented is then made. The divination blocks may be thrown to verify that the offerings are pleasing to the god. When the incense has been allowed to burn down something over half its length in the incense burner the divine patron and guest is asked, by means of the divination blocks, whether he is pleased, and a special favour is asked or a generalised plea for protection made. On the less important dates of regular domestic worship, this form may be simplified into a more perfunctory burning of incense to introduce whatever offerings are made, leaving out the divination blocks.

Without divination blocks, incense may itself be the medium as well as the introduction of communication. A man who makes a partial living from the fish, prawn and eels he catches in the creeks of Mountainstreet, said he could tell his traps were full by burning incense. They were full if all three sticks burned down absolutely evenly. Once, before the results of a lottery were announced in the press he used the same technique to tell, to the astonishment of his neighbours, that he had won.

Incense itself is thought to be capable of initiating communication in what is known as 'flaring incense' (*fa lu*) or 'flaring fire' (*fa huo*), when the incense sticks in the burner, instead of smouldering down, suddenly flare up from the bottom. This is taken as a warning, and as a sign that some ritual precaution must be taken. The ancestral incense-burner in the house of a goldminer in the northeast coastal region of Taiwan flared, so his Mountainstreet cousin said, and that day his pick hit some unexploded gunpowder and his hands were burned in the explosion. All the other occurrences of flaring incense about which I heard were in temple incense burners. It was said that incense in Mountainstreet temple's incense-burner used to flare in pioneering days when aborigines were about to attack. More recently, in the last few years, the incense in the burner for Xian Gong in Mountainstreet temple flared, and ritual precautions were taken so that nothing untoward happened.

Incense is, in short, treated as a medium of communication in its own right as well as a symbol of deference. In both senses it has the effect of singling out the social unit which owns the burner. From the examples given, it is apparent that the unit is singled out for the particular effect on it which eventualities implying a larger, and inclusive unit will have: the Mountainstreet creeks, unowned and common property, on the trapper; the mine, or an anonymous carelessness of one of its workers, on this particular miner; foreign attackers on one Chinese temple area. The message is more than an answer to 'why me'. The 'me' is also defined as a social unit: an incense-burner is corporate property. And the 'why' is not a selection of the unit by completely non-social natural forces, though that is possible in some cases such as the eventuality of a pestilence. The forces are, rather, social forces in units of such generality or inclusiveness as to appear to the incense-burner group as natural forces.

By burning incense, and through its medium, a social unit identifies itself and is identified. Once recognised it is enabled as a subject to act through similar ritual mediation upon the projected circumstance in relation to which it is singled out. There are three points of reference in this drama of communication and effect; the social subject, the greater force or circumstance or eventuality to which it is subjected, and the ideal, supernatural subject. The last ideal term, which may be multiplied as a hierarchy of subject beings, is linked to the third person which is the force, circumstance or eventuality. It may be its administrator (for instance controller of forces that can beat back *the aborigines*) or its essential being (for instance a point of concentration or a particular manifestation of *financial luck*). By means of addressing the ideal term, the third can be treated as a subject with which the first subject can interact as if the two were commensurate, albeit one more powerful than the other. This elementary form provides one way in which a person can know and represent the structure in which he or she exists.

The first term is always a collectivity. The domestic incense-burner unit is the whole family or household (*he jia* or *jia nei*). While the temple incense-burner unit is the village (*zhuangtou* or *cun nei*). If not in the inauguration of the domestic gods' incense-burner, then in the exchange of incense when the local temple burner is taken past every household in procession on festivals, the former is a subdivision of the latter's ash. A further division of incense ash to a single individual is possible. But then it is no longer a medium of communication. It is the agency of protection itself. Incense ash from the burner of an effective god is taken as medicine, mixed with water and drunk. Or it is worn around the neck in a sachet when travelling long distances or staying away from home for a long time. Boys conscripted for military service are often prevailed upon by their parents to wear an incense sachet.

In a frequently cited legend of the foundation of Lung Shan Si, the largest of the Taibei city temples, such an incense sachet worn by an immigrant, was the foundation of the new cult centre, but only when transformed into an incense-burner. The smallest unit of worship is either a voluntary association of individuals or a household. It may itself be associated with other households territorially and possibly in other, more voluntary kinds of association, as a subdivision of a shared incense-burner, but however small, the minimal unit is collective. The performance of regular worship is itself a shared act. There is delegation of ritual labour, from the essential work of holding incense in deference and communication to the throwing of the blocks to discover whether the offerings are satisfactory. The laying of the offerings themselves, the burning of spirit-money, and the firing of crackers, may all be delegated to juniors.

Furthermore, the division of incense ash links domestic ritual units into a larger territorial unit. The rotation of responsibility for an incense-burner links an association of individuals or of ritual subunits, and the combined territorial and compatriot ritual unity of Mountainstreet is itself, as we have seen, linked through such a rotation as well as through the division of incense ash to more centrally placed temples. One thing to note here about the organisation of ritual units is the combination of several levels of inclusion, with a lack of ultimate centralisation. They are neither joined in a single unified cult, nor in a single territorial entity if we exclude, as both historically and institutionally separated, the organisation of state cults. Nevertheless, this is inclusion of units with each other at levels which are progressively general (household, ward, festival area, town's region, region of origin and the diaspora of its migrants). This inclusion is both a means of organisation and ideologically a symbolic device by which mediation between a first person unit is possible with a third person as interacting subjects even though the third person be a set of social relations or a social-cum-natural eventuality that includes the first.

## PATRONS

The relation between the manager of the corporate property of a temple and the temple's community is much like the relation of god to feast members. It is one of patronage.

Donations in excess of the standard levied amount for temple building, furnishing, festival and theatre, as well as taking the responsibility for the expenses of a local band, lion or theatrical troupe, is the channel for conversion of wealth to local notability and possible management of the temple. I listed all the names of donors inscribed on the Mountainstreet temple furnishings provided since 1950 – boards of eulogy to the gods, altar tables, side tables, set of divination lots, and so on – and of the twelve names which occurred more than once, eight were on the temple's management committee.[2] In Mountainstreet, this amounts only to confirmation of patronage. But in Taibei city the equivalent position brings considerable power of its own since the temple's resources and links are far more substantial.

The distinction between them and the rest of the community is there potentially from the first donation. Frequently it is the donation by a household head of the use of his domestic altar statue to others not members of the household. A household is both a unit of neighbourhood and a unit of grouping by descent. Its altar is divided for the worship of gods on one side and ancestors on the other. Nevertheless, despite the division in ritual, the household is a single social unit. Should a household let it be known that a god on its altar is very effective and responsive, and invite neighbours to communicate with the god, that side of the household altar can develop into a separate altar, entirely for the worship of the god and additional gods, and perhaps eventually into a temple. This seems to have occurred in the early history of Mengjia, now part of Taibei, and of what eventually became some of its most popular temples (see Feuchtwang 1974b). It can also occur when the domestic altar of a spirit medium becomes the centre of a successful practice.

Each proposal to build, rebuild or make a major repair to a temple is the creation of an opportunity to donate a large enough sum to become a main sponsor and thus achieve a position of importance in the management of the general subscription fund for building or repair, or for the ensuing consecration and henceforward in the management of the temple and its property. Each renewal and its subscription appeal is also a formalisation of the temple's following, and the consecration gives it a territorial definition.

The greater the number of generations in the history of a cult and the greater its popularity, the looser the claims to be descended from its originator or originators are likely to be. But they are nevertheless made in some instances of long-established and very popular and central local temples. A city god temple in Taibei for instance was run by men who claim descent from the shop-keeper whose household god the central figure of the temple originally was, four or five generations ago.

At its most general and implicit, descent works as the mere reckoning of generational time of residence in a place defined territorially as the area of a local temple's festivals. It is more prominent when the area's first settlers defined themselves and their settlement according to a place of common origin, and enough resident households can claim descent from it to form a larger group than any other ritually definable group in the area. It is yet more explicit if the temple, like the Palisades' Ang Gong, was built by an association of residents who defined their association not only according to a common place of origin but also by a common surname.

For the organisation of the Palisades' Ang Gong the vocabulary of kinship segmentation was used. Each regional section was suffixed *zu* (ancestor) referring to the subfigures taken out from the root temple annually to make a tour of visits through each region. The regions were subdivisions of three so-called *fang* (sublineages). The first great *fang*, and possibly the third (but I lack information about it), had estates in its name, and there were estates of sub-*fang*. From these estates came the largest contributions to the rebuilding of the Palisades temple in 1960. In each case the estate bore the name of a specified ancestor, whose name and genealogical position was in the surname association's register. By the donation of estates in the name of their ancestors, the wealthy constituted the areas in which they had accumulated or invested their wealth as regional segments of a compatriot organisation. Among the other participants in the surname association's festivals there were those like the three wealthy Gao families of Mountainstreet who contributed in the name of a branch temple. They were also members of Mountainstreet's temple committee.

Those that contributed in the name of a branch temple were exercising a residual right of the same type as the right exercised by the families of the relevant surname to manage the Palisades temple. They managed it, as descendants of its founders, even though it was also a local temple with festivals in the name of and financed by the households of *all* surnames in its area.

The geographical distribution of Ang Gong temples marks a pattern of concentrations of settlement by descendants of immigrants from Anxi.[3] A modern extension of this is the high frequency of Ang Gong festivals in the eastern suburbs of Taibei city. They occur not only where the first settlements of Anxi compatriots were founded but also where urban immigrants from the areas of later rural settlement by Anxi descendants have begun to reach the stage of building temples. For instance, I saw in one such area the inauguration of a standing incense-burner in what had been a Locality God (Tudi Gong) temple and had already been enlarged with a new canopy in front of the original rural shrine. The old Tudi Gong figure was quite hidden behind an altar table on which the new figures of Guan Yin, Ang Gong and Qingshui Zu Shi Gong had been placed.

Thus suburban localities are identified by the god of the place of origin of a section of its inhabitants. A number of suburban residents decide to start a festival, quite possibly because they want an occasion for commercial entertaining. They will then invite the figure of a god from a nearby large temple, of which there are a number at this time. The selection will depend on the connections already established and brought to the suburb by the initiating group, even if none of them actually has the god installed on his domestic altar.

The root-branch tree shape used as an analogy for this kind of organisation is suitable to its articulation both spatially and temporally from a point of origin and the kinship vocabulary of segmentation fits the analogy. But it is less suited to the fact that this is also a structure of territorial units which do not intertwine, nor overlap. The analogy used to describe this is the nested subdivision of state administration.

All the Ang Gong temples in the Taibei basin outside the city, including the root temples, are also territorial temples of the places in which they are built. By an effective combination of the two analogies, of kinship root and of territorial administration, patronage takes the form of a local hegemony with generational continuity. Either it is of one compatriot group and its notables governing the territory of its temple which includes people from other origins who may well outnumber them. Or it is of one surname group over those of several other surnames, as in the case of Palisades' temple's territorial area. And it is in making this combination that patrons vie, and structure the social landscape into segments.

In a place which is a central point of accumulation of surplus, more than one compatriot group of its resident notables can afford to build its own temple – which will be the root of an extensive network reaching into the place's hinterland. When only one of them can become the place's territorial temple, that leaves the other or others as purely compatriot temples. This seems to me to be the sense of the history of Taibei city's major local temples until that point in their development when some of their patrons were powerful enough to accumulate on a qualitatively different geographic scale as merchants or as officials. At that point they would try to convert their temples into centres of more pan-Chinese ideology or else leave the temples to other lesser patrons who were their clients and through whose temples they could keep a foothold in a home base. After this point of development the compatriot temples of the most powerful patrons detached themselves from a territorial definition while maintaining the more geographically extensive local network of compatriots, which could be fitted into the China-wide network of compatriots easily by reference to prefectural or provincial area of origin and its most central places.

This was the structure of the system in which Mountainstreet's temple was formed. Its temple combined territorial and compatriot functions, with the former dominant because the town was never an important enough place to become the point of accumulation of enough surplus for it to have been invested with an estate which would be the material basis for hereditary hegemony and continuous interest. The last two local notables who donated to and managed the temple and the market scales before the Japanese standardised weights and abolished this institution, were not of the same surname.[4] The narrowest definition of their patronage which the ideology could offer was that of Anxi origin, which was shared with the majority of the population without the patrons having in addition a more exclusive claim of origin.

## PROTECTION AND LONG LIFE

The local temple is an extended and more complex material formation of the elementary incense-burner. In it the rule of descent works upon the rule of territorial definition. An incense-burner is used to treat a place in the universe as a subject. Whether it be for their legendary mortal life or for their active presence, deference to gods is an act of communication between subjects. A local temple as compared to a domestic altar is a more socially mediated construction around an incense-burner, a centre in which domestic altars are included. It is an incense-burner identifying a greater place and a more exemplary or effective presence as a subject of communication. And the social principles of territorial residence and of descent mediated by property are translated into patronage and personal reputation in the construction and maintenance of the temple.

A local temple is the result of a process in which a god's reputation for efficacy (*ling*) has spread. Most of the Mountainstreet people interviewed, when asked which god is most *ling*, said it was a matter of personal choice. Any god could be, and the one which is most chosen is most *ling*. 'All gods for whom incense is burnt are *ling-gan*'; 'People make their own choice'; '*Ling-gan* is everybody's talk'. The answers vary only in the degree of scepticism about the whole question of efficacy: 'the one that one trusts most is most responsive'; '*ling* is where there is most activity, most incense burnt'. It follows that *ling* is a concept of something that is socially made, like reputation, out of acts of personal motivation. The difference between *ling* and reputation is that *ling* is made around a projected subject, whereas reputation in its various forms, of countenance (*fengse*) or face (*mianzi*), is made around a subject identified with a concrete individual, living or dead. Neither a living individual, nor an ancestor is ever conceived to be *ling*. Nor is the past life of a god ever decribed as *ling*, though certainly it may be described as the life of a person of high reputation. When rituals were explained to me, gratitude to an ancestor and respect for an exemplary life were sharply distinguished as commemoration (*jinian*) from the act of pleading (*xiayuan*, or *qiu*) the favour of a god.

The two, *ling* and reputation, are nevertheless closely linked in the building of a temple. A household, in the name of its head inscribed on the donated part of the temple and in lists of contributors, makes its reputation as a prominent donor. At the same time donation is seen as an act of thanks for the protection of the god and to vouchsafe further protection. I and my assistant asked Mountainstreet residents why they thought people contributed toward the building of temples. Invariably they answered that it is the rich who can afford to spare the wealth for it. But these answers varied in their subsequent explanations of donations. One repeated explanation referred to the social motivation of the donor: either to his good and/or grateful heart (*hao xin* or *xi xin*) in performing what was a social duty, or to his show of good-heartedness for the sake of showing off and social gain. Some explanations referred to religious motivation: that donation was for the protection of the donor's peace (*ping'an*) or out of sincerity of belief in (*zhengxin*) or respect of (*jing*) the god. Other explanations were less in terms of donors' motives than of a temple's functions. Those most often mentioned were that it is a meeting place which can become, if its reputation spreads, a centre of social activity, of entertainment (*renao*) and commerce, that it is a moral centre where people can find consolation (*anhui*), and that a temple is the gods' dwelling, for the protection of the peace of the area or locality (*difang*) and the centre (*zhongxin*) uniting the locality.

A local temple and its organisation, then, constitute a form of patronage combining person and place as patron and community just as the god is a combination of person with place. In Mountainstreet the office of master of the incense-burner is elected from most house heads in the territory. But for the procession festivals of centres wealthier than Mountainstreet, the list of candidates is confined to those who have volunteered to underwrite the great expense involved and have their own names publicised in the name of the god of the locality. And the donor-managers of the temple select themselves in the festival of Xian Gong's birthday and the ninth-month *dou* festival. The latter is a festival of petition for long life. But the *dou* is a symbol of a spatial unit as well as temporal fortune. The self-selection of the wealthy in Mountainstreet is similar to that which occurs on a greater scale at the Xian Gong root temple. There the same festival in 1967 included over a thousand household fee-payers and their *dou* were ranked in status and cost, the central *dou* being the most expensive, then the four *dou* of the quarters, then some special *dou* and then a multitude of common *dou* tubs. The fee for the central *dou* was the equivalent of 750 US dollars, well over a Mountainstreet miner's annual wage at the time. It was reserved in advance by the manager of the temple. In other words, the *dou* at the festival for long life is less a representation of the community within a bounded region than the self-selection of individual households, those whose heads are wealthy and nearing old age, as a Buddhist priest told me. Xian Gong is treated as a saviour god and in his cult the wealthy are on their way out of the community altogether. At the same time they maintain a symbolism for the community itself in which they appear as its patrons.

## POLITICS AND PATRONAGE

To present a large donation and organise the collection of further donations for local public works, such as roads, bridges, schools and temples, has long been an activity instigated by the wealthier members of a village or town as an act of patronage and an enhancement of status. The inscriptions of their names, the amounts donated, and the date they were made, form rolls of honour and a documentation of local history.

Property and economic activity are far less important in the foundation and activities of what I am calling local temples than in the foundation of Buddhist or Daoist temples of retreat or in the foundation and upkeep of ancestral halls. Of course, the donation of land and other gifts to these other types of temple are also recorded and exhibited, as acts of patronage, but not to a local community. They are recorded as acts of piety in the tenets and purposes of the religious institution itself, whereas the building and refurbishing of a local temple is the provision to a local community of a number of services, of divination, celebration and recreation, openly available to all residents and visitors. Of course, the foundations of temples of retreat may fund charitable and other services, available without restriction. Ancestral trusts may fund schools and scholarships and provide selectively for the welfare of members of a local lineage. Local temples or the halls of local lineages can also become the centres for the organisation by their current patrons of the village bands of crop- and night-watchers (see Duara 1988:105, 123). They can be corporate owners of land and aquacultural rights, the shares of which are held by the resident households of its territory (Wilkerson 1994). But in addition, local temples are themselves a donated service, and the main activities associated with them are festivals, which must be funded on each occasion by a further collection of donations in the locality. So, donation and upkeep of a local temple has the same merit and obligation as the building and repair of a bridge, used by all in the locality. The travellers and visitors who make use of them are expected to respect them as a recognition of the pride of the place and its hospitality.

If we take for granted a steady acceptance of local temples, then the state of their repair and the splendour of their activities will rise and fall like those of other public facilities with the rise and fall in the general prosperity of the locality. But of course we cannot take steady acceptance for granted. Local temples have in the first place an intrinsic sensitivity to changes in the residential composition of the locality and to whichever deity's cult is celebrated for its efficacy (*ling*). New deities may be added, old ones and their festivals decline in importance. Each addition, each major new construction creates an opportunity for new patronage and leadership, or is an opportunity created by a new bidder for leadership.

Gary Seaman's remarkably detailed description (1978) of a spirit-writing cult in post-war Taiwan clearly shows the relationship between public patronage, local politics and the imperial bureaucracy of the deities invoked in local temples. It describes events leading from the establishment of a spirit-writing cult in the home of a trader and interpreter who had returned to Pearl Mountain village during the war from court service in Japan, to its expansion and re-establishment at the core of a new temple constructed in 1960. It is the story of a spirit-writing cult becoming a local temple cult.

The temple was built at a place near a stream which divided the two, rival parts of a village. After it was built, a second public work, the building of a bridge across the stream, made this place the commercial centre of the village. But before that, the growing membership of the spirit-writing cult and the rise to prominence of the brother of its spirit-medium as an arbiter in disputes between the two parts of the village made possible the donations and agreements for both these construction projects. The cult membership and his own skills as an arbiter and political entrepreneur were the basis for the brother's election as village leader. On the basis of his membership of the cult and its links to other cults based on the local town, he established an alliance with the town's mayor, a member of one of the related cults. By this connection and as vote broker for candidates to higher political representation, he was able to arrange a number of public works contracts, partially voluntary and partially government-funded. Among them were two which added a village administrative office and a store-room and stage to the temple building.

Changes in local leadership and changes in the popularity of cults, the introduction or invention of new cults may affect the decline and rise of local temples. These changes will themselves be responses to changes in the nature of economic activities and economic organisation. For instance, the commercialisation of agriculture and development of small rural businesses seem to have been the conditions in which the figure of Ma Zu was first brought inland to a Mountainstreet hamlet from a large and well-known temple in a coastal town. Her local reputation for quelling crop pestilence was an adaptation and striking departure from her established association with the protection of sea travellers and traders. Another example, this one of changing economic and political conditions affecting local temple cults in the eighties and in Fujian is given by Guo (1985). Irrigation engineering and the reliability of water supply meant the disappearance of rain-seeking rituals. Two developments, one the provision of preventive health care facilities, the other the establishment of new inter-village relations after liberation bringing village feuds to an end, between them reduced the importance of the demon-quelling gods of the village temple. But they and the Locality God have acquired a new importance as protectors of wealth and against accidents for the small factories and commercial establishments which now predominate in the village. And a new deity has been introduced for the protection of vehicles – Che Gong.

So, local temples and their cults change with changing political and economic circumstances. The institution remains, but its interpretation changes. A recent survey of temple cults in Taiwan found that the number of cults in a single temple had increased and that the nature of these cults had changed the character of temple worship itself. It is now much more individualistic, the cults having far more to do with the chance of individual or family achievements than in the more communal past (Li Yiyuan 1988). Nevertheless, they are contained in the local temple, its imagery and its festivals. The survey also found a growth, parallel to these worldly and individualistic cults, of sects much more devoted to the revitalisation of moral life. Many of them are spirit-writing cults such as the one described by Gary Seaman. And as we have seen in that example, local temples can result from such sects, the very temples which also contain the apparently less ethical, and less spiritual cults of the first tendency noted by Li. The two tendencies, and the retention of procession festivals, have a long duration.

More radical political and cultural change, other ways of cooperating, other ways of giving and accepting leadership, may replace those to which the institution of local temples is suited. The collective organisation of rural economy and politics in the People's Republic and the ideology of scientific socialism which accompanied it promised such a change. But

147

It was with the profoundest sorrow that we were brought to acknowledge that, more than thirty years after the construction of the PRC and despite the overthrow of the feudal system, feudal superstitious activities still prevail. Particularly in certain economically and culturally low-level areas, they are an increasingly serious tendency. (Zhou Ying 1988)

An eighty-year-old woman in 1982 dreamed the gods of her village in southern Fujian, in the People's Republic of China, came into her body and through her said they had no place to live and so were suffering. The villagers should build a new home for them. A couple of months later, a group of old religious activists went round the village to collect donations, and organised the village into four areas for further collection of standard, basic donations per household, each with its responsible collector. A temple was completed six months later. Altogether, three annual festivals for each of three of these gods were re-started, and a fourth was resurrected for a visiting god figure who comes in a series of processions from a nearby town. People donated because, as they said, not to donate would be to lose face. In the military metaphor they used, they 'spend men not to lose the front'(*shu ren bu shu zhen*). It was partly just a revival of popular custom (*minjian guanxi*) and of the inertia (*duoxing*) of tradition and partly of donation towards an occasion for theatre and procession. Culture bureaux officials are charged with the task of education and propaganda. The article (Guo 1985) which described the revival of this temple and its festivals in the journal of a department of Xiamen University ends on a similar note. The task for the sake of progress is to inject a more scientific and healthy content into the traditional forms and transform them from within. As one culture bureau director said to me when I visited Xiamen in 1988,

Some aspects of superstition are bad, some good because they can be guided in the approved direction. For instance, we can make sure that the content of the theatrical performance or of the film shown is helpful for the civilisation of the village. For another instance, the spirit mediums who show off by cutting and piercing themselves without coming to harm, who cut their tongues and write talismans with the blood, dance (*wudao*), and perform magic (*moshu*) like a conjurer. Their show is a cheat, which is bad, but it is also a demonstration of skills, in acrobatics and in *qigong* [the strengthening of internal energy].

The task of culture centres is, one official told me, to organise, aid, train and research local cultural activities. Thus they preserve and improve the performing arts of lion and dragon dancing, theatre and music which are part of the festival tradition, by organising annual competitions and spending some money on their equipment, while seeking to eliminate the superstitious contents. I was cited an instance of how research is used for this purpose. The historical origin of the cult of a god with the title of a general was investigated. It was found that he had been one of the generals sent against the Ming Chinese patriot Zheng Cheng-gong (Koxinga) by the Manchu conquerors, and the worship of his memory had been imposed by their dynasty. 'In superstition, people are blind to the history of their gods, but when in this instance the history of their god was explained they ceased to worship him.'

With rising living standards many prefer modern sports, fine arts and musical instruments to the traditional performing and gymnastic arts. The culture bureaux encourage participation in both, not as spectacles, as in a festival, but as recreation in which villagers take an active part, producing, training and rehearsing for evening shows in which they entertain each other. Ancestral halls and village temples are themselves culture centres, including entirely secular facilities like a television room and card tables. The tendency reported to me and plainly encouraged by culture officials, is for the evening shows to be self-financing, like festivals, and for the halls and temples to become cultural centres without any superstitious elements. Beyond that, 'civilisation' (*wenming*) is promoted by the culture bureaux, which would include scientific education and agricultural or horticultural shows together with traditional and modem arts and sports.

In sum, culture bureau policy is to turn popular religious activities into folk arts and assimilate them into organised and separate, leisure-time recreation. Its implementation entails considerable familiarity with popular religion. The collection of relics for museums, and the compilation of local histories are also within its remit and they include the histories of local temple cults and the preservation of their artistic products. The persistence of popular religious practices is a fact of local culture, and culture bureaux personnel, museum curators and local historians are sources of information about them. But culture bureau policy is driven by notions of progressive health, skill, and knowledge which do not require an interpretation of the culture of religious practices except to condemn them as backward. This, then, is the quite different ideology and institution which has replaced the imperial cults with a republican calendar and its history of positive progress.

Between high concern to find a concept of Chinese culture to help fill an ideological vacuum and local implementation of cultural policy, popular religion and the historicisation that it performs are signs of backwardness. Some analyses of the current situation and the revival of popular religion insist, as does the anthropologist Guo (1985), on the basic tendency of people's reliance on their own abilities and knowledge and therefore the decline of dependency upon supernatural authority. But they find it difficult to account for the inertia of traditional religious practices, and their adaptability to new circumstances. The whole thesis of secularisation implied by this view contains a notion of technological progress, or of increasing possibilities of control and decreasing dependency upon uncertain and dangerous natural conditions. But it cannot deny new kinds of uncertainty and danger, social or political, man-made if not natural.

The means of tolerating uncertainty and of taking responsibility and decisions without certainty of outcomes, the guiding sense of authority, may still not be provided by or entrusted to official, state institutions and school education. Security may be sought in revelations of *ling*.

## LING, SPIRIT-WRITING AND PATRONAGE

Seaman's Pearl Mountain temple started as a spirit-writing cult in its founder's home, and the cult members remained an inner group within the temple's organisation. So were the participants in Mountainstreet's festival of Xian Gong in an inner group when compared with the mass participation of the temple's other main festival, though Xian Gong was no longer invoked in spirit-writing seances. The relationship between an inner group of founders and major donors and an outer mass of festival participants is typical of the institution of local temples.

A local temple is one which houses a territorial guardian and thus includes all the households in its area, literally marked out in procession festivals. But local temples also house other deities which may not have this festival. Accretion of new cults, and new reputations for efficacy are always possible. Spirit-writing is the literate means of establishing a new reputation and it contains a claim to a new orthodoxy and to moral leadership. The fortunes of the spirit-writing association are, however, like the fortunes of the spirit-medium who simply writes talismans in contract with a deity and its *ling*.

*Ling* is the dangerous quality, belief in which imperial and republican regimes sought to control. Daoists also had an orthodox version of *ling*. To classically trained Daoists, *ling* is of celestial origin, but true only of the Middle, that is the Human. Daoism is the cultivation of the power to accomplish without having to act. Lagerwey (1987: 6–9) cites Daoist philosophical texts to demonstrate an association, in refined Daoism, with *ling*, which he translates as 'potency' with the male principle of primordial energy in mind. But it can also be a property of the cults of female deities.

Parallel to a deferential gathering around the incense-burner which transmits petition to and response from this power to bring things about, is the relationship of sponsoring the building and organisation of a cult.

The way of reaching consensus within the cult, of sealing political alliances outside it, of making deals for the use of public funds, or of persuading donors to make important contributions is a mixture of respect for merit and the cultivation of personal loyalties typical of patron-client faction formation. 'Cult organization is a complex blend of ritual offices and personal networks, of political entrepreneurship and the intervention of gods' (Seaman 1978: 81).

The 'intervention of gods' is at the core of spirit-writing cults, for they are revelations and reminders of an order based on virtue summed up by Seaman as

> an ideal order based on the true meritocracy of the celestial empire of the Jade Emperor. The gods in heaven judge merit and dispense fortune according to a truly honest appraisal of a man's actions and intentions, not according to official whim and crass political considerations as do the powers of this world. (Seaman 1978: 7)

A refined calculus of merit was the subject of one of the cult's 'good books' (*shanshu*). Rewards for meritorious conduct in a lifetime constituted one path to the avoidance of courts of purgatory and appointment to the position of a temple god (Seaman 1978: Chapter 9). The accumulation of merit by a descendant for an ancestor's appointment was also possible. In other words, merit must not be understood simply as an individual achievement, it is lineal and filial. The virtues counted are indeed the standard virtues often described as 'Confucian'.

But one of the two other paths to deification mentioned by Seaman's informants was to have been an historical personality with such potency that it remained effective after death. Such gods were distinguished from those of the imperial bureaucracy as semi-independent 'kings' (*wangye*) or as dark gods (*yinshen*) (Seaman 1978:55). There would seem to be a space left by the canons of virtue for the strength and strategy of military leadership and political entrepreneurship, for these are typically demon-quelling and dangerously powerful gods. The third path to deification mentioned was by more secret arts of self-cultivation than public or filial deeds, namely the disciplines of Daoist or Buddhist retreat (Seaman 1978: 53). So the order of meritocracy as expounded in the texts and statements of the cult studied by Seaman includes the panthei of the gods of popular religion and it includes all three of the ethics of lineal and public service, of personal strategy, and of the disciplines of meditation and magic.

In the construction and organisation of the temple there is an exclusive room for the seances, the blue gowns of their participants standing for their purity and inner positions in the cult. It is repeated in the relation between the cult and the ordinary donors to a local temple and its festivals. Here the inner cult of virtue combines with wealth, which defines patronage as an ideal.

As I and others (for instance, Brim 1970 and Guo 1985) have already observed, in smaller and less wealthy areas, the procession festivals of local temples and often the reconstruction of temples themselves are financed by a standard donation collected from every household which has permanent residence in the temple area. Furthermore, the annual leaders for the festival – the master of the incense-burner and leaders of each residential section – are chosen by divination block from a complete list of heads of households. Each has an equal chance of being chosen. The temple records are a census, and the means of selection egalitarian. But those who volunteer above-standard donations are more prominently displayed on the published lists of donors. Their capacity to give, however it was gained, thus achieves both merit in the temple's internal order and recognition for contributing a public good to the standard donors and their households. In the wealthier areas, there is indeed an effective wealth qualification before a man can be chosen to be a festival's leader. But the whole area enjoys the spectacle he has provided for it. The patron's wealth becomes a virtue.

Not all local temples were formed out of spirit-writing cults. Not all temples of spirit-writing cults become local temples. On the contrary, they seem more often to have a more general appeal (see Overmyer 1985 and Jordan and Overmyer 1986). But I am sure that many examples could be added to the examples I have given of a local temple housing an inner cult.

What I wish to draw out of such examples is the thought that the more spiritual or overtly ethical quality of a sect is continued, more implicitly, in the relationship of deference to the *ling* of a hero and the stories told about it. The transmission and reputation of extraordinary gifts (*ling*) is the central feature of local temple cults, their festivals, and the attention they receive every day in divination and pledge from individuals and households. The implicit ethics of that relationship can be seen in the organisation and morality books of the spirit-writing cult. In both cases, authority is due to their being forms of transmission from a past and both form a present collectivity in receiving that transmission. Their social and political implication can be seen in the way the temple and festival disposes participants in circles of inner and outer access and leadership. But at base is the organisation of force around the extraordinary gift, demonic power against demons.

In an incense-burner association, equal households are joined and organised in deference to a protector, whether they form a voluntary and exclusive organisation or an inclusive territorial organisation. Incense, divination blocks, and the stories of *ling* defer what might be conflicting decisions and choices of who should be leader. The principle of equality can be upheld, at least in feast association and in smaller territorial festivals. But its universality is one of consensus around the divine agent, averting the democratic division into majority and minority.

## CHANCE AND TRADITION

Entering the Guan Di temple in Quanzhou city one evening in 1988 accompanied by my hosts, I admired the new wooden carvings and beams and the figures of deities in the side and front halls and then went on to the darker main hall at the back. There I recognised a tube of divination sticks (*qian*). Near them was a lamp-lit table with an old lady sitting at it, a large old book of standard interpretations in front of her. Seeing me notice this, one of my hosts asked if I wanted to pick out my luck. So with a sense of awkwardness, I asked if I should burn incense first as others were doing. Possibly to save embarrassment, I was told this was not necessary and instead went straight to shake the tube. But by its omission I had removed myself from local practice. I was reminded to ask a question. I did, and took out the lot which came to hand. Then I stood in front of the shrine of the main god, whose figure was shrouded by curtains. Divination blocks were ready, on the altar table. I picked them up, held them for a moment in a gesture of respect, and dropped them to the floor. The throw being positive, I took the stick to the old lady. What had I asked? As she looked up the entry for the lot's number I told her my question was whether I would be able to return here. After reading, she answered, 'Well, perhaps, perhaps not!'

I had received an easy, if true answer. But that was not all. I had also silently put a question outside of my own doubts and entered it into a standard procedure, familiar to my hosts. It was also familiar to me as part of what I had known and studied as an observor. Since my question was about wanting to continue those observations, asking it made my cultural and academic distance waver and the participation not just an act of curiosity. It felt more intimate than a show of participation, since the question expressed a wish appropriate to the small act of faith I had put on. I did want to repeat my visit and continue my observation and description of this and other linked practices which had long fascinated me. Indeed, I wanted to make of them an important part of my foreseeable life. I felt I had put on an exhibition of a wish and an uncertainty.

From previous study I had already concluded that for its principal actor, an act of divination such as this is a standardisation and an externalisation of uncertainty. In the minor religious practice I undertook, chance, in the broad sense of unforeseeable eventualities, including those already experienced, is inserted into a ritual procedure. This ritual, contrary to chance, has the quality of tradition, which is to say of repetition and of familiarity in a local cultural environment.

Since it was not my local environment, but one I was visiting from a great distance, the translation into a familiar ritual of my uncertainty and of the new chance of pursuing my interest in studying a constantly changing Chinese society was across a wide and awkward gap. To a local person, the translation would be across a finer gap. But the ritual, and the imagery provided by the temple environment, translates even for the most frequent and familiar devotee a present and changing situation which is spoken about and calculated in quite other ways outside that discourse of temple divination. What the imagery and practices of temple festival, worship and divination convey is a kind of authority.

In January 1967 a woman came to Mountainstreet's temple to seek guidance by drawing lots. She was in serious financial straits which had driven her into thinking of selling one of her two young sons into another family. But she had understandable doubts about taking this course. Not knowing the procedure of drawing lots after burning incense she consulted a woman friend who went to the temple with her. This woman friend and her husband were also my friends and I asked them afterwards how they had guided the troubled woman through the procedure. First the situation in question, or an actual question must be kept in mind, they said. Next the divination blocks are taken and held in the hands in a gesture of respect, as for greeting a superior or a guest, and the god, who was in this case Xian Gong, should be told the address and the name of the head of the household, the situation in question, and the question or the desired outcome. If on then throwing the blocks the answer is either indefinite or negative, the supplicant has to ask or suggest why this was the response. She goes on in this way until the blocks show a positive response to the modified question or desire. The sticks are then shaken and the one which emerges is taken out and the blocks thrown again until a stick receives a positive response. This was the procedure.

The appropriate slip of paper from the pads hanging on the wall of the temple was then torn off and the couplet on it interpreted as an answer to the question or about the desired course of action and its outcome. The troubled woman's answer was one which indicated a good outcome for either course, keeping or selling her son.

I do not know what she eventually did. But I think the procedure helped her to reflect upon and to state the situation in a certain way. This was by far the most common form of divination, costless, simple and not very time consuming compared with spirit-writing or consulation of a *tongji* spirit medium or other kinds of diviner. Among these other modes of divination, it is the one which relies most heavily upon the existence of a local temple. Indeed, I would say it is part of the institution of a local temple to provide this kind of divination. In any case, by recourse to it, a social subject, its situation and sense of direction in that situation is stated in a certain procedure.

That procedure includes the context of a local temple and its cast of persons: the supplicant, those to whom she refers or on whose behalf she comes (her household) with or without their knowledge, those who help her in the procedure, the gods addressed and by implication the community of donors which provided the gods' thrones and halls. The imagery of the procedure is a kind of drama and is indeed repeated in the depiction of other situations in the theatre and for the location at large in the procession on festival days. It is an imagery of another time. The historical accuracy of the depiction is not at issue, except when another kind of historicity intervenes as a rival authority to the cult and its temple. Cult and temple, its divination blocks and its festival days construct a different authority with its own construct of an anterior time.

Divination is the presentation of a decision publicly, that is through others, and in a standard form. The situation is one in which other forms of calculation known to the participant have left a sense of uncertainty. So it is a situation heightened by incalculability or uncertainty, of weather or of market or of political future. Incalculability or luck is by divination turned into a defined temporality, given a sense of time, and a decision or outcome is given an authority. The situation and its outcome are turned into the working and response of extraordinary virtue and knowledge (*ling*) or of fate (*ming*) and corrections of fate by appeal to *ling*. But note that this does not imply fatalism; there is no resignation to let things happen because after all the object is to reach a decision. And if a decision is offered it may not be accepted. If it is, then the decision and the activity have been authorised, identified in a certain way, placed in a sense of time, under a certain form of agency and thereby given a certain form of authority and identity.

This does not mean that all activities of the subject identified will thenceforth have this identification or seek recognition by this kind of authority. Other activities or the same but in other situations may be calculated by other means, depending on what means are available or have been learned and what conditions of uncertainty remain. Indeed, an historical analysis of the changing means and conditions of calculating important eventualities, and what count as important eventualities would be the most appropriate way of studying changes in the prevalence and practices of divination.

But let me in the meantime conclude by one further comment on the authorisation which divination in a local temple provides.

The gods are images of political authority and of judgement. But they are always of the not-present. They are historic metaphors or analogies of authority, protection and judgement. They are also figures in the temporal continuity of the supplicant subject. They and the temple define a containing social subject linked to the supplicant and her situation in a relation of deference. She represents one of the following:

1 a household and line of descent in a surname locality and their shared security (*pingan*);
2 a household in a territorial locality of domestic altars and their shared security;
3 a household in a universalising cult and its restoration of virtue.

A local temple combines all three. But dominant in its establishment is the authority of *ling* within which selected salvation, protection and success is sought.

What kind of responsibility and what unities and differences of combined activity does its establishment form and recognise? My answer to this question is derived from both an examination of the drama of divination and worship, and from the organisation of local temples and festivals as public works. They stand for a local history and its culture in a network of local histories and cultural differences; they stand for competitive communalism and personal patronage; they also stand ambiguously for egalitarian association and for deference to an inner circle of patron-leaders. Changing conditions of uncertainty and incalculability change the contents and the nature of the cults. But their authority is constructed in the same way, by the historicity of the transmission of *ling* and the privilege of access to it.

With this authority are transmitted the ethics of lineal and public service and of self-cultivation. With the same authority another ethic of self-defence and local loyalty is also transmitted.

Whether this way of dealing with chance by tradition will disappear in the processes of modernisation is not easy to say. Taiwan and southern Fujian show how the institution of local temples has so far accommodated these processes; the authority and ethics of local temples may provide a balancing sense of security and a reminder of social responsibility. On the other hand, alternative knowledges of history and senses of direction, other forms of collective responsibility, and other kinds of public celebration and recreation may supplant those of local temples.

## REPRESENTATION

To describe the act of incense-burning as one of a number of instances of opening communication is helpful in saying what it is *like*. But we have reached a point where we should no longer ignore the fact that incense is burned, rather than an invitation card or cigarette offered or, as another analogy had it, a telephone rung. Burning incense is distinct from forms of deferential communication such as the toast, the offer and receipt of gifts, the kowtow and petition, none of which are accompanied or prefaced by the burning of incense when they are directed to a responding person.

This difference could be described, if not as opening communication then as a representation of the opening of communication. But this still leaves unanswered the question of the accurate description of what is represented and how to describe the relation of representation performed.

'Communication' clearly implies the immediate or deferred presence of one or more corresponding subjects to whom the initiating subject directs a message. In short, it implies the transmission of meanings between subjects. On the contrary, asymmetry of response, initiated by deference, immediately calls response itself into question. Angry silence or dissatisfied honour could be registered by *lack* of response. On the other hand, the same lack could be registered as the absence of the possibility of response.

Yet that possibility is excluded in every exegesis of incense-burning. Indeed, many describe incense as the mark to which the attention of a responsing subject is called. And invariably the simple verbal as well as the elaborate written accompaniment to burning incense is a naming and placing (addressing) of the initiator who offers the incense. Thus one of the opening Daoist rites of temple festivals (and mortuary rituals) is often called *fa biao*, 'sending a memorial'.

Let *biao* be noted more carefully than the occasionally accurate translation 'memorial'. It is a word with a very similar range of connotation to 'representation': prayer or petition, externalised desire, delegated or transferred political will, submission. The initiation of an act of will, then, the burning of incense 'expects' completion. It 'expects' in a syntax of ritual, completion being marked by the explosion of fire-crackers. Completion is but the completion of a formal act of petition and thanks for its acceptance. It is a ritual, and must be completed. Though the petition must be directed to a subject named and much more elaborately identified than its initiator, the petitioner none the less provides all the means of response to the petition as well as its submission. Here, then, is what differentiates the act of 'communication' initiated by incense from any other. It brings the possibility of response into question and compensates by the very plenitude of its provision for the response.

The same ritual sequence might as well be not so much petition as commemoration and eulogy, where the act is not an initiation but a record in which the named and eulogised subject is represented as the presence of a past, as a memory or a history or as a genealogical point.

In the naming and selection of the subject addressed for its 'responsiveness' or for its 'name', in the circumscribed time between the always completed but cyclical stages of ritual when the response is registered between, for instance, a festival and its recurrence or in the very restricted registration of chance by divination blocks during the rituals, what is to be completed? Representation or memorial? Divination or record?

These questions are not for answering. They describe the act initiated by the burning of incense: the fire and smoke, the smouldering incense and its scent providing both representation and response, identification and record, the insistence on communication but the completion by the communicant of all its stages; the lit fire that might flare, the wish that might (not) be fulfilled. The fire which might flare also lights the 'eyes' of the image and is reflected in the mirror of the *dou* ensemble. There is an over-doing of communication, the representation of communication itself rendering communication redundant while insisting upon it.

What incense-burning suggests here is the first part of a more general conception of ritual which is religious. Religious ritual addresses a postulated subject. Religious ritual represents that subject by an extravagant completion of address, performing both the petition and the response, even while it brings response into question and in many instances defers it. Its syntax expects response, and ritually completes it.

It also suggests the second part of a concept of religious ritual, the asymmetry and indirect nature of the syntax of addressing a postulated subject which is not just far larger, but which encompasses the initiating subject. The burning of incense and its expected completion are identifications of a point both of activity and also of passivity in reference to a second person whose response is already provided. The 'self' in question is defined in the ritual statement, and not merely by name and address, but by the very principles which make possible the formulation of ritual statements. The peculiar character of these ritual statements is that by addressing a second-person, the postulated subject, that subject is held to represent a third, inclusive condition of the existence of the first. In providing the response or record of the second, the ritual defines the first as a subject for recognition. These ritual statements define a subject initiating and accepting response. They have a transitivity.

159

Transitivity describes the position and relation of the subject as to a second person. There is a differentiation between three kinds of transitivity, those of effectivity, adjustment and commemoration. *Effective:* second-person command over or intervention in the condition within which the first person is recognised, is the disposition of fate, the cosmos of planetary forces or the hierarchy of purgatorial administration. *Adjustive:* no distinction is made between a second person and the condition in which the first person is to be recognised; the condition is treated directly as in magic or instrumental ritual. *Commemorative:* celebrates the second person as memory or history for the definition of name and fame or descent as distinct from pleading effective intervention in fate or purgatory.

Let me put this forward as a concept which could be tested for its general validity. Religious ritual is a performance of completed communication, which addresses a postulated subject. The performance is one of effect, adjustment or commemoration upon a third, including condition in which the performing subject is defined and recognised.

Definition is by reference to the subject addressed, the second person. In Chinese religious rituals, there is a differentiation within the inclusive condition between three principles of historical inscription, those of effect, repute and descent; that is to say, between second persons defined a) as guardians of territory or of fate, b) as heroes and c) as ancestors. Heroes and ancestors are the agencies of obligation and honour rather than effective response or instrumental result. By these three principles, Daoists are differentiated from masters of (historical or ancestral) ceremonial. In a more complex fashion, local or popular cults are also differentiated from both official and ancestral cults, as guardians of territory or fate through present effects.

Representation or memorial? Divination or record? These are questions whose answers stress one or other of the alternatives among the religious systems of imperial China. Territorial cults stress the Daoist alternative more than any other, and so it is to Daoism I now turn.

# Chapter Six

# Daoism and its clients

The procession festivals of local territorial guardian gods are minor versions of a great Daoist rite. This is the rite of cosmic re-adjustment known as a *jiao*. As people in Mountainstreet said, even the twice-monthly domestic feeding of gods' soldiers was a substitute for a *jiao* that should have been performed when the temple was extended and rebuilt.

I have already pointed out key contrasting differences between the ritual and organisation of imperial state cults and this Daoist rite. The *jiao* is the chief rite of an alternative and empire-wide territorial definition and identification. It too is a tradition authenticated by texts. But the texts are themselves authenticated by the aura of revelation.

There are by now several recordings and expositions of the *jiao*, made in Taiwan and Fujian (they are listed in Lagerwey 1987, but see also Saso 1972). The full exposition of its programme, which is the most elaborate and important of the rituals for the living in the Daoist canon, takes several volumes. Many have indeed been written by Japanese and Western scholars, particularly those associated in one way or another with the construction of a concordance of the Daoist canon, a project conducted by Kristofer Schipper at the Ecole Pratique des Hautes Etudes in Paris and at the University of Leiden. I too have benefited from conversations with Kristofer Schipper and from his book *Le Corps Taoiste*. The work of Schipper and his associates is essential for any understanding of Chinese popular religions. But I am not one of the sinologists of the Daoist canon, whose work is to combine textual scholarship with records of close observation of the rites performed by Daoist masters. Instead I will have recourse to Lagerwey's interpretative exposition of the *jiao*. He runs through all its rites as performed by the Daoist master Chen, of Tainan city, Taiwan. I will not repeat it, nor run through the whole sequence of a *jiao*. I refer the reader to Lagerwey for that.

Lagerwey's exposition is from inside, from the perspective of the Daoist master, while I wish to maintain a distance sufficient to indicate the differences between that perspective and the perspective of the contributors to the territorial cults which the Daoist serves.

Daoists are masters who serve. For, while the Daoists who can perform a *jiao* are led by an initiate into Daoist techniques and mysteries which require a long and literate apprenticeship, he and they are nevertheless employed by the representatives of a locality to consecrate the temple of its territorial cult. The performance of the *jiao* turns the territorial cult itself inside out, bringing into its centre the Daoist's own altar and furthering the Daoist master's initiation into his esoteric knowledge. The objects of the cult normally at its centre are displaced into positions of supplicant community representatives and underlings in a cosmological hierarchy of purity. Even so, unlike the officials and the scholars who conducted themselves through the exclusive state cults, the Daoist masters and their troupes are hired, and the mastery for which they are hired provides them with no authority beyond the conduct of the *jiao* itself.

## ORTHODOX UNITY

There are several centres and traditions of Daoism, but the one to which I shall refer is that of Orthodox Unity (*Zheng Yi*). It traces its genealogy of instruction from revelations made to Zhang Daoling (also known simply as Zhang Ling) who lived in the second century (of the Christian era). As founder of the Daoism known as Orthodox Unity, he is reckoned to be the first heavenly master (Tian Shi).

The current heavenly master claiming direct succession from him more than sixty generations later, is a figurehead of a motley of registered Daoists in Taiwan. He has little left of the orthodox Daoist authority of his ancestors, removed as he is from the temples of the Dragon and Tiger Mountain (Long Hu Shan) of Jiangxi province, centre of the heavenly masters from the tenth century onwards. His predecessor was expelled from this centre of Orthodox Unity in 1931 by Communist forces establishing one of their earliest liberated areas in the border region which includes Dragon and Tiger Mountain.

In any case, Orthodox Unity itself has several lines of apprenticeship in which variant and often rival ritual practices, liturgies and meditative techniques are transmitted. By various paths of authentication, and often through a master's graduation at Dragon and Tiger Mountain, they trace their authority to the revelations which Lao Zi, legendary author of the first classical text of Daoism – *The Way and Its Power* – made through the first heavenly master.

Beside this genealogy to an originating revelation, and, from the tenth century, to a mountain centre of heavenly master descent, what characterises Orthodox Unity Daoists is that they live as married members of households, making a profession of being employed for their exorcising and healing skills, including the communal exorcism and cosmic readjustment which is performed in the *jiao*. Other centres of Daoism, such as the school of Mao Shan, are monastic orders. They are as much heirs through transmission by instruction and the study of a textual tradition, over tens of generations, from the ultimate founder of that tradition, the author of *The Way and Its Power*. His name, Lao Zi or Old Infant, is central to the mystical returns to and from an originating nothingness which form the core of Daoist liturgy and history. Mao Shan and other schools of monastic Daoism recognise in the heavenly masters a line of Daoist inspiration. But their liturgies and their meditative and bodily exercises are for individual purification and for pilgrims, not in service to a community and a clientele.

The textual scholar of Chinese culture and custom often describes popular religion as a mixture of rather confused interpretations of Daoism at the hands of half-literate healers, exorcisers and interpreters of mediums. These are called minor magicians (*xiaofashi*) distinguished from masters of both classical Daoist liturgy (*jing*) and of the commands, dances and other performative acts (*ke*) of magical method (*fa*). A master of *fa* in northern Taiwan told me he belonged to the Sannai School of Daoism which specialises in *fa*, and stems from the Sect of the Two Gates of Daoist Method (Dao Fa Er Men), whereas most southern Taiwanese masters are of the Efficaceous Treasure Sect (Ling Bao Pai). Both sects are part of Orthodox Unity, and masters of both have the authority and learning to perform the great rite of cosmic adjustment (the *jiao*) which minor magicians cannot perform. The great rite includes both the intoning of classical texts and the performative acts of *fa*. But the latter are accompanied by vernacular speech, not the classical, high pronunciation of texts, and its subjects are the gods of popular religion, not the more abstract Venerable Celestials (Tian Zun) of high Daoism. When they perform *fa*, Daoist masters approach the practices of minor magicians embedded in their local cultures.

The Daoist seeks to establish a relationship of authority to both magicians and to the popular cults which he attends according to his own, Daoist literacy. Just as the *savants* of official literacy in the imperial era and, according to another conception of knowledge and historical truth, the intelligentsia in the republican era regarded popular religion as confused, so the Daoist master also regards popular cults and magicians as vulgar, sensate, and confused. Yet the Daoist *savant* has, of all the other upholders of textual tradition and the sorters of recorded truths and origins, a far more intimate commerce and involvement with popular cults.

## EMPERORS AND DAOISTS

A succession of revelations of the Dao from its source in the energies of Chaos (*hundun*) inspired the authors of several histories preserved in the Daoist canon. These texts describe a series of Lao Zi's re-appearances from the Chaos to which he had returned. Others include revelations from other pure spirits. In any case, revelation is the characterstic authority of Daoism and Daoist history (according to Schipper 1985: 25 and Lagerwey 1987: 255). Revelations are the exclusive source of Daoism. They are Daoism's claim on the imperial state. But Orthodox Unity can also present itself as an idealised local state, which has a precedent in the early history of the heavenly masters.

By the time of the third heavenly master, in the last years of the Han dynasty, the Daoism of Orthodox Unity had become a theocratic state in what is now the province of Sichuan. It came about as a result of an uprising, known as that of the Yellow Turbans or the Way of the Five Dippers or Pecks of Rice, which was the name the heavenly master gave to his teaching. His regime was made up of cells ruled by local Daoist masters, centred upon houses of purification and incarceration for sickness and sin. They were also centres of military organisation, for the Daoist masters were both exorcists and commanders (see Mather 1979: 105–6, Welch 1958: 116ff, and Lagerwey 1987: 255–6). The theocracy of Daoists on their own authority was shortlived. But the idea of local territorial cults as centres of healing, military organisation and correction or purification has become part of the institution of Orthodox Unity Daoism. And the authority of Daoism for political establishment continued vicariously.

A number of dynasties in the fragments of the empire after the fall of the Han dynasty, between the third and sixth centuries, and a number of the reigns of the re-unified empire during the Tang and

Song dynasties, began with an initiation by Daoist masters. This initiation was that of an instruction by revelation through a Daoist master to the emperor, establishing the emperor as a sage or saint (*sheng*) and so re-establishing the era of saintly or sage rule which is part of both Confucian and Daoist classical myth (Lagerwey 1987: 254, and Mather 1979: 112–13).

These were at the same time re-establishments of a calendar and a cosmological order marked by correct sacrifices in official cults. But these were not the calendars and cults which were eventually adopted in later dynasties. They are far closer to the calendars of the occasions for local religious ritual. One of them is expounded by Stein (1979: 70–1). It was marked out by five so-called *la* – of Heaven, Earth, Way and Power, Popular Year (New Year), and Kings and Lords – and by three so-called *yuan*. The three *yuan* have since become the markers of the tripartite universe and calendar of popular almanacs. In Daoist codes the three yuan were assemblies (*hui*) of communities and of spirits addressing themselves to each of Three Offices and their Officials (San Guan). They were occasions when registers of births, marriages, and deaths, and confession-records of crimes were reported through local cults of earth and stove (Stein 1979: 72–7). The Three are the officials of Heaven, Earth, and Water: Heaven, the fifteenth day of the first month, now popular as the Lantern Festival; Earth, or within-the-earth, fifteenth day of seventh month, since associated with the general salvation of orphan souls; and Water, or flow, in the earth but linking earth to heaven, and associated calendrically with the fifteenth day of the tenth month, which in Mountainstreet and possibly elsewhere is an important date marking a season of territorial temple festivals. For Daoists it is the season for most *jiao* (Lagerwey 1987: 21).

Nevertheless, each instance of the initiation of an imperial reign by a Daoist was also a re-installation of the heavenly master and his succession as an orthodoxy. As such, Daoism was engaged in debates with Buddhists, Confucians and Legalists over questions of propriety and impropriety, the ways of the sages and their deterioration, and in denunciations of impure cults among the common people. Daoism was particularly vulnerable in this last point, for, as Stein (1979) points out, the cults of the common people, including 'excessive' (*yin*) cults of possession, were often so close to the families of Daoists who professed a purer release from them, as to make the line of distinction difficult to draw. Nevertheless, a distinction was drawn and the means of drawing it was by a written code. This consisted in a register or hierarchy and a history which was addressed either to sage emperors of actual dynasties or to the hope of ones to come.

One such hierarchy is described by Michel Strickmann (1979: 179ff). It is part of the incorporation into the canon and practice of the heavenly masters from the fourth century onwards of texts stemming from the monastic Daoist centre of Mao Shan. The *Concealed Instructions for Ascent to Perfection (Deng-zhen Yin-jue)* by Tao Hong-jing (456–536) 'synthesized the data on the bureaucratic hierarchy of the invisible world found in the Mao Shan revelations and other Taoist and secular literature current in his day' (Strickmann 1979: 179). One chapter in this work concerns 'the ranks and functions of the perfected and other powers', and has since been transmitted in the usual way of writing, copying and printing, as an independent work. In it the invisible world is divided into seven ranks of celestial beings. The top two are the levels of the Pure, which are eternal spirits, first those who have not yet and second those who already have in various ways manifested themselves on earth. The next three are those of the Perfected and of Immortals, who through merit and various prescribed methods of purification have achieved their true place in the well-ordered cosmos. The sixth is that of Cavern-heavens, beneath the earth, peopled by those who have achieved immortality but are still connected to their terrestrial souls. The lowest is that of the Six Heavens of the Yin world and of Night. It contains the Three Offices.

As expounded in this text, the Three Offices are courts of judgement and authority over the ghosts of the dead, including those who have become gods of popular cults, impure in their continued absorption with the bloody and terrestrial business of flesh, meat and violent death.

> After judgement had been pronounced on the newly dead by the Three Offices, they might be given some minor administrative post among the other shades, or assigned to retributive corvee labour; shifting rocks at the Yellow River's source is mentioned. In their obscure exile the dead were nourished by blood offerings, made either in their public temples or (for those who had not yet attained otherworldy ennoblement) by their descendants among the living. (Strickmann 1979:18 1).

Texts such as these, compiled in the Daoist canon, are frequently entitled *Concealed* or *Hidden* or *Secret*, because they were the prescriptions and registers for initiation into the succession of Daoist families and their profession as adepts in the liturgies of purification. Purification was also to be achieved by gaining merit, by proper, filial and moderate conduct and by acts of service to the community. The gaining of merit was 'public', including the *use* of the secret liturgies and prescriptions for diet, breathing, alchemy and meditation in promoting propriety and to save, by exorcism, the vulgar and excessive. But the skills which the adept put at the disposal of the people of his community were those of an initiation into esoteric knowledge transmitted through descent and then instruction, each level of which was more hidden, less manifest, and more pure than the lower.

Many of the gods worshipped by the impure, and many of the cults of wild and excited possession by them, were (and are still) held by these Daoist *literati* to be the causes not the curers of disease and wrong-doing. In contrast, the cult-houses of the communal earth and stove gods, the lowest ranks of the correct, were, according to the texts of Orthodox Unity, isolated chambers of quietness with a single, south-facing window. They were furnished with a writing table and an incense-burner. At the table a petition was to be written, begging dissolution of disease, which was also moral failing, by confession to the local god, and ultimately to the Three Offices.

The Offices are, according to the *Concealed Instructions*, situated in the north whence also old, worn out breaths (*gu qi*) emanate, causing disease, evil, and calamity (Stein 1979:67). The Daoist keeper of these houses acted as recorder, reporter, and defendant of the households in the territory, having access to the accumulation of merit or demerit down their ancestral lines, as well as using his knowledge of acupuncture, pharmacy and liturgy to cure diseases. He was contracted with the local god of soil or stove, but also as an adept could gain access higher up the order in the service of the Three Offices. The Three Offices were themselves in the same position as the sources of evil and harm, holding them back, and the Daoist was a master and an expert in the causes of destruction and punishment. The line of distinction, and the ambivalence of its guardians is patent. From the perspective of the imperial dynasty and the rivalry between Confucian, Buddhist, Legalist and Daoist traditions of authority, Daoists' closeness to the impure was important but also manifestly ambivalent. They served both the pure and the impure, the imperial dynasties and those subject to aberrant cults.

As Lagerwey says, the Daoist orthodoxy and its history is a history of revelation, and it is revelation through possession or dream.

Daoists, unlike Confucian *literati*, corrected by exorcism. What they exorcised, according to their canon, was what they pressed back into the northeast, souls congealed in earth or subterranean impurity, baleful or stale emanations which took 'excessive' (*yin*) or 'aberrant' (*xie*) possession *contra* the pure possession of the correct and high-ranked spirits in the canonic registers taught as part of a Daoist initiation into secret and professional knowledge. As Schipper (1985) is at pains to point out, the Daoist does not use the trance techniques of spirit mediums. He uses meditation and bodily techniques to reach a state of purity. In this state revelations are also said to have been vouchsafed. These pure revelations could be a source of authority to a reigning monarch, but also to a challenger and could therefore be a danger to current imperial rule.

The Mao Shan revelations which include the *Concealed Instructions* are described by Strickmann as being messianic and suicidal, for they prescribed a diet identical with that of the Perfected themselves:

> The stellar essences on which the Perfected delicately feasted were deadly poisons here below, in a world that openly reversed all celestial values. Yet by what better means could one effect the essential transition from corrupt mortality to luminous perfection? Thus, when the sign was finally given by the unseen world, the adept would complete his program of practice by preparing and swallowing the stellar nutriment of the Perfected. In partaking of that communion, he would at last die entirely to his mundane life, and be that much further advanced toward his ultimate goal of full participation in the harmonious movement of the stars (Strickmann 1979: 190).

The same revelations of signs furnished the authority of Daoists who enjoyed the patronage of emperors. For them, the sign of fulfilling an auspicious destiny was the sign of the arrival of a sage emperor, not for taking poison. Immortality could also be gained without suicide.

During the Tang and Song dynasties certain emperors – Lagerwey mentions the first and the sixth Tang emperors, and the first, third and eighth Song emperors – named or re-named their reigns after hearing of a revelation through a medium or finding a written document, in either case interpreted by a Mao Shan Daoist master of long and respectable lineage. These revelations and the accompanying signs were always a discovery to the emperor of his own heretofore unknown ancestry in one of the Perfected or the Pure of the highest levels of the Daoist hierarchy.

In subsequent dynasties, the Orthodox heavenly masters of Dragon and Tiger Mountain in Jiangxi province were the accepted interpreters of authenticating or restoring signs. They were given lavish imperial patronage for this service. 'The titles accorded them, and eventually accorded their wives and mothers as well, grew longer and longer, their land holdings richer and richer, and they even came to be allied to the imperial house by marriage' (Lagerwey 1987:259).

The change from the monastic, Mao Shan Daoism of purification and immortality to the heavenly masters was also a change in the relation between emperors and Daoists. Imperial adoption of the heavenly masters was not so much to authenticate the dynasty or the reign as to serve the emperor or his rule with the health-saving techniques of the Daoists and the popular cults to which they lent their authority. For these later dynasties, official cults claimed authority from a less mystical tradition, and were placed as centres of moral correction at an exclusive distance from popular cults, upon which controls by education and instruction were exerted through the institution of the village pact (see chapter 3).

Lagerwey provides a key example to illustrate the Ming dynasty relation to Daoist orthodoxy. It is the imperial adoption by inscription in 1417 of a popular cult of two brothers named Xu. Their cult had started in Fujian province in 983. It received an inscription in 1263 by a Song emperor. But the Ming inscription brought the cult to the imperial capital. It was like many other adoptions of popular cults into the lowest level of the hierarchy of officially celebrated deities, but Lagerwey shows clearly that it had a special significance for the Orthodox Unity Daoist succession.

Imperial adoption of the cult was, as usual, by means of an inscription in stone over the name of the emperor, but the inscription was soon to be published as a preface to a Daoist text. On its own the inscription is no different from other imperial inscriptions officially entitling the City God, or Guan Di, or Ma Zu (see Zito 1987:344–8, and Watson 1985:299). The inscription praises the merit of the two brothers, in the first place as an acknowledgement of their having become immortals and having received appointments from heaven. But the occasion celebrated by the inscription, the one which has brought about his gratitude and recompense, a conferring of new titles upon the brothers to add to the ones already given by heaven, is the manifestation of their power in a medical treatment which brought the emperor personally back to life.

169

Due to the close relation of Orthodox Unity Daoism with the third Ming emperor who conferred these titles, a new compilation of Daoist texts, the re-edition of a Daoist canon, was authorised in 1445. It included the liturgy of a complete Daoist ritual for the cult of the brothers Xu. This Lagerwey takes to show how important the cult and Daoism was to the Ming imperial family (1987: 261). The other way around, how important the Ming imperial family was to orthodox Daoism, must certainly be true. Imperial authority was important to the heavenly masters and their orthodoxy. But what was the importance of Daoism to imperial rule?

Certain emperors, from the fifth century on, 'viewed their mandate as the reflection of a larger Taoist dispensation' and ordered the collection of Daoist texts and their distribution (Bolz 1987: 5). But the compilation under the third Ming emperor was not because of any Daoist lineal authentication of his reign, as it had been for some of the Tang and Song emperors. By his own authority, the dynasty instead claimed recognition of its celestial mandate through official cults which did not owe their sanctity to the Daoist canon. Rather, it was he that conferred titles on the brothers Xu, not the other way around. Furthermore, when popular cults were included into official imperial sanction, it was not through Daoist channels, but through the mechanisms of the imperial hierarchy of rites and cults which by the Ming dynasty had their own textual tradition, more associated with a Confucian classical canon than with the Daoist canon. Many cults were themselves more or less closely associated with Daoist liturgical services, but imperial favour recognised their Daoism only as an act of control and of synthesis with Buddhist metaphysics and Confucian ethics. The quotation Lagerwey provides from the first Ming emperor's introduction to *The Standard Rituals for Offerings and Fasts of the Celestial Religion of the Great Ming* in 1374 states this quite plainly:

Chan [Buddhism] and Integral Reality [Daoism] devote themselves to the cultivation of the person and the improvement of the individual endowment: they are just for the self. The [Buddhist] Teaching [possible reference to the White Lotus sect] and Orthodox Unity [Daoism] focus on salvation and lay special emphasis on filial children and compassionate parents. They improve human relations and enrich local customs: great indeed is their merit! (Lagerwey 1987: 260)

Lagerwey returns this synthesis to Daoism, by pointing to a key text in the Daoist compilation which similarly synthesises Buddhist metaphysics and Confucian ethics with a Daoist view of popular mediumism. The text is *The Perfect Scripture of the Jade Emperor*, a 'key Daoist text from its first appearance in the Song dynasty until now in Taiwan' (Lagerwey 1987: 263). It is addressed to the Jade Emperor, head of the popular pantheon. According to Daoist history it was, Lagerwey notes, first recited by the Xu brothers. This leads him to a partisan Daoist conclusion that the Ming imperial adoption of the cult of the Xu brothers and of Orthodox Unity Daoist masters made Daoism the state religion and at the same time incorporated the whole of the popular pantheon to it (1987: 263–4). But his claim depends on an assertion that 'all the cults of popular religion belong' to Daoism (p. 264), and incidentally on assuming that the 'alien' Qing dynasty did not adopt Daoism as a religion of state, because the Qing was Manchu, not Chinese. All these claims are wrong. But his making of them is very instructive, not least because it indicates a way in which Daoists themselves may have sought authority.

It is wrong to imply, as Lagerwey does and high Daoists might, that all popular cults were adopted by the Ming emperors. The only way such an implication can be sustained is by excluding from the designation 'popular cults' all those not recognised in the Daoist canon and all those not adopted into the official cults by imperial inscription and conferment of titles. They are in this view inconsiderable because they are wild and heterodox. Lagerwey accepts the Daoist claim to authority over all popular cults, which is to dismiss, as the Daoist canonical texts do, the 'excessive' and to include the rest by definition into the lowest level of a Daoist hierarchy of purity and orthodoxy, whether or not the cults' adherents refer to the Daoist textual canon as their authority.

Further, he appears to claim that whatever was adopted by imperial authority was also adopted into the Daoist orthodoxy, which is, perhaps, how Daoist orthodoxy augmented itself. Lagerwey claims authority over emperors for Daoist orthodoxy. But emperors' acceptance of Daoist revelations of their own dynastic authority was occasional, not constant. By the time of the Ming adoption of the heavenly masters as their official registrars of communal Daoism, emperors had adopted a neo-Confucian synthesis and a hierarchy of official altars and a calendar which may have included Daoist elements, but was not dependent on Daoist authentication.

Orthodox Unity Daoism was an important purchase on popular, communal cults. The official cults of state administration were another. These two imperial channels of moral control joined in the

171

adopted cults since in most cases they would have been consecrated by Daoists of Orthodox Unity lineage. But most popular cults were not imperially recognised. They either came under the tenuous moral control of magistrates through the system of City Gods and of the village pact. Or they came under the even less direct control of their own employment of Daoists, whose reliance on authentication from the Celestial Masters was at best sporadic and was scrutinised, if at all, only through professional rivalry among Daoist families.

Daoist compilations under imperial authority ceased with the Ming, but that does not mean that the Qing emperors, despite their personal adherence to a Manchu religion, ceased the imperial practice of authorising popular cults by the conferment of titles on their deities in recognition of their meritorious efficacy. On the contrary, this went on just as it had under the Ming emperors. As emperors, the Manchu dynasty participated in the same set of official cults.

The compilation of Daoist revelations into an imperially authorised canon preserved as it attempted to control a volatile traditionality. Daoism, in the very compilations authorised by emperors, laid claim to a revelation of original power beyond that of the emperor, however sage. It could therefore claim, as in the fifth to thirteenth centuries, a superior distance, an authenticating knowledge or prescience about the mandate of an emperor to rule in a well-ordered universe. The Orthodox Unity Daoists sought to control what they considered false possessions and revelations, in rival cults of reception through dreams, spirit-mediums and other instruments of written truth, just as did the emperors and their officials. They could be revelations of a new dynasty. But the Daoist orthodoxy was itself one such source of rival access to a primal Chaos or womb of original truth.

The Jade Emperor, equivalent of the terrestial emperor, is included in the Daoist liturgy as the head of the popular pantheon. But in the Daoist altar which reconstructs the Daoist hierarchy, he is placed to the side, lesser than Lao Zi and the Three Pure Ones (Lagerwey 1987:37–9). The Daoist hierarchy and the registers of positions in it, including the one from which the Daoist master starts, are like a bureaucratic hierarchy. The liturgy prescribes formulations, written orders, and symbols of rank – seals, gowns, crowns, swords – which are like those used in imperial courts. But they refer to a cosmology which had, by the time of the Ming dynasty at least, departed from the calendar, the astronomy, and the altars of imperial rites. The rites of the Daoist orthodoxy were in any case, at all times, distinctive in being rites of exorcism and purification.

The imperial rites, while based on the same numerology and patterns as the Daoist cosmology, were a purification only by being correct and in harmony with an originating and basic order of resonance. The imperial mediation of heaven with earth in the rites at the altars and temples of the imperial capital, were a prerogative over the lower, delegated rites at the altars and temples of administrative centres, and maintained a strict hierarchy of control over other cults. But the control was by exclusive prerogative and example, and by the surveillance exercised by those who were educated to pass examinations in a *corpus* of classics which avoided anything to do with possession, revelation and exorcism. The act of exorcism is a commanding, military evocation and performance, which the imperial military forces actually undertook in pacifying parts of the imperial realm. But the communal service of purification which the Daoists undertook in the employment of the leaders of a popular cult and the households in its territory had its actuality in the militia which performed in procession some of the same steps which the Daoist master performed in far more elaborate and secret rituals inside the temple. Beside these displays, local militia bands might act on behalf of local gentry and leaders supporting an imperial order. But they were as likely to be organised in activities of smuggling, brigandry, plunder or defence against the militia of other localities which could become the concern of the imperial forces. In such situations, and even more so when they linked up with other militia in defence against the depredations of imperial agents, they became the forces of disorder, or rather of an alternative order to those of the current imperial rule.

Daoist exorcism represents the revelation or re-establishment of an originating purity, not the rites and practices of imperial rule which it resembles. A messianic inspiration, carried in the liturgy of orthodox Daoism, but also in other textual traditions such as that of the White Lotus in the north of China, could inspire and lend authority to such rebellious organisations of local militia. China's history of uprisings, from the Yellow Turbans onwards, is one inspired by such revelations.

Orthodox Daoism has an ambivalent relation to this history, stretched between its authority in imperially ordered compilations of its liturgy and its intimate relation with popular cults of *ling*, an exercise of revelation through local repute for effectiveness. I can think of no better illustration of this ambivalence than that provided by one of the the most popular collections of narratives in the history of uprising. The *Water Margin* (*Shui Hu Zhuan*) provided one of the models of guerilla warfare and of strategy to Mao Zedong, among others. Its 108 heroes are bandits, but of them the most appealing are portrayed as righteous bandits, who have freed themselves from the clutches of a cruel, if not unrighteous regime. And the remarkable point is that the regime from which they have escaped is a Daoist temple of one of the heavenly masters. The 108 bandits are presented as the 108 stellar influences, 36 heavenly and 72 earthly, which cause disorder in certain conjunctions or when their paths across the notional sky are contrary to their normal ones. They make up the celestial camps of gods' soldiers (see Chapter 2).

This point is drawn to our attention by Hou Ching-lang, a Taiwanese scholar linking beliefs and practices current in Taiwan with historical records of the same objects of belief and practice made two thousand years ago. He calls these stellar influences 'baleful stars'.

The belief in the baleful stars had spread before the founding of the earliest Taoist organizations, and they adopted it without adding much of their own. This explains the fact that, in the Taoist Canon and other Taoist writings, there is no systematic theory with respect to this belief. There are simply rituals and collections of petitions (*yiwen ji*) – an entire arsenal of practices intended to protect the faithful [from them]. (Hou 1979:226)

These are the practices of Daoist exorcism, for the baleful stars come into the category which includes restricted souls and stale emanations whose place is in the quarter guarded by the Three Offices and to which they are confined by petition of superior powers in the hierarchy, by command and by sword-play in Daoist rites, including the communal offering that is the *jiao*.

Three of these baleful stellar influences are particularly feared objects of exorcism in Taiwan today: the Great Year (Tai Sui), the White Tiger (Bai Hu) and the Heavenly Dog (Tian Gou). They feature prominently in the warnings for the year given in popular almanacs. Their feared conjunctions are also called 'passes', crossed by the stellar influences of a person's birth, or by those which mark the occasions for important family events, such as marriage and burial, or by those which rule the date and geomantic siting for the establishment or refurbishing of a house or a communal building such as a temple. In each case, a crossing which clashes with the baleful star requires avoidance or a remedying, exorcising rite. But of the three, only the Heavenly Dog is unmitigated harm. The Great Year can be petitioned for protection, like so many other ambivalent demonic influences. And the White Tiger is the stellar influence and emblem of the Western Quarter associated with the corresponding one of the Five Phases (Wu Xing) which must always be encountered, but kept contained or pacified. They are, in the appropriate analogy used by Hou, like imperial officials with whose passage one can accidently clash and cause offence (Hou 1979: 228). For Daoist orthodoxy, they are extraneous demons of the lower orders, to be exorcised and confined, and this service coincides with the popular conception of defence against them.

Daoist orthodoxy retains certain elements of the theocracy on which it is founded: an aspiration to authority and an encompassing inclusion of the cosmological system and the popular cults of the empire; a model of local cults as cells of Daoist rule and purification; texts whose origin is various forms of inspiration; the compilation of such texts into a canon authorised by emperors and so containing records of knowledge and practice which have been transmitted, partly by reference to this authorised collection and partly by independent lines of descent and instruction from the centres of Daoist learning and initiation since their foundation. But the link with imperial authority has been an alternative and potentially rival source of authorisation.

## THE DAOIST ALTAR IN THE TEMPLE – THE *JIAO* OFFERING

The altar placed at the centre of a temple by Daoists is, like the open altars of the official cult, superior to the cults which it displaces. But unlike those of the official cults it is not fixed. The Daoist master can place it where needs be, and the liturgy of his greatest ritual, the *jiao*, places him within it and in the position of a journey of meditation by which he is transformed, passing through several gates, including the gate of the Jade Emperor himself. The end to which this meditational journey is performed ties the Daoist to the terrestrial community, for he journeys as its representative through layers of figuration. What he achieves by it is a purification of the temple's area and its residents of the baleful emanations and spirits by means of reports to the Three Offices and an audience with the Jade Emperor. Outside the temple, the five camps of spirit soldiers and their generals are addressed in a similar journey using the local gods and the more vernacular rites of the Daoism of *fashi* magicians (Schipper 1985: 28–9).

The Daoist master at the centre of the *jiao* practises the art into which he has been initiated to ascend the meditational terraces of heaven for an audience with the Jade Emperor. But he then engages in an act which is the central mystery of the *jiao*. From his low position in the Daoist heavenly hierarchy he identifies himself with Lao Zi and so with a source of power well beyond that of the Jade Emperor, namely with the source of power of which the Jade Emperor is a manifestation and a particular.

In a meditation in which he finally takes up a crouching position with his head near the ground, his back like a shell, the turtle position, he enacts the attainment of immortality, the suicide of former Mao Shan adepts. All this he does by disciplined breathing and interior speech, concentrating upon images and the appropriate parts of his body treated as a microcosm, while around him his assistants step out in movement what he is silently invoking. Visualising a new-born infant in his lower belly, the Cinnabar Field or alchemical crucible (*dantian*), he moves to his heart where the infant becomes a Real Man, a civil official flanked by two generals, and they travel up the trachea, a twelve-storey tower, to the mouth, lower crucible of the head, to the nose, middle crucible, to the eyes, sun and moon gates, to the space between them and from there up through the top of the head to a crown in the shape of a flame fixed on its top-knot. There they present the announcement of the *jiao* offering to the Jade Emperor. But that is only the half-way point, for they return to the lower belly at which point, in the turtle position, the Real Man has become a venerable Lord of Long Life. At this point of consummation, which is called 'killing the turtle', the passage has become a cycling back of the floodwaters to their origin in maternal creation, an identification with the act of Yu the Great whose control of the waters allowed the earth and the features of the land to appear under heaven. The turtle is the north, the place of exorcism and control, its shell the surface of the earth. Also in the north is the tomb of Yu's father who had failed to control the waters, but to which Yu himself returned at his death. The Daoist has returned in identification with the originating chaos, the mother and father of all things. (See Schipper 1982: 134–5, and Lagerwey 1987: 132–4.)

The Daoist ritual area is called *daochang*, the bounded area of the Dao. This is also the name for any occasion in which a Daoist altar is set up, whether it be for the living, when it is a full or minor form of *jiao*, or for the dead, when it is a merit-making ceremony with an equal range of duration and liturgical complexity.

To the Daoist it is a replication of the mountain retreat, a site of mediation between earth and heaven, but an internal, not an open and exposed one as it would be on a mountain top. Its design is always the same. The Daoist's equipment includes all the pictorial representations and ritual implements necessary for its reconstruction. At its centre, as in the cult-houses of the Daoist theocracy in which the earliest heavenly masters established their authority, is an incense-burner whose shape and flames represent a mountain and the purifying passage of communion and eventual reunion with the pure dwelling of immortals, situated on the map of the Chinese world in the far western range of mountains called Kunlun (Schipper 1982: 125–6). But unlike his monastic cousins, the Orthodox Unity Daoist remains among the people, and undertakes his retreat within their communities, indeed at their centres, not on mountains outside them.

Like the emperor at the open altars (*tan*) outside the imperial city, the Daoist master is the central figure in a ranked order of deities. But the Daoist altar is not tiered and so is not ranked by level, but instead is ranked, as is the imperial city, by disposition around a north-south axis in which the north is the supreme position, facing south, and east superior to west. The circumference of the altar is notionally open at eight or ten gates, and the diagonal axes between them are passages of influence and transformation, always with the northern point as the higher.

At its centre, the Daoist master is within the mountain and bears the title of Gao Gong Fashi (Magician of High Merit). The title includes the designation *fashi*, even when he performs a rite reserved only to the Daoists of classical learning, all of which goes to show that it is not easy to separate, at least by designation, the claimants to the orthodox tradition and the local, more vernacular, Daoists. In Taiwan, the rites he performs within the altar eventually bring him to a point where he exchanges that terrestrial title for the title of Zhong Zun (Venerable of the Centre), which Schipper interprets as 'Great Master, universal inspector of merit, appointed to spread civilisation in accordance with the principles of nature' (Schipper 1982: 129, illustration p.128). By the rites he performs in a *jiao* or in a minor form for an annual territorial festival the Daoist master re-creates an ordered universe. And in presenting a memorial on which are listed the representatives of the community on whose behalf he is acting he also effects a reunion with Yu the Great, making the re-enactment a re-appearance of Yu (Lagerwey 1987: 154).

In short, the Daoist master is placed by Daoist liturgy at a position equivalent to the emperor. Indeed the same word is used for Daoists' altars as for the official altars, *tan*. But every Daoist master accomplishes a transformation to this imperial height, whereas the officials who performed rites at the open altars of the imperial administrative capitals were delegates of the one and only emperor. They were not equivalents because the emperor existed and performed the highest rites himself.

Surrounding the Daoist *tan* is an outer boundary marked by portraits and large free-standing figures whose names are like, but are not the same as those celebrated at the altars of the imperial administration. Lagerwey's photographs from Taiwan show the following: four marshals (black Kang in the north, blue Wen in the east, white Gao in the west, and red Zhao in the south) who are guardians of the inner altar; various feudally entitled commanders of the natural elements (Count of the Wind, Master of the Rain, Duke of Thunder, Mother of Lightning); and a number of untitled spirits (Soil, Metal-armour, Hills).

Beyond these are the spirits of the unworshipped dead invited to feast, be saved, and to return to the other world in the general salvation which is the outermost and most spectacular rite of the *jiao*. They are invited by lanterns which are, if possible, floated on the water of a canal, stream or lake at the boundary of the temple's territory to disperse invitations to the scattered ghosts. At the outermost boundaries of the temple's territory are images of the four marshals of the quarters, each in his quarter guarding by terror against the disorder and malicious influences otherwise associated with the hungry dead.

So, from the territorial boundary of the temple's actual area, to the central altar within it, a series of concentric layers builds up to the point where the Daoist master meditates, hidden within his body and within the walls of the temple, whose doors are closed. Beyond the outermost boundary are the area's ghosts.

Between the concentric layers of this arrangement around the Daoist master, at the lowest (southern) point of the inner altar space, is the altar of the Three Offices. Behind that, further south are placed the representatives of the community assembled for the rites. Arrayed in a similar position in the south on either side of the living representatives are the images of the cults of the temple in which the Daoist has implanted his altar, and next to them the images of the minor temples and domestic cults brought there from altars in the area. They, the living representatives and the images of their cults, are under the gaze of the demon-controlling Offices before which their merit is being argued and their positioning ordered according to the principles of Daoist nature.

The liturgy which at the centre is secret and esoteric, has detailed outer implications, for which instructions are issued which order the community for the duration of the *jiao*. They are issued by the committee in charge of the *jiao* and also in charge of the employment of the Daoists themselves. For instance, at a *jiao* which I observed in Shulin *zhen*, northern Taiwan, in 1967, a number of documents were issued on pink paper containing lists and guides to show the heads of the territorially defined community their places and identities in a ritual order. They give a good idea of the scale of the undertaking, and that it does effectively identify and order, for the duration of the rites, the whole of a community.

## THE OUTER ORDER

This was a three-day *jiao* (a more elaborate one takes five days) performed for the repair and refurbishing of a temple called Jian Gong (Temple of Relief and Peace). It was the main temple of Shulin, a thriving market town not far from Taibei city.[1] The local cult to its main deity, Bao Sheng Da Di, had started nearby in 1788. It was, virtually from its foundation, a territorial cult with a procession festival every year. In 1927 it was relocated to what had become the new commercial centre of the area consequent upon the building of a railway. And the *jiao* I attended was to seal its refurbishment, forty years later. (See the history of this town as marked by its temples and their cults, written by one of its natives, Wang Shih-ch'ing (1974).)

In order of publication, the first document issued by the *jiao* office (*jiao ju*), was a calendar of the most important times, and the horoscopes of those who should avoid them in order not to clash and bring about a baleful stellar influence. This public notice (*gong qi*), posted on walls and handed out in numbers sufficient for every household to take note, also contained instructions for the purification of every household, starting three days before the *jiao* proper began. Household heads were told to paste up new and edifying door couplets and paper decorations, and to sprinkle, sweep, and cleanse their homes and the areas in front of them, fit for domestic prayer every day from then until the day after the final rite. Like New Year, this is a time to avoid divisions, quarrels, and bad words. One quarrel did, in the event, occur in my hearing, and it arose from an alleged misuse of the contributions from one of the constituent neighbour-hoods. Its chief and representative at the *jiao* threatened to withdraw.

But he was dissuaded by a retired civil servant on the grounds that such quarrelling would destroy the whole sense of the *jiao*.

*Fourteen important times for which to avoid clashes:*

1 A preliminary soliciting of Heaven, five months before the *jiao*, when every household should be prepared and clean for formal attendance at the temple.

2 Twenty-two days before the rites of the *jiao* commence, the construction of four outside altars is inaugurated, one or more for the three heavenly realms of the universe, and one for the central offering of this *jiao*. The outer ones were huge and colourful constructions, the height of a four-storey building, which housed the images and artifacts from the domestic altars of wealthy households in the temple area, to which in pride of place some of them added figures from favoured shrines which they had personally invited. To the south of the central altar were three masts for the three heavenly realms. It was to this altar that the officiating Daoists emerged, to invite the celestial gods, and to present the memorial petition. The heaven masts were to the superior side of the lantern masts for the orphan souls (see no. 4 below) and were to invite and show the way to the spirits of the celestial courts, each with a single light, in contrast to the many lights of the seven constellations (*dou*) of north, south, east, west, upper and lower earthly courts for the mass of souls (so one of the Daoists explained to me). On the third day, the central outside altar, which had a stage platform at its base, was mounted by the Daoists for the presentation of the memorial on which were listed the names and positions of the community's representatives.

3 Two days before the eve of the *jiao* (when the rites begin), the gods of every place in the territory should be invited and brought into the temple at the centre of the *jiao*. From this day until the last day of the rites, every household was expected to make offerings to the gods' soldiers (*kao jun*).

4 On the same day, the lantern masts were to be raised. These were very high masts, one at each of the four quarters, called 'thousand-lantern masts' because on cross-bars running up their length were hung paper lanterns which invited orphan souls from a great distance to take their part of the offering at a rite of general salvation on the third day. On the day of their establishment, every household, properly clean, was to present offerings at the foot of one of the masts.

5 On the eve of the first of the three full days of the *jiao*, fasting begins. This is fasting from alcohol and meat, until midday of the last full day of the rites. Butchers must also stop their work from this day, but can start again on the last day of the rites, which is the day of feeding the orphan souls and for general domestic feasting in the evening.

6 On the same day, the lamps of the stars of the dippers (*dou*) in the four quarters of the sky, were to be settled and lit in the temple. These are the lamps of the living representatives of the area and its households (see no. 14 in the *Agenda of Duties* below).

7 Later on the same day, the starting of the drums and the announcement. This is the first great rite conducted by the Daoists, summoning spirits with powers to cleanse the altar and its area of filth (see Lagerwey 1987: Chapter 6).

8 In the evening of the second day of the *jiao* proper, the lanterns for orphan souls would be released on to water at the outskirts of the temple area. The masts were carried to the temple and then taken in procession to the water's edge for the lanterns to be released, each on its little raft, dispersing on the dark water. The masts are then returned to their places, as beacons.

9 From the first hour of the third day, that is from midnight, alcohol can be brewed and offering pigs can be brought out. These were pigs bred domestically for the occasion, slaughtered in the morning to be dressed and brought to the temple for a competition in which the heaviest wins, and to be presented to the gods of the temple and the other local cults whose images are assembled there.

10 Early in the morning of the third day, obeisance in thankful recompense for Heaven's mercy and the fulfilment of virtuous vows. This was the presentation of the memorial (Lagerwey 1987: Chapter 9).

11 Early in the afternoon of the third day, the general salvation of orphan souls.

12 After all the other rites have been performed, but the altars have not been closed, the settling of the dragon and the thanks-dismissal of the tiger of the temple area. This was a secret rite of exorcism.

13 Later on the same night, thanks-dismissal of the altars and of the lantern masts.

14 Early the next morning, sincere hearts accompany the gathered gods of the area back to their shrines.

This, then, was the preparatory and most generally distributed of the instructions issued by the managing committee of the *jiao*. It indicates how and in what aspects of the rites ordinary householders of the area were involved.

Another important document issued by the management committee was the agenda of a meeting two months before the ceremonies. It is important because it indicates what were the priorities for the organisers themselves. The meeting was called by a management committee of five. But the meeting itself was the occasion for an extension of the committee, adding the other main financial contributors to the commissioning of the *jiao*, bringing the total membership of the committee to more than twenty.

The agenda is an assignment of duties for the ceremonies involved in the *jiao*. It starts with a list of those taking up the main ritual roles of collective representation: the master of the incense-burner (*lu zhu*), taken by the head of the management committee; four assistant masters of the incense-burner, one of whom was also assistant manager; the host of the assembly (*zhu hui*) and three assistants; the host of the offering (*zhu jiao*) and three assistants; and the person in charge of sacrificial ceremonies (*ji dian bu*). The rest is the list of duties themselves.

*Agenda of duties*:

1 The arrangements for going, two months later, to the root temples (in Taibei and other nearby cities) of the main cults in Shulin, and to bear figures of their deities back in sedan chairs, for most of the way by lorry, but at the border of Shulin to be met and carried by foot to the main temple; the troupes of musicians, martial arts gymnasts and actors to be invited to participate from the twelve neighbourhoods comprising the temple's territory; their order in procession; and the marshals for the various contingents participating in the procession to invite the gods of the area to the temple.

2 The allocation of responsibility for erecting the lantern masts and tables for the offerings to the hungry ghosts: these were placed under the authority of one of the management committee members, and under him, as submanager, one of the vice-principals of the incense-burner who was in charge of sacrificial ceremonies; allocation of the two main ritual roles remaining: the host of the altars (*zhu tan*), which were the elaborate and colourful tiered platforms, almost as high as the lantern masts, in honour of

the heavenly deities outside the temple building; and the host of the general salvation (*zhu pu*), in charge of the tables of offerings for the hungry ghosts.

These two heads, or hosts, made up the complement of what were called the Four Great Pillars (Si Da Zhu). They were represented by four large paper figures outside the temple, repeated at each of the outside altars of the heavenly courts. But they, or their patron deities, were also represented in the inner altar, where the committee members acted as their living representatives as well as the beneficiaries of the representations made to the courts of the four quarters by the officiating Daoists.

Of the four pillars, the host of the offering itself stood third in rank from the master of the incense-burner. But I was told the deity commanding this pillar was the dark warrior, also popularly known by the title Obscure Heaven Imperial Ruler (Xuan Tian Shang Di), the supreme exorcising deity. This identifies the pillar of the offering with the northern of the Four Sages (Si Sheng) of the quarters. They are frequently and in various forms addressed in the inner altar. In another manifestation, they could be the Four Potentates (Si Ling), monstrously fearful martial guardians whose figures stood outside the temple and at four outer bastions of the temple area for the duration of the *jiao*. The exposition of these sets of four varies according to the tradition of the Daoist one asks, and according to the ritual context. But all agree that the northern one is the sombre warrior, subject of one of the most important of the liturgical texts of the Daoist canon, where he is named Wen and entitled Marshal among numerous other titles.

The patron deities named to me for the other three pillars varies from those given Lagerwey for the Four Sages or Potentates. The four were, in order of the rank of their positions around the Master of the Incense-Burner, the Host of the Assembly who is the heavenly master (of Orthodox Unity); the Host of the Offering, who is the Obscure Heaven Imperial Ruler; the Host of the Altar, who is Guan Yin, the Goddess of Mercy (this is what I wrote down, but it strikes me that this saviour deity would be more appropriate for the last pillar, and the deity I wrote down for it more appropriate for this one!); the Host of the Salvation, who is the Correct Spirit of Fortune and Virtue, the formal title of the god of the soil and locality. (I can not find this or any other mention of the set of Four Great Pillars in Lagerwey's or any other exposition of an observed *jiao*.)

183

3  Arranging the images of the local gods on each of the altars; responsibility for this was given to the Four Pillar roles and one of the assistant masters of the incense-burner.

4  The allocation of expenses for purchasing the offerings and furnishings on the altar tables: for offerings 128,500 Taiwanese dollars (£1,147, or US$3,212 at the contemporary exchange rates); for furnishings 109,700 Taiwanese dollars (£979 or US$2,742).

5  The arrangements for taking the lantern masts to the water's edge and the positions on the bank for floating them off on their rafts (to be decided after investigations on the spot).

6  Obeisance to Heaven and the general distribution of offerings to the hungry ghosts, whether thanks to the heavens should be held in the temple or outside at each of the altars to heaven; they could be simultaneously in the temple and at the outside altars.

7  Congratulatory activities: gymnastic team – 20,000 Taiwanese dollars; health team – 2,000 Taiwanese dollars; exhibition team – 13,000 Taiwanese dollars; commemoration affairs team – 85,000 Taiwanese dollars; and the award of prizes amounting to some 60,000 Taiwanese dollars.

8  Commemorative memorial listing of the names of all the representatives of the community and contributors to the finances of the *jiao*, to be published as well as posted on the walls of the temple.

I was told that the total fund for the *jiao* contributed by this committee and by the temple's management committee was between 500 and 600 thousand Taiwanese dollars (£4464–£5357 or US$ 12500–US$ 15000). This was on top of the fund for the repair of the temple, which the *jiao* commemorated and completed. The temple repair fund was about one million Taiwanese dollars. The position of principal of the incense-burner went to the person who had contributed most to both funds. The rest of the management committee of the *jiao* was made up of those who had contributed the next largest amounts to both funds, for the temple and for the *jiao*. But the *jiao* management committee, at least in its enlarged form, was not the same as the temple's management committee. It existed simply for the *jiao*.

The total cost of the *jiao* was far greater than the fund contributed by this committee's members. One estimate of the total cost, made by the son of one of the neighbourhood chiefs, was 15 million Taiwanese dollars. The local newspaper reported it had cost 30 million. Certainly, it was likely to be a multiple of the fund so far mentioned because of two important facts. Every neighbourhood chief collected a contribution of a fixed amount of 20 Taiwanese dollars per head of population from every household in his or her neighbourhood. In addition there were subscriptions for over 200 *dou* (see no. 14 below).

The preparation for the *jiao* involved a census, a tax, and a social pressure which few if any households resisted. This pressure came from a combination of secular and religious authority. The *jiao's* managers and leaders were already locally powerful and their selection had been vouchsafed by divination, that is by the throwing of divination blocks before the main temple cult's deity, from the names of household heads who were, by previous selection, candidates for *jiao* representation.

9 Commemorative gifts.
10 Emergency arrangements.
11 Electrical equipment
12 Construction of an honorific arch. (I assume this was simply for the honour of the area and its temple.)
13 Service points (where people could find help and information).
14 Chart of arrangements to make clear where the lanterns for the living should be placed on tables in the temple.

Beside those of the master of the incense-burner and the four pillars, this chart names lesser positions, further to the south of the Daoist altar. The positions are named after the celestial beings addressed in the course of the rites to be performed. In each position is also the personal name of the representative who will occupy it. In all, 221 positions and names are charted. First are those of the management committee in the roles already given. Next are the representatives of the twelve neighbourhoods in the temple area. The rest are individuals representing their families, having paid a subscription to be so included. The least prominent position cost 600 Taiwanese dollars, the most prominent 12,000. The 221 did not themselves attend all the rites. Attendance for one or more in the programme of thirty-eight rites over the three days was distributed among the lantern positions.

The lanterns (*deng*) themselves were oil lamps placed in a tub and with a named flag, a mirror reflecting the lamp, a ruler which represented a sword and a measure of the proper span of life (Saso 1972: 108 shows a sword and scales instead), and a pair of scissors representing the danger of the light being cut off. These tubs were also called *dou* (dippers). The flame represented the connecting link between the named terrestrial unit and the light of a stellar position called the 'original conjunction' (*yuan zhen*). This is where the fate and merit of the household, neighbourhood or community named on the flag resides. Its light is vulnerable to assault by obscure and unclean spirits, or it might cut itself off, and the same 108 baleful stars which might otherwise threaten it are invoked to return it to its place (as I was told by a *daoshi* in Taibei). The *jiao*, being a comprehensive purifying and exorcising ritual, includes rites for the brightening, the cleansing and securing, of the light of the whole community, the lights of its representatives, and the lights of households who have contributed enough to be represented.

15 Carrying the *dou* lanterns in procession.
16 Fasting and the closure of the temple doors.

The management committee issued supplements later, one of them naming those with the duties of organising and assisting with the ghost-lantern masts, another identifying the route and timing of two days' procession past every temple in the area to invite their spirits (and images) to the central temple. It noted where they should be met and greeted with incense. It also announced the dates for giving recompense to heaven, for fasts, and for other prohibitions to be observed at the main temple and two other temples linked with it.

Not mentioned in the *jiao* committee's documents summarised above are the theatrical performances which took place for several days, for the entertainment of the gods and the community. The first item mentions troupes of local actors. But these would have been for the procession, dressed up to represent scenes from popular dramas. Performances of the dramas themselves, on stages in the evenings, might have been on an agenda of another meeting or of another committee altogether. In any case, most of the performances would have been funded by contributions made directly in payments to the players, the amounts and sponsors' names displayed near the stages. They would not have gone through the *jiao* committee.

These documents indicate the parts of a *jiao* which are important for those outside the inner circle: the processions bringing in the figures from surrounding temples, the outside altars, the lantern masts, the procession to the waterside and the lanterns' release, the *dou* lamps and the commemorative memorial of the community and

186

its representatives, the offerings and rites performed at the outside altar to Heaven, the furnishings of this and the altars in the temple.

In addition to these are the theatre performances, the weights of the sacred offering pigs, and most involving of all, the rite of general salvation and the propitiation of hungry ghosts on the third day when hundreds of meters of tables were laden with offerings brought from every household and not supplied by the *jiao* fund.

They are furthest out in terms of a lack of interest in the ordering liturgy and in being left entirely to community representatives. They are occasions of great spectacle and for noting who is jostling whom for prominence through patronage in local politics. In particular, the young, junior members of local households, and most of all those educated beyond compulsory school-leaving age in the new literacy of republican Taiwan, participated in the Shulin *jiao* as unbelieving spectators. For them, the *jiao* was 'good to watch' (*hao kan*), a scene of great life and activity (*renao*). Just so, it was still the greatest show put on by their home town or village and one to which all its households contributed. In the evenings, the townspeople promenaded around its sights.

The night of the second day of rites, before and after the procession of lanterns to the water, was most crowded with vivid, sometimes lurid scenes. A glimmering lady saxophonist turned in the light from gold to green, accompanied by trumpet, two-stringed violin and rattling gourds. On the way across an open space to the distant fairy-palace lights of one of the heaven altars, a gas-flame threw more shadow than light on a woman who sat in front of a begging tin and breast-fed one child while others lay limp around her in the grass. She was sitting there, moaning, every time I passed, one of a great number of beggars, many of them grotesquely disabled. (The next day some of them would insist on their right to help themselves from the offerings brought by households to 'feed' the hungry ghosts.) The brush-stroke leaves left at the top of a thousand-lantern bamboo mast, nodded in the wind against the dark. The night air carried sensations from all directions. The tattoo of a big drum and the swirl of pipes and cymbals came from the direction of a long dragon of lights being taken to the river. Each lamp was in a paper house, a small version of the spirit houses built for the souls of the dead at their merit-making ceremonies, but the doorways of these, instead of good wishes for the passage to Paradise, bore couplets which were 1000–mile passes from the Courts of the Earth. In another direction a squad of white warriors carrying halberds and swords performed to the thuds of another big drum. The stink of rancid bean-curd frying in peanut oil floated from another direction. On stage, a brilliant history of warring states was rather casually played to the rattle of a hard drum. It lasted well into the night.

These were the connections and junctures of my impressions. Another's attentions will have been caught and drawn to other juxtapositions and speculations, reminders, contrasts. But there is no question that the spectacles, sounds and smells drew attention and therefore reminders and references. Neither is there any doubt that they were organised around a centre, the temple, bounded by the area of residence to which guests were invited, and limited to the three days and nights of the occasion.

## DANGER AND EXORCISM

Meanwhile, Daoists specially invited from the port city of Keelung (Jilong) on the other side of the island for this rite were sealing the altar. This too was an exciting performance of acrobatic charges, twirls, and sword-play. But it was heard and seen only by the other Daoists, their friends and by the lantern representatives scheduled for this rite, behind the closed doors of the temple. It is the drama of thrusting a sword and spraying from the mouth pure water in each of the five (four outer, one central) directions, explained in a long incantation facing south, calling on the agents of the four quarters and the local god of the soil to 'get rid of filth'. I did not note the text used, but it will have differed little from one used in southern Taiwan, where the Daoist master follows the incantation with a direct address to the community representatives. As 'son of the most high, grandson of the original sovereign' bearing the three terraces of the Red Bird of the south on his head, treading the Dark Warrior of the north underfoot, straddling the Green-Blue Dragon of the east and bringing the White Tiger of the west to heel, the Daoist orders the representatives, 'officials of the Offering, heads of the assembly', to receive his purifying spirit water through all the pores and regions of their bodies. He then reads a 'letter', one of a number of letters, contracts and offerings written and burned in the course of the jiao by the Daoist-bureaucrats, sealing relations with the highest celestial forces in the manner of the original 'covenant' of Orthodox Unity (Lagerwey 1987: 97). This one is addressed to a general of the south, who destroys filth with incense.

In the course of their investiture as Daoists, the masters conclude alliances with gods who are spirits and demons (*guishen*). The spirit-demons agree to obey the master's commands. It is an act of merit to help the living and so gain promotion in the ranks of heavenly government. 'The career that the *fashi* offers to demon spirits is the one that has been followed successfully by all "historical" Gods of the pantheon' (Schipper 1985: 28). A similar covenant is secured by Daoists of higher learning. It is a covenant with the more abstract entities of the Daoist classical cosmos. Nevertheless, these Daoists, the masters called *daoshi*, are also engaged in an act of exorcism.

In southern Taiwan, but not in the Shulin and another northern Taiwanese *jiao* which I attended, the purification of the altar reaches a dramatic climax with the irruption of a demonic tiger (one of the Daoists in a tiger mask). To furious gonging and drumming, the Daoist master rushes into the altar space. With a bowl of ritually purified spirit water in his left hand and a sword in his right he takes giant steps across the space, then swivels and, facing north, from his mouth sprays water taken from the bowl. Several strings of firecrackers are set off, and then, to piercing shawms, the devil, barefoot and dressed in tiger-striped rags, rushes from the northeast corner on to the altar space. The master makes way for the demon, who runs from one end of the altar space to the other, doing somersaults and looking under the altar hangings. Suddenly he smells what he is after. He snatches up the community incense-burner and runs away with it. The master comes after him and charges him several times with his sword, nearly running him through. When that proves insufficient, he glowers and sprays at the tiger, and at last succeeds in driving him back into the northeast corner, whereupon the master triumphantly calls out 'now I close the border to the east'. Finally, the master fixes the tiger demon there by writing the character 'demon' on rice in a bucket in which the tiger mask has been placed. He traps 'demon' there by drawing with his sword five horizontal and four vertical lines over the character like a net, and then presses it down by tracing with his sword a symbol composed of the character for demon under the character for mountain and planting his sword upright in the rice. Now he adds the flame-crown from his head and the seal of his authority to the contents of the bucket, and from then onwards, the tiger demon has been converted into a guardian of the gate through which he invaded the altar-space. Incense and candles are lit in the bucket, and spirit-money is burned in offering to him. (The details of this whole sequence are taken from Lagerwey 1987: 99, 102.)

In northern Taiwan, a similar drama of exorcising the tiger is enacted, but it is a separate rite, Settling the Dragon and Seeing-off the Tiger (An Long Song Hu), in addition to sealing the altar. Indeed it has a more permanent purpose than the sealing of the Daoist altar, which is after all only temporarily in the temple. The dragon is the site upon which the temple is built, and to settle it is to settle the geomantic order of the temple's area itself. In Shulin this was done as the last but one rite, late on the last night, after the Daoist's altar had been dismantled but before the outside altars had been dismantled and burned with the large guardian figures outside the temple in an immense bonfire. In the other *jiao* I attended, the dragon was pacified early on the morning of the first day, before the Daoists' altar had been set up.

The dragon of the locality (*di long*) was represented by a shape of rice behind the main altar table. Its ears were folded gold spirit money, its whiskers sticks of incense, its eyes eggs, on its forehead a third egg and the character for 'king', its eyebrows china spoons, its tongue a lit oil-lamp, its claws and back scales thirty-six coins, the point of its tail and its six feet a further seven flames of oil lamps. Around it were placed twenty-four bowls, each with offerings of meat and wine in them, a full set of offerings added at the head. To its left was a small paper figure of a dragon, the dragon of the eastern quarter, and a blue cloth on which was written 'Announcement of the receipt of commands from the venerable of upper heaven for the rite of pacifying the left, blue dragon'. To its right was a paper figure of a tiger and a white cloth with a similar announcement for sending off the right, white tiger. Offerings and incense were placed before each of them.

Just to the left of the site-dragon's head was placed a tile covered by a black cloth.

On the altar table were measures of rice (*dou*), one for each of the four quarters and the centre, with talismans in the appropriate colours placed in each, accompanied by the usual scissors, ruler, and mirror indicating the conjunctions of the quarters and centre of the temple's territory and its assembly of residents.

One of three temple-keepers, who were *fashi*, beat twenty-four drum-strokes. He bowed with incense and wine for the dragon and the tiger. This introduced one of the Daoists who had helped the master perform the *jiao* and had remained behind to perform this rite, not included in the main *jiao* liturgy. He performed the steps of Yu, marking out the stars of the Dipper, then stamped on the tile to break it. He wrote commands with sword-strokes in the air over the site dragon, and sprayed it and the left-dragon with spirit-water. Taking a live chicken, he bit its comb and used the gouts of blood to dot, first the emblem of the eight trigrams taken from the *dou* which stood on the altar of the celestial masters and the teachers of the *jiao* Daoists, then the talismans in the five *dou* of the temple's area, then the left-dragon, and finally the site-dragon on its forehead, eyebrows, eyes, snout, tongue, whiskers, spine, paws and tail. Just so a statue is dotted to bring it to life as the vessel of a spiritual power. (See Feuchtwang 1977:589.)

From a tub on the altar table, the Daoist then took handfuls of rice, nails and coins, throwing them in the four directions and into the middle of the temple, each time caught for luck by the temple-keepers, just as mourners catch the rice (crop fertility), nails (male progeny), and coins (wealth) thrown from the auspicious site of a grave just after the burial of a new ancestor.

The band, playing as it went, marched out of the temple. Firecrackers were let off both inside and outside the temple, to announce the next act. But as for the first act within the temple, only the designated representatives were there to see, for it was late in the evening and what would emerge was something to be avoided. The Daoist took up and brandished his sword again, this time over the tiger, and with fierce commands, grabbed it and strode out, placing it under his arm to hide it as he emerged. Accompanied only by one temple-keeper, he went to the edge of town, where he trapped it with his sword. The paper figure was lit, and as it burned he ordered it to keep out. The blue dragon, on the other hand, was buried, with the eggs which had been the forehead and two eyes of the site-dragon, secretly at a spot behind the temple.

One temple-keeper told me that if the spot were known the whole area would be vulnerable to the negative version of the exorcism and purification which had been completed. Someone could disorder and damage the geomantic fortunes of the residents of the temple area by burying a copper nail, a dog's blood and human urine at the spot which is the head of the site-dragon. The local minor Daoist who worked in a nearby temple had done this, he told me. People lost money. Spirits would not come to spirit-mediums. The gods' statues began to peel. Wind blew bits off the temple. People in the neighbourhood felt ill. The Daoist was denounced by his pupils, beaten, and taken to court. One has to be very careful to whom, as a Daoist, one teaches these secrets because they can be used to cheat society, said the temple-keeper, perhaps meaning to praise the bad Daoist at least for his pupils.

Whether they are major or minor magicians, the service for which Daoists are employed is exorcism. The *jiao* itself is an elaborate purification in the orthodox tradition, reading and enacting a liturgy which engages all the senses in passages through cosmological levels and stages in the generation of cosmic order, a theatre of the Daoist universe to purify body and place of extraneous, intrusive, disordering conjunctions and influences. It puts them in their place, as in the sealing of the altar, where they serve to guard the gate from further intrusions. The only difference between this and the lesser rite of exorcism, is that in terms of the temple area itself, the tiger is despatched, rather than converted into a guardian. But this is only a difference of emphasis. What is fixed in its place can become intrusive, what is expelled can invade. The image of the guardian is little different from the image of the tormentor. The Daoist's esoteric knowledge can be used to order or to disorder. So can the emperor's.

## THE *JIAO* AS POLITICAL ORDER

The distinctions between higher and lower, inner and outer, are maintained by the marking of boundaries. But the boundaries kept in a *jiao* are not only the Daoist altar space, the temple doors, and the territorial borders of the temple area. They themselves bring others in train. Among these are the distinction kept by greater literacy and authentication of transmission by instruction and descent between orthodox purification and exorcism, and between a more classical and a more vernacular and located exorcism. They define by purity, avoidance, selection, and privileged entry, distinguishing between secret orthodox rites and outer spectacle. They set up a relation of representation between the purifying order of Orthodox Unity, the magician's performance (*fa*), and the physical reality of health or the social realities of familial, economic, or political fortune which are represented in discourses and formalities to which the *jiao* is a wasteful and backward distraction. Each of these distinctions also sets up problems of discrepancy or of intrusion, rather than simply of metaphoric representation. Each intrudes upon the other side.

Divine selection of the representatives of the area's assembly of households was limited by a short-listing according to wealth and status. The orthodox master was employed by the town's wealth and in particular by those seeking political status, converting their wealth into votes via prominent funding of the temple's repair and sponsorship of its *jiao*. The winning candidate in elections for township mayor, which took place soon after the *jiao*, had no ritual role in it. He did not even kill a pig for his feast. He deplored the extravagance of the occasion, adopting the official Nationalist (Guomindang) view of it as wasteful, while his election agents made quite sure voters would also know that he had contributed substantially to the rebuilding of this and every other temple in the town. He was a member of the temple committee, but not a manager of the *jiao*. His rival, on the other hand, was a manager of the *jiao* and acquired one of the leading ritual roles in it.

A similar discrepancy but interaction between leading ritual roles in Daoist *jiao*, heterodox popular spectacle, and official state abstention could have produced a similar choice of tactics in imperial times. Ritual leadership was related to political leadership. But it was itself a political leadership as well. It was never a rehearsal nor a representation of it. The *jiao* was and is a version of political leadership. The history and order which it invokes is another order from either the late imperial, the nationalist, or for that matter the socialist republican orders, histories and canons of leadership.

The organisation and the most spectacular elements of the *jiao* are hardly mentioned in the Daoist liturgy: The management of the *jiao*, the definition of its constituent neighbourhoods, the listing of their households and the membership of each for the collection of a head tax to fund the celebrations and hire the Daoists, the erection of the outer altars and the display of valuables and lights upon them, the processions and theatrical performances, the construction of the huge guardian figures, the raising of the masts of a thousand lights, and the extravagant feasting preceded by the presentation of pigs to the gods and food to the ghosts. Yet most of the expenses are those involved in the mounting of these outer spectacles and feasts. They are the attractions which feature, after finely worded sentiments of auspicious beauty, on invitations sent out by residents to visit, tour, and sit at their tables.

Procession, territorial cult, feasting and theatre are as fixed and organised a tradition as the more textual traditions of the *jiao* and the imperial official cults. But of the latter, it is the *jiao* and not the official cults which provides the closest, inner, if also imposed and discrepant, orthodox referent to this popular tradition.

# Chapter Seven

# Ang Gong, or
# the truth of puppets

The god of the first local cult set up in the settlement of Mountainstreet as a small town is generally called Ang Gong. In Chapter 4, I described how every year a figure of Ang Gong from a more central temple to his cult, in a larger town down the road, is brought in procession to a number of neighbouring localities, and to Mountainstreet on the fifteenth day of the tenth month itself. Every household contributes towards the costs of the procession and almost every household feasts. So almost every resident, even a young school-child who describes the festival as nothing more than theatre, spectacle and activity (*hao kan, re nao*), identifies the temple's cult and the festival as that of Ang Gong.

A dictionary definition of Ang Gong is almost anonymous: 'the old god', 'the figure' or 'idol' as the missionary definition has it (Douglas 1899). That may be all there is to say about the object of the festival for many of its participants. Further enquiry adds information, for observer or participant alike, but it leads in various directions of reference, and the interesting question to ask is not which of them is true, but what authority is invested in each of them. What I am about to describe for Ang Gong is typical; a similar set of references could be drawn from any other local cult figure.

Starting with the image itself, in the front shrine of Mountainstreet temple, there is the one main figure, in imperial and military costume and colours, wielding a sword. It has before it one main incense pot. But on either side of it are two smaller ones, also included in the designation Ang Gong. The central incense pot and one of the smaller ones is marked with the longer title: Venerable King, Protector of Propriety (Bao Yi Zun Wang). The incense pot on the other side, however, is marked Great Minister, Protector of Propriety (Bao Yi Da Fu). Further inquiry, from anyone who knows and remembers the annual calendar of temple festivals in Mountainstreet, identifies the

194

first as a general whose festival procession on the fifteenth day of the tenth month is the biggest annual occasion in Mountainstreet, and the second as the general's supply officer, who has a separate, smaller, procession festival on the sixth day of the second month. So the singular image has divided into two identities and occasions, and into two honorific titles.

Since each festival involves its own visiting figure, met at the border of the festival area and paraded around and through it in a place of honour with the figure and one or other incense pot from Mountainstreet's own temple, this line of inquiry takes us to two separate temples. Each is an older temple, in an older and, in the case of the general, a larger town. They are the 'root' temples from which the incense of Mountainstreet's two pots was divided, establishing them as branch centres of the two cults. And when this is followed further, by asking the temple keeper of the larger town's temple, the trail of divisions of incense stretches further to the county across the Taiwan straits and inland from which the first settlers came, and to a story of another division. This is not a division of the cult into several cults, nor of a single god into two, but of three men who brought to Taiwan from the mainland a figure of Ang Gong, another of his wife and a single incense pot. They divided up the three objects and each became the centre of a separate, branch cult, associated with the family name of each of the three companions: Zhang, Chen and Gao, according to most Mountainstreet versions; Zhang, Lin and Gao according to one variant. (The confusion between Lin and Chen is not surprising because only the other two surname groups are still active in maintaining separate celebrations of Ang Gong.)

So, by a mixture of surname and place of origin, the residents of Mountainstreet and a number of towns and villages in northern Taiwan, link their festivals to each other in rivalry and in connection. Some are reminded by the festivals of their special privilege by surname to identification with one or other of the root temples. Others are reminded by the series of processions of the figure from the root temple simply of a common place of origin. Others are just included as residents in the local procession festival. Beyond are the cults of root temples of other places of origin, such that the whole region can be mapped into linked and rivalrous temple areas in this way.

Such is the history of multiplications of cults traced by annual festivals and invitations to each others' feasts. Its authority rests in the truth of the festivals and cults themselves. The stories of their foundation are the myths of the questions posed in divination and the outcomes noted as responses from the figures of these cults. They include the safety of crossing the mountains and founding settlements in southern Fujian or, later, of crossing the straits and founding settlements in Taiwan. The responsive gods carried for security are remembered in their festivals, I was told by several old men, because the huge phantom shapes of their soldiers scared away attacks from the 'barbarian' (*huan-a* in Taiwanese) mountain people. Their incense flared in warning of the impending attacks, alerting the militia organisation of the settlers.

Another route of reference is that of literary information. By this route the family and given names of Ang Gong are disclosed. There is a mismatch between them and the names of the three surname groups whose three ancestors divided the relics of Ang Gong in Taiwan. The names of the general and his supply officer are said to have been Xu Yuan and Zhang Xun, though which is which alternates according to different informants. In any case, only the Zhang would have their claim authenticated on this account. The personal names of Ang Gong take us into another kind of authentication than the holding of festivals.

A teacher at Mountainstreet primary school and a number of its graduates told me the story they had from a school history, in which Generals Xu and Zhang were besieged, defending the last city of the Song dynasty empire against the Mongols. To feed their soldiers they first had their horses slaughtered. Still besieged, General Xu then had his wife (concubine in another version) fed to the troops. Finally Xu was captured but refused to capitulate, grinding his teeth so hard that he spat blood in scorn at his captors, and was put to death.

One of the local school-children who re-told this story made no connection between it and Ang Gong in the temple. Another, older graduate of the school did associate it with Ang Gong but she also insisted that the main statue in the temple which others called Ang Gong was a more China-wide and official cult deity, Shen Nong, patron deity of agriculture popularly known as the Five Crops King. Some such link had been made before. I found in the temple a copy from a limited edition of a book about Shen Nong and the temples to his cult in other parts of Taibei county. The book was prefaced with what must have been spirit-written testimonials of his worth by the supreme deities of the Daoist altar. This young woman's family head, the local doctor, identified the two procession festivals for Ang Gong with giving thanks to the Jade Emperor for the two crops and hopes for the two sowings of the year, but did not himself name Shen Nong.

I mention this as an example of one of the ways, through spirit-writing, through re-attribution of the figure's iconography, and through the other points of departure which I have described here, the same cult can simultaneously lead in several narrative directions.

Returning to the reference via school history, it can be checked with dynastic histories. There the names Zhang Xun and Xu Yuan appear not in the Song but in the Tang dynasty. In *The History of the Later Tang* (Hou Tang Shu) it is Zhang Xun who is prominent. He is an exemplary warrior leader, and Xu Yuan is merely one of his generals. Zhang Xun is above all noted for his profound seriousness about ties of friendship and for the discipline and loyalty which he inspired in his troops. The enthusiasm with which he went into battle is made evident by his habit of shouting with such vigour that his mouth bled and he gnashed his teeth with such determination that they broke. Then, in this most classical of literary sources we find again the vivid elements of gruesome heroics that we were told about in Mountainstreet, only in greater detail and amplitude. Zhang Xun led several generals to defend the cities of a large region for the ruling emperor against the forces of An Lushan, rebel and imperial pretender, now assassinated and usurped by his own son. The rebel forces besieged the cities and after a year most of them fell. But Zhang Xun and his troops held out in their city. When food ran out, the troops took to killing children and eating them. Zhang Xun is reported to have been so ashamed of retaining a concubine while his troops had to resort to such desperate measures that he killed her and offered her body to them. Still under siege, the leader's example was followed and all the women in the city were killed and eaten, and after them the old men. Finally they had to surrender. But before giving himself up to the rebels, Zhang Xun shouted and gnashed his teeth with especial fervour and knelt on the ground facing west towards the emperor saying he could do no more, but he would go on fighting even as a ghost (*gui*) after death. When the rebel leader forced open his mouth, only three teeth were left. Impressed by his loyalty, the rebels gave Zhang Xun an honourable funeral.

Not surprisingly, in the records of their Tang campaigns and in dynastic and other records of campaigns to defend cities and dynasties, these generals and their spirits are celebrated, in some cases by imperial inscription and adoption for official worship. For instance, in searching the local histories of Ningbo city and prefecture (Zhejiang province) for their records of official cults, I found a longish entry noting two imperial endorsements for a temple dedicated to these generals. The first emperor of the southern Song dynasty (who reigned from 1127 to 1163), retreating from the Tartar armies which had conquered the northern half of his empire, hid in this temple. Looking up he saw the banners of the generals in the sky, and thereupon spiders' webs grew over the doors of the temple such that the Tartar armies swept by, convinced there could be no-one behind them. In recompense, the emperor had new figures of the generals made and installed in the temple. In the reign of Ming Wanli (1573–1620) the temple burned down and was left in ruins. This was reported to the prefect and magistrate, who were authorised by imperial decree to use property confiscated from corrupt officials and thieves to pay for the re-building (Tanmiao, Xie Zhong *miao*, 1560).[1]

This route of reference has taken us to histories of loyalty and defence of official rule, the authentication of dynastic lines and of propriety. Both the titles associated with Ang Gong include the defence or protection of propriety. No doubt the terrifying extremity of their loyalty and of their patriarchal principles to the point of cannibalism gives the story its almost demonic power. The Mountainstreet doctor's literate reference to explain the title was a story that the imperial Pavilion of Propriety was set alight. Two spirit shapes were seen in the air and recognised as those of Generals Xu and Zhang. Immediately the fire went out. In thanks the emperor gave them their present titles, based on both the name of the pavilion and their action. But the cult of Ang Gong in Mountainstreet was not for this reason part of the imperial official cults. Mountainsireet temple was set up and continues to hold its festivals like most other temples, without official endorsements. The doctor, in line with his partly classical Chinese education, simply took his line of reference in that direction.

The character which I have translated as 'propriety' (*yi*) is also used to refer to the principle cosmic forces, Yin and Yang, the Five Phases, and so on. This indicates another direction of reference.

The wife of one of two main grocers of Mountainstreet told me the same story of the burning pavilion as did the doctor in reference to Ang Gong. She also told the story of Zun Wang, the title of the main general, having sacrificed his favourite concubine. But in her version he does not allow himself to be captured. Instead, he commits suicide by eating gold. This combines loyalty to the dynasty with an act reminiscent of the achievement of immortality by Daoist techniques.

Reference in that direction was indeed drawn by Schipper, who told me in 1967 that the touring marionette puppet troupe he had studied, based in the northeastern Taiwanese coastal town of Ilan, had three clown figures in their repertory which were usually called 'the three brothers' but were also known as the three Tang dynasty generals, Zhang Xun, Xu Yuan and Lei Wan-chun. In his short article on the marionette troupe he records his own investigations into the identity of the three jesters in Daoist texts, concluding that they are the three marshals who command the Wind-and-Fire Department in heaven, according to a Ming dynasty compilation of Orthodox Unity exorcism rituals (Schipper 1966: 86–8).

As marionettes, the three marshals are part of a repertory whose complete cast consists in principle of seventy-two heads and thirty-six bodies. These numbers identify them with the 108 stellar influences, baleful or protective, but which Schipper also represents as 'the total of the spirits in the universe', which accords with the Daoist incorporation of the popular belief in them (Schipper 1966: 81).

Of this cast, the three jesters stand apart as the patrons of the whole art of acting and puppetry.

> Before every show, a short ceremony takes place backstage. The three jesters are hung behind a table with offerings, and a ritual is performed in order to 'open the eyes' of the puppets (kai guang), that is: to give them a soul and turn them into spiritual beings. (Schipper 1966:81)

A similar ceremony is performed in respect of Guan Di, God of War and Commerce, by a company of actors before a play in which one of them will act his part. The paint, the mask, the puppet are respected as a representation which is itself filled with power. But in the case of the marionettes, the representations are used for exorcism. In Mountainstreet there were a number of coal mines. The owner and manager of the largest of them employed many Mountainstreet men. It was not a model of safety standards and there were frequent fatal accidents. After one of them in the 1950s, I was told, the miners refused to enter the shaft until the owner had hired a marionette troupe to exorcise the baleful influences, now augmented by the ghost of the latest killed miner. The exorcising puppet was Zhong Kui, a great warrior who figures prominently on temple doors and in prints pasted on domestic doors all over China.

The Daoist and exorcist line of reference could have started from the very name 'Ang Gong'. When I asked for this name to be written, the Gong was always the character usually translated as 'god' or simply as 'figure'. This leads us only to the anonymous honorific of any god. But 'Ang' was rich in traces. By some it was written as 'red' (*hong* in the common language, but *ang* in Taiwanese and Amoy dialects). Perhaps this was simply a reflection of the ruddy, loyal and military face of the temple figure itself. Most often 'Ang' was written 'old man' (*weng* in the common language), a respectful reference to an ancestral or originating presence. But another way of writing 'Ang' was a character (pronounced *wang* in the common language) which is rare and has not been easy to translate.[2] Neither Douglas' Amoy dictionary nor its supplement, by Barclay, include it at all. The *Ci Hai* (Chinese-Chinese dictionary) cites an authority for it referring to a limping person, or one who is short or emaciated, and Mathews' *Chinese-English Dictionary* (1956:7038) has a sentence for its usage which he translates: 'an emaciated person exposed in the sun to move Heaven to pity'.

The emaciated figure is, according to Granet, that of a feudal prince or a medium who through exposure to rain or heat had the power to move heaven to end a flood or drought. The limp, on the other hand, refers to the limping and leaping gait of Yu the Great whose control of floods is repeated by Daoists in *jiao* and lesser rites. (Granet 1953: 247). In later imperial times both Daoist rites and the exposure of praying officials and the statues themselves of the Dragon King or the City God were used to make or end rain. (See Feuchtwang 1977: 603.)

'Ang' in Taiwanese is, in fact, used to speak of puppets.

Each version of Ang Gong shows a multiplication of identities and narratives held to be their truth. But the Daoist version indicates that each representation is its own identity and power. The Daoist line of reference takes us back to the simplest, almost anonymous designation of the 'idol' as such. It has also led, on Schipper's trail of literacy, to the Daoist orthodoxy of a celestial hierarchy of offices, where the imperial titles of propriety would also mean the principle forces of the cosmos. But each representation, the Daoist leaping like Yu, the puppet exorcising the ghosts, the incense of Ang Gong flaring to warn of an impending attack, tells of the immediate object having the power to act. It responds to divination as well as mediating response.

## WRITING, IMAGE, ACTING, AND METAPHOR

*Wu* is the character for the dance of possession or of inspiration. It is usually translated as 'sorcery'. Mediums are called sorcerors derogatively by those with literate and scientific learning. The Daoist literate treat the statues of the popular cults and their spirit mediums alike as puppets which it is their task to interpret.

Each orthodoxy in its own direction of authenticity and authority moves through a series of representations, the highest of which is writing, to an ultimate point. For Daoism, this ultimate is chaos. For the imperial cults it is Heaven's order. For scientific republicanism it is progressive, positive knowledge and the history of the current regime's version of national culture.

In the course of these moves, representations are rejected in favour of the ultimate, authoritative truth itself, of the natural or political order. The most vulgar is also the least informed representation, the most erroneous and the most bound-up in representation – the statues, the puppets, the mediums, the spectacle, the procession, the theatre. Better that they be interpreted into the orthodoxy of writing and words. Better still that these be passages to the secret knowledge of which the writing is itself a reminder.

The moves from one to another kind of representation, from spectacle to writing, to aural and enacted transmission of truth among initiates or seniors, are not only across relations of representation. They are also across relations of correction and denial.

We have come in the course of this book to Daoism as an inner representation and denial of territorial cults and their festivals because, of all the orders of representation – the imperial, the republican, and the Buddhist or salvationist – the Daoist is the most involved, the most committed to serving territorial cults. But like the others it is also a removal from them.

The text of Daoist liturgies placed on the altar, its pages turned for the master by one of his orthodox Daoist helpers, is itself only an *aide memoire* for the rhythm of movements, the drumming and playing of string and wind instruments, words written in the air, and the images called to mind by the master in the prescribed course of a rite (Schipper 1982: 130). The often still and meditative form of the master at the centre of these movements and sounds is the point of concentration of all that they invoke. In his mind the Daoist imagines the points of his body as an image of the universe. Through a disciplined bringing of images to mind in their cosmologically appropriate colours, each point in the compass having its corresponding colour, accompanied by breathing and concentration on channels of bodily energy, and with silent recitations, he conducts an internal ritual parallel to the one acted outside on the altar's stage.

Alternatively, the points on his hands are maps of the universe and he touches them in secret hand movements parallel to the actions of his assistants.

As Schipper observes:

> yet again we find, at the heart of the great Daoist rite, this re-doubling of the master and his puppet, of the barefoot master-interpreter and his medium, of the inseparable couple in which what one thinks the other says. . . .

The Daoist Grand-master, by ritual meditation at the centre of the space which he has set up, becomes the Zhong Zun (Venerable of the Centre). He is doubled by an acolyte who speaks-chants his thoughts and silent speech, as the external to his internal action. To inaugurate the incense burner and at the same time to become Zhong Zun, the Grand-master, after preliminary concentration upon the three-times-eight *qi* (pneuma) and actual breathing motion, takes the community's incense burner in his right hand and starts the rite of illumination thus (chanted by the double):

> High and ancient lords of the three breaths – the Obscure, the Originary, and the Primordial – of the Three Supreme Heavens, call from within my body the meritorious appointees of the Three (spheres) and the Five (phases), emissaries of the incense, messengers astride dragons, the Golden Boy who guards the incense, the Jade Girl who transmits the spoken word, the appointed officials of the symbols of the Five Emperors at hand today, thirty-six in all. Come forth each, with appropriate costume and ceremony to present yourselves before the sacred officer, god of the locality of this place to inform him that I am now here, burning incense, in order to ascend the altar and practise the Dao for the sake of [named] place. I intend the cosmic breaths of life to come down and spread through my body in order that my sincere wishes may be communicated speedily to the throne of the Jade Emperor of the Golden Gate in the vast heavens. (Translated from Schipper 1982: 131–2)

The actions, rhythms and sounds performed by his assistants stand for the quiet movements and internal representations conducted by the meditating master. The master's body in which these take place stands for a concentration which is also a movement of transforma-tion. Of and to what? The master is, according to his own description, transformed from an ordinary human body to whatever it is that is entitled the Venerable of the Centre. The point in the ritual where this transformation is accomplished is marked by the master placing on top of his head, on to a top-knot which is therefore just above his physical scalp, the image of a flame which doubles the flame of the incense in its burner. He has gone outside himself and renounced his name, place and terrestrial position, in short, according to Daoist doctrine, he has become immortal and as such begins to move through various steps which represent his further metamorphosis to accomplish an ultimate union. This ultimate point of centrality and doubled representation is both birth and venerable age, personified in the name Lao Zi, founder of Daoism and its re-appearances.

You could call this removal one of spiritual accomplishment, achievement of union with the source of order, removal from image, history, biography, from self and from a location and its inhabitants. But this would be one-sided. The purification is not so much a distancing from the worldy and vulgar. It is paired with them.

A master Daoist performing the great rite itself, is a microcosm uniting itself with the macrocosmic order. He, his body, and the locality in which it is situated are ordered by the same principles, phases and forces that form the whole universe according to Daoist metaphysics. So much is easily recognisable as religion or as religious philosophy practised in ritual and meditational activities. It introduces to the local and immediate an embracing, indeed cosmic, vision of the ultimate nature of things. But even in his own classical liturgy the Daoist master 'communicates' by means of his body and on behalf of the locality. He is tied to them, and to the systems of demon-spirits (the gods, their soldiers, baleful stars, ghosts, and the filth, as it is sometimes called in Daoist texts) of popular, vulgar imagery. His own virtuosity is in combining these with the classical liturgy into which he has been initiated. This skill, his own secret knowledge, he transmits to the next generation, much as Chinese traditional medical practitioners transmit their art.

The trick for a Daoist and indeed for a diviner using the system in which she or he is expert, is in establishing a point of view in relation to a client and a situation. It is the point through which are combined for a particular situation the variety of systems of correlation and representation or diagnosis brought to attention in two relationships, one of learning from a master a metaphysical system and a liturgy and the other of service to a client and the several stories and imageries of local festivals, cures, and preventions. The location served by the

Daoist for his own merit is also a *locus* in which are combined several systems as well as the one of replicating Daoist orthodoxy in microcosm.[3] They are none of them governed by one of the others.

The master Daoist and his classical written memory is paired not only with his similarly trained acolyte, but also with the vernacular memory of the magician (*fashi*). He conducts exorcism as a magician, as well as purification as a grand-master. The venerable celestials in the classical liturgy are invoked impersonally. But the Daoist also calls upon gods and has covenants with them, invoked by short epic ballads rendering their histories. These ballads are simply shorter versions of those told by storytellers in teahouses and played by actors on stages (Schipper 1985: 31–2).

The Daoist performs. The performance is one of a command hierarchy bearing a sufficient likeness to the imperial regime to appear archaic and historical. But the Daoist is not a magistrate in an imperial regime and its state cults. He has no powers to discipline or to exact controlling measures. His is more like the performance of the theatre opposite the temple than the ceremonial of authoritative power and its sanctions. Both the Daoist's theatre and the theatre for entertainment were subjects of suspicion and control by imperial and, now, republican regimes. Daoist and theatre musicians can and do substitute for each other. Both theatre and ritual purport to reproduce the arts of battle and the protocols of court audience. Actors themselves perform exorcisms (Ward 1979). Theatrical performances are offerings to the gods at festivals as well as being entertainment for the people. But the ritual performance has a mystique distinct from both popular entertainment and from military art and court gesture.

Consider again the performance of writing in the expulsion of the white tiger, an ambivalently powerful, dangerous but necessary force, from a temple. It is an act of exorcism in which writing with a sword the character for demon and then the lines of a net over it, pins the demon tiger in his place. This act of writing is both military and civil. But it is quite unlike any actual military order or civil promise ever issued.

Sword-written characters in air, or on rice, are clear though insubstantial. Another ritual produces talismans (*fu*). These are commands and permits, and are substantial, written on paper. But they are obscure, even less comprehensible than the writing of classical texts. They are not even in the knowable styles of ancient script, as on the bones and bronzes of the first two thousand years of Chinese historiography and divination. They are the marks of the most secret knowledge of magician or adept. Their characters are an

204

Performance of the short opening play, which is also a ritual of blessing, before the main theatrical entertainment on the temporary stage opposite the Shiding temple, 15 of 10, 1967.

invention in archaism, transmitted from master to apprentice in a tradition of what is by now itself many centuries long. The writing of covenant and command between gods, demons and their inter-mediaries is mysterious. But the performance of the Daoist when invoking the gods is in the most popular and clear literacy of ballads or of rhyming couplets. Again we find a paring of the inner and the outer, the esoteric and the exoteric.

Yet another ritual writing is that of merit-making exhortations composed in spirit-writing sessions, a more refined and salvationist ritual and divination than that associated with demons and exorcism. Its compositions are in the same catchy ballad style as Daoists use for the invocation of gods. But in both, and in the plain and the cryptic forms of literacy they use, through the archaism of its forms and the mode of its transmission, the writing exercises the authority of a revealed sign. It augurs an original truth, universal or local. It is also the record and repetition of the revelation of that truth, the re-inauguration of its tradition.

Festivals of territorial cults themselves are repetitions of revelations of miraculous responses and the local traditions which stem from them. The procession festival and the territorial cult is a mode of transmission, informed by the more personal acts of divination performed by householders before the image of the god in a local temple in the course of the year.

Spirit-writing combines moral tract with personal wish (Jordan and Overmyer 1986). It founds and renews a tradition of communication which parallels but seeks to transcend the festival renewal of local traditions of territorial cults. It is more sectarian. While the local festival is inscribed by the annual rhythm of performances, spirit-writing in one way, Daoist orthodoxy in another, more elaborate way, proclaim their authority by a revealed writing.

Daoism, its writing and other gestures gain authority, according to its own liturgy, from an innermost revelation. The master's learning and ritual point towards an originating source of all form and movement. But at the other extreme, the Daoist's performances gain authority from the outermost spectacles for which the whole location of a festival is mapped and mobilised in the raising of finances and in the expenditure and enjoyment of feasting and theatre.

One attraction of the spectacle to the least involved is the social pressure of the occasion. They know at least that this occasion is a test of their own and of others' depth and expense of involvement. They register the uses made of that involvement, the external politics into whose service it is pressed, and the temporary politics into which they are organised for the occasion itself. Another draw is the entertainment on offer, on stage and off, moving in procession or standing in displays on external altars. Both the pressure and the entertainment are based on a minimal recognition of the traditionality of the occasion and its activities. The imagery conveys traditionality by its archaism, whether outside or inside the temple.

A Daoist performs an archaic image of command and control. He acts and tells stories but the rites are not tales. They do not take place in a narrative sequence nor on a stage. Their completion is not a moral, a triumphant, or a tragic conclusion. They are not legends: their place is in a liturgical sequence and their stage is a geographical space; their conclusion is simply the completion of a properly conducted act.

It is announced by incense. The Daoist's 'communication' with spiritual agencies is through the incense of the local temple. The burning of incense bears no metaphoric relation to any other image. It is and stands for the authority of a communication with an honoured past and of deference to it. The imagery of other authorities can be enacted around it. Incense initiates memorial honour to ancestors in lineage halls and domestic shrines. It initiates the same in official cults to sages and heroes of official histories. But in the local temple and its festivals, incense initiates not only honour and deference. It adds the completion of response from another legendary authority.

## INCENSE AND FLAME

The liturgy of local festivals is a cosmic adjustment and an exorcism of demonic influences from a residential territory. Households as well as the territorial community itself are represented as incense and as a flame or lantern. The symbol which represents either a household or a residential territory and the opening of communication with the figure of its local guardian is the lantern and mirror placed in a measure of rice, called a bushel or a dipper (*dou*).

The whole set of symbols which make up the bushel lantern (*dou deng*) appears in the quite distinct contexts of the great rite of cosmic adjustment and the more salvationist rituals of the syncretist cults of The Immortal in Mountainstreet and Taibei. But in both contexts, the symbols are for protecting, whether it be the area centred on the altar or a household bringing its fortune to the altar, by means of renewing the flame of the area's or household's primordial conjunction and

The bushel lantern; a set of symbols standing for local cosmic adjustment – a mirror in front of which an oil-lamp flame represents the benign stellar light. The ruler and scissors are instruments for warding off threats from baleful stellar influences. They, and a casual packet of cigarettes, are placed in a measure of rice. The measure and the side inscriptions on the crowned flag which stands in it refer to the Bushel (or Dipper) constellations in each of the quarters of the cosmos and of the local territory. On the pelmet just under the crown of the flag is written: 'security within the completed boundaries of the area' (*pingan he jing*). The area is that of Mountainstreet, and the altar table on which the symbol stands is in the shrine of Ang Gong.

208

defending it against the attacks of baleful influences. In Daoist ritual the flame is associated with the performance of the 'distribution of lamps' (*fen deng*). This rite is included not only in the *jiao* but also in special acts of exorcism called 'seeing off the baleful star' (*song xiung xing*) (Hou Ching-lang, 1979: 194–9) performed as antidotes to the influences of the 108 baleful stars.

Both the classical Daoist and the strict devotee of salvationist cults may distinguish sharply between such vulgar and misleading acts of exorcism and the more abstract and moralising meanings of a restored harmony. But the distinction between the pure lights of primordial conjunctions and the influences of baleful stars is more blurred or at least ambivalent for the uninitiated, who employ *fashi* to conduct exorcisms or perform simpler versions for themselves.

It is an ambivalence clearly evident in a story told to me by a master *fashi* about the origin of the bushel lantern symbols. There were seven heavenly immortals. One of them, Lü Dongbin, was sexually attracted by another immortal who was an adept still bound to earth. She and her brother He were both earth immortals, but Lü Dongbin wanted to take the sister to heaven and make her the eighth immortal, so completing the set of eight which is depicted everywhere in China. He contrived, by the method which is now the bushel lantern, to detain Lü Dongbin on earth. The symbols were a means of reducing Lü's line of communication and return to heaven. He did this for three years to keep his sister with him, but eventually Lü Dongbin overcame the earthly immortal's method and took He's sister to heaven.

Lü Dongbin is also the historical character of the deity known as The Immortal (*Xian Gong*) in Mountainstreet and in the main temple of his cult in Taiwan, a very popular mountain temple near Taibei city, where young men are told stories of the danger of holding hands with their girlfriends unless they want them to be seduced by the god. In all versions, he is responsive. Flame and incense are the minimal and essential symbols for the 'opening' of the eyes of images and for expecting and receiving communication from an image or any other focus of what is known to possess responsive *ling*.

*Ling* is power, intelligence, effectiveness of a more than ordinary kind; the power to intervene, cure or turn fortune, by reference to which individual householders reach decisions or reduce uncertainty, for instance in gambling or taking examinations. In a tripartite division of the cosmos into celestial, human, and (sub)terranean, *ling* is identified with humans. It is associated in particular with those who have led extraordinary lives and died extraordinary deaths. It is the power which has to be controlled and separated (exorcised) in funeral rites from the ancestral and the grave locations of the remembered dead, and from their living descendants and their households, before they and their ancestors are re-integrated into a residential neighbourhood. *Ling* is by the same token the power most identified with the unremembered dead: ghosts. *Ling* is therefore I think most appropriately translated as the demonic power of humans. But it is a term used to describe only the use of that power to benefit or to protect and thus to indicate that the ghost is upright, a god. Malign power is unspoken, just as demons (*mogui*) and ghosts (*gui*) are mentioned aloud only by euphemism or as objects of correction and salvation.

Incense and the petition or divination which it communicates expects and reaches a ritual completion of response. It marks a ritual, which in the local cults of common people is one of responsiveness from *ling*.

Incense and flame mark the internal space protected from the threatening exertion of demonic power, the space from which unspoken, threatening *ling* is warded off by celebrated and spoken, protective *ling*. Incense, flame, and the ritual theatre of processions link the households and mark the boundaries of the space. They also trace it to places of origin and pilgrimage, the older centres of the cult, centres from which settlers came or centres to which residents go or refer in their trading and political transactions.

The objects of these cults are titles, treated as possessors of *ling*, manifest in powerful deliverances from pestilence, epidemic, and other misfortunes. The empty words of good fortune (*fu*) and security (*pingan*) used in annual festivals, are vehicles for these remembered events and for the particular questions and urgent uncertainties with which householders address the titles of these cults during the year.

From donor inscriptions to divination manuals, a written record of the ritual spiral of annual commemorations, new cults and the problems brought to bear in them, is precipitated. Such records constitute the annals of a local history of the uncertain preservation of good fortune and security. They are also the monuments, along with the building which houses the cults, of a place's civic pride, its identity and its affinity with other places and their rival festivals. The procession festival day is a date unique to the god and often also to the calendar of that place. Other days are thought to be China-wide festivals.

Temples and the festivals of local cults are a mixture of self-organisation and of patronage, by which the wealthier residents acquire representational status as benefactors to the other residents and as givers of thanks for local guardian gods' *ling*, protecting the locality's as well as their own energies of good fortune (*fu qi*). They are celebrations of theatrical, musical and martial art. The bands of performers of neighbouring villages and towns are invited and paid. The band of the place itself is prominent and performs in the procession without recompense. At other times members of the band act as the local fire-watch, crop-watch, or militia, the profane versions of exorcism. They are protectors of their own locality, but they may be plunderers as seen from other places.

The ambivalence of upright, demonic *ling* becomes a much sharper division and separation when higher and lower reaches of the imperial cosmocracy are represented. Even within an apparent replication of imperial rule, the local cults of common people are distinct and heterodox.

The imperial cosmocracy is either a command hierarchy or a salvation hierarchy. The higher gods may be upright commanders, protectors of cosmic harmony itself. These include exorcisers of demonic intrusion like the Three Offices of Heaven, the ultimately commanding Jade Emperor of Heaven himself, and the most renowned and imperially adopted cult objects such as the God of Military and Commercial Arts (Guandi). They command inferior controllers of the human *ling*, particularly those pictured in the limbo and the courts of (sub)terranean purgatory. Or else the higher gods are saviours, more Buddhist figures like the Goddess of Mercy (Guanyin), or the most revelatory immortals of Daoist purity who have mastered the harmony and energies of universal motion (like Lü Dongbin). They are capable of intervention on behalf of merit or of instruction in the cultivation of the concentration of energies.

Incense and flame are openings to the presentation of both, the upright commanders on high and the merciful saviours on high. But the highest are not offered the meat and rice with which the possessors of *ling* are presented. Only sweet and light 'food', if any food at all, accompany their incense, candles and wine. But much more elaborate spirit-lanterns and petitions are burnt before their images. The texts of their rituals are the internal and higher learning of ritual experts, who are employed to insert them into the most central and internal area of the festivals of local cults.

Both kinds of higher god have no sense outside a relation to lower subjects of their powers: the malign stellar influences, the demonic ghosts, the condemned and the confused. But their uprightness (*zhengyi*), their merit (*gongde*), or their purity (*qing*) are rarely if ever described as responsive power (*ling-gan*).

The higher gods which command are identified in a structure of imperial administration which is more associated with military rule than with the Confucian ethic of civil superiority by which the imperial administration represented itself. Intervention by saviour deities and by upright post-holders in the lower ranks are in several instances against the exertion of destructive righteousness, against the terror of military punishment. The most popular and common festival of the all-China calendar, the turn of the lunar year, is an annual repetition of such an act of deferred wrath.

The more orthodox version of imperial military command pictures the courts of purgatorial trial and punishment in a separated, celestial (Tian) and terranean (Di) world. It is a world identified by a structure of City (Chenghuang) and Locality or Earth (Tudi) Gods. Beside them are the demon-commander kings (such as Yenlo Wang) and the shrines to the unknown dead. Beyond them were the exclusively official altars of imperial administrative cities, ending with the altar of heaven itself, at which the celebrant was the emperor in his title of Son of Heaven (Tianzi). But the local cult gods, with their title names, their individuated festivals, and their reputations for responsiveness, constitute a network between the levels of this hierarchy, above the Locality Gods and equivalent to the City Gods. Local histories, linked to cult centres are interposed within and counterposed to a unified and single-centred history of dynastic China.

What sense can we make then of the single-centred structure of representations as a history? It is eventful, while being represented as an eternity. Stories are told about the incumbents of its posts, such as the story of the man induced by his wife to take, in unprecedented audacity and uprightness, a corrupt Locality God (Tudi Gong) to the imperial high court. He and his wife become the new Tudi Gong and Ma.

But eventfulness, such as that story, is an attribute only of the middle term of the tripartite universe, that of humanity (Ren). The stories of the turn of the year concern the entire destruction of this middle term, averted.

What sense do local cults and their networks have as histories? They are the commemorations of miraculous changes of fortune and of thanks for good fortune, real events attributed to the responsiveness of possessors of demonic power. An upright enhancing of demonic power keeps not only malign demonic power at bay, it also keeps the power of the emperor at bay.

## IN WHAT SENSE ARE THESE HISTORIES RELIGIOUS?

Local cults and the historical character of their gods are represented in the tense of eternity, beyond death and of death. Interruptions, destructive or benign, are the interruptions of the ordinary by the extraordinary, by the feared or the desired but unexpected event. The event becomes a symbol and a ritual occasion, its historicity becomes a metaphor for other events and potential disasters or promises. The symbols and occasions include, centrally, the symbols of the performance of completed communication, of response: incense and flame. The historical metaphor and its festivals are sacred by virtue of bearing an unlikely resemblance to past political persons and practices. At the same time they commemorate and recognise a present self-organisation, patronage and linkage of localities as having a past, archaicised.

Communication and linkage suppose boundaries and separations. The boundaries of local festivals are those of territories and their constituent households. They are also the boundaries of interiority in the festival rituals, the most internal being the exclusive altar of the Daoist. But at the other extreme, in the greatest inclusiveness of the festival, its involvement of the populace in theatre, stories, divinations and feasts, the authority of regular well-being, changing in its contents and fashions, constitutes another pole of authority and identification. To cross these boundaries, from household to locality, from one locality as guest to another, from outside to inside the temple, to communicate or transgress, is to reach higher orders of authority and greater orders of natural and social condition. What gives authority is, however, always posed in temporal terms, the crossing of boundaries to a higher, past, order. It is also one of response back, or intervention in the present and smaller, local order.

It would be wrong, or one-sided to describe this crossing of boundaries as harmonious. I hope I have shown that there is also a threatening converse transgression. It would also be wrong to describe the identification provided by local festivals as integrative in the sense of having a supportive complementarity with the political order of a current regime and its rituals. I hope I have indicated the tensions which can result in a split precisely where there was a replication of the imperial order. The dissimilarity with the imperial imagery of courts, coinage, and military regalia is as significant as the similarity.

213

# Chapter Eight

# The politics of religion and political ritual

Even over the years spanned by the research for this book, every sphere of Chinese life has undergone tremendous change. Political order and its revolutions is one constituting influence. Territorial cults with their imagery of imperial courts make up another. There has also been radical economic transformation. It is time, therefore, to say something at last about those changes. What has happened to territorial cults in the midst of these changes? How have they themselves changed?

Freed from the assertion of imperial canonical, ritual and cosmological authority, religious traditions and movements in China now renew themselves under another kind of authority. With varying emphasis they present themselves as a heritage, scientific or cultural, localised or in a public space. They historicise themselves, the most ambitious ones within a grand narrative of the Chinese people or peoples. In part this is a deliberate policy of state. However different their regimes are in other respects, both the PRC and Taiwan have established a politics of culture which has made local history and its appearance more self-conscious, reflected in many outside views, including those of government departments of culture, the press, overseas Chinese and other visitors, as well as sectarian movements which challenge them.

Territoriality suggests geography, but there are many conceivable maps of China. Territorial cults with their centres of pilgrimage and regional cultures trace one map. Another is the map of economic hierarchies, with large cities at their centres – such as Shanghai, Guangzhou, Hong Kong, Chongqing, Tianjin, and Taibei. These very large cities are the quarters of several ranges of economy, trans-national, national, and regional. One recent change is the increasing transport and other links between peripheral zones and centres and across national borders. But between 1890 and 1990 there has been no

214

diminishing of spatial differentiations within and between regions (Skinner 2000).

A third is the map of political hierarchy with its two centres, Beijing and Taibei. The long twentieth century in China has seen the formation on its Qing imperial territory of two modern states, that of the PRC on the mainland and that of a republic on Taiwan which is still formally entitled Republic of China. The process of forming a modern state began under the imperial dynasty in the nineteenth century, and it continues in the twenty-first century with the awkwardness of Chinese terms which do not exactly fit the Western orthodoxy of sovereign states in a world system. 'China' is at once a civilisation, a nation, two states and a special autonomous region (Hong Kong)[1]. The significance of this for cultural policy and the redefinition of locality and therefore of local customary and religious heritage is great.

None of these maps is stable and they are not isomorphic. For instance the Taiwanese economy is increasingly linked through investment from Taiwan with the mainland, affecting most of its provinces. On the other hand, through visits and exchanges with their ancestral places of origin and regional centres of culture in Fujian province, Taiwanese are re-establishing a Fujian-Taiwan cultural region. At the same time, however, Taiwan politically as well as culturally is asserting its own identity and unity as a centre between Japan and China. Finding a way to combine these three different geographies of relations between Taiwan and the mainland will occupy politicians for many years., even as they change.

Having noted these complexities, I will now select from them salient features of the transformation of China's maps as they affect territorial cults and the fate of location.

## THE REGULATION OF RELIGION

Up to the end of the nineteenth century the most serious risings against the imperial dynasty were inseparably religious and political: Muslim risings in the northwest, the syncretic Christian Taiping rebellion which set up a kingdom over several provinces for a few years, and the anti-imperialist Boxers who were a network of religious community militia[2]. But in the end it was a secular republican movement for self-strengthening progress, not a religious movement which did away with the imperial state, its cosmological rites, and its neo-Confucian orthodoxy.

The political parties which ascended through the republican movement, the Nationalist and the Communist, fought a devastating civil war interrupted by the eight years of Japanese invasion and occupation (1937–1945). But they had and still have two things in common. One is the profession of representing 'the people' rather than a celestial mandate to rule harmoniously. The other is the promotion of mass literacy and a scientific education. Both have imported and domesticated from Japan and from Europe and North America ideas of modern education and political constitution which have included a secular and constitutional definition of religion. 'Religion' (*zongjiao*) is a well organised institution of beliefs and textual authority. They have added concepts of secular modernity and its state to the imperial state's suspicion and condemnation of the carnal, theatrical and martial festivals of local temples.

In short, under the modern states of mainland China (Communist) and Taiwan (Nationalist), there has been an institutional separation of politics from religion. Indeed the very category of religion has been introduced as part of this institutional separation. The new word used to import the category 'religion' *zongjiao* combines 'ancestral tradition' with 'teaching'. Institutions which fit this category, such as monasteries and churches, so long as they are patriotic, are registered and granted religious freedom. Everything else is liable to be 'superstition', or 'errant beliefs' (*mixin*), another European category[3]. In Taiwan 'superstition' is a pejorative category spread through schools to so effective an extent that on my arrival in 1966 in answer to my enquiries about festival rites I was sometimes told that 'we are devoted to superstition' (*xin mixin*) before being told stories and interpretations of rituals.

In the mainland 'superstition' is not just a negative category. It is also a term used in the various criminal codes of the People's Republic of China alongside older categories of prohibition on forming secret societies and using heterodox teachings to organise movements which cause unrest or other criminal and sexually licentious acts. Religious freedom is guaranteed in the constitution of the PRC, but that freedom is under the surveillance of the Religious Bureaux with which religious organisations, places of worship, and religious festivals have to register. Religious activities and organisations are treated as a threat by the policing organisations of the Chinese state in several ways: as harming citizens physically or by fraud, as disturbance of public order, or most severely as sabotaging the law, subverting state power and aiming to overthrow the socialist system. Or else they are regarded simply as 'backward'. Organisations to exercise for the gathering and reinforcement of breaths or energies (*qi*) have also to be registered, with the Qigong regulatory bureau and to do so they have to be accepted as 'scientific', otherwise they too are treated legally as criminal or as superstitious activity. Superstitious activities and unregistered religious activities are subject to being forbidden by police, who can stop meetings and destroy buildings, but more often they are tolerated in a kind of legal and ideological limbo of uncertainty as far as official policy and its terms are concerned.

'Superstition' is a portmanteau condemnation of several aspects of popular culture as backward. It can contain anything that does not suit the ideals of a scientific and democratic governance and its project of modernisation. Backwardness shames. So cadres use the local police to destroy or curtail popular rituals. At the same time 'superstition' overlaps with other, less condemned terms such as 'custom' (*fengsu*) or 'culture' (*wenhua*) which are legitimate. Modernity's ideologues treat popular religion either as a way of promoting modern civilisation, as heritage and local custom to be preserved, or as an attraction to tourists and to the nostalgia of urban and overseas visitors for their origins. Rituals, festivals, and buildings, even spirit-possession can be turned into a show and a skill, or into tradition and culture. According to the law, 'superstitious' activities use the gullibility of the backward to harm or defraud them. So when the police act it is always with the additional legal charges of fraud or harm (Feuchtwang 1989).

In one way or the other, the major change from imperial times is that religious activities are now reflected in the mirror of legitimation by non-religious institutions, principal among which are the agencies of a secular state. On the mainland the collectivisation of land and state administration of industry into units, which were for its workers both work and home, created a monopoly for socialist political culture, which marginalised and privatised religious teachings and practices. Another change is that condemnation of superstition in twentieth-century China is implemented by governments with far larger apparatuses of policing than those of the imperial state.

## DESTRUCTION OF RELIGIOUS INSTITUTIONS AND ACTIVITIES BUT REINFORCEMENT OF LOCALITY

Leaving aside the stormy and violent first half of the twentieth century, the political administration of the mainland under its longest single government, that of the Chinese Communist Party, has itself changed several times. First there was the change from military regions to a full administration of ministries and their units in the cities between 1949 and 1953. In the same time redistribution of land made China into a countryside of small-holders and took away and redistributed the trust lands of lineages and the communal land of local temples (as well as the land of large temples, monasteries, churches and mosques).

Then villages and small towns became collectivised into large communes until the disaster of over-collectivisation and the starvation which followed in 1958–61 led to their being diminished and tiered. After a brief interlude, during which some temples and halls were rebuilt, fourteen years from 1964–1978 of intense mass mobilisation politics eliminated all local temples, halls and their open rituals.

Collectivisation brought the maps of economic, political, and residential units and their connections into correspondence with each other. Locality was reinforced, even if its previous public buildings and activities were abolished. Since 1978, however, there has been a return to something like the situation of land redistribution before collectivisation. The major difference is enormous growth of wage labour and commerce. Some of the wealth generated by economic reforms after 1978 has been used in widespread, but not universal, rebuilding of temples and halls and the revitalisation of rituals. The maps of economic hierarchy, political centrality, residence and territorial cult and pilgrimage have gone out of synchrony again. In addition, mobility and interconnection have dramatically increased, so that the local is lived far more than before with a view from or a memory of other places and with the presence of people returned or coming from elsewhere. But before turning to this, current situation, what happened in the decades of reinforced locality has to be understood. It was a long period during which political rituals replaced religious rituals. And the most intense period of political rituals has come to form a total event in the historical memory of mainland China.

It is rare to have so marked a discontinuity, a line between before and after so clear and dramatic that it looks like a line of death and revival. This remarkable event in the history of ritual and religion in China was the sustained campaigning against religious and super-stitious activities and buildings from 1964 starting with the Socialist Education Movement and continuing with the campaign against the Four Olds – old thinking, culture, customs and ways of life. Ten of these years, starting from 1966, have a single name: 'Wen'ge'

218

('Cultural Revolution'). They are vital for any account of popular religion in China. Fortunately, there are enough indicative studies to begin to gauge the significance of collectivisation and to understand what might have been the effects of the political rituals of those years.

The attack on religious activities in itself was nothing new. More remarkable were its thoroughness and its spread. Everywhere under the state of the People's Republic of China (PRC) was affected. Sustained over a period of time the attacks were sufficient to have thrust nearly all religious activity out of public sight and to have destroyed or converted to other uses nearly all the religious buildings which still remained in 1964, except for a few preserved as national artistic monuments. After the destruction there was no open religious activity until the beginning of reforms and the repudiation of the politics of mass mobilisation in 1978. The revival of the four olds after 1978 in every province was a local, not a nationally coordinated event, but since it came after what was known to have been a universal event it is accurately described in the singular. Nevertheless this is not a story of pasts securely separated from each other, the collective past of religious traditions from the political past of mass mobilisation. The two co-existed for many years, and political rituals built on as well as replaced religious traditions. Now the collectivist ideals and senses of self that had been induced by political rituals have themselves become a tradition over which the revivals have been laid.

The fourteen years of mass campaigns between 1964 and 1978 are remarkable for the intensity of political rituals that were of a new, congregational kind. They were at a greater level of frequency and of a longer duration than for any other rituals performed by Chinese people and they affected everyone. The fourteen years were themselves the culmination of a politics of mass mobilisation which had begun with campaigns to confiscate land from rich peasants and landlords and redistribute it through the formation of peasant associations in every village. But, despite the confiscation and redistribution of their land, temples and halls remained. By means of subscriptions from village households, festivals could still be held, though to a diminished extent. The stories of responsive, powerful and upright gods celebrated in festivals coexisted in tension with the newer political rituals of mass mobilisation (yundong) which spread the morality and manner of revolutionary performance. Schools formed ideological subjects with ideals of service to the people and of mass participation in revolutionary transformation. The idea of revolution and of the masses being the masters was proclaimed and performed, but constrained by the necessity for discipline and deference to the leadership of the Chinese Communist Party (CCP), which became personalised in the figure of Mao. Children's dances and songs were routines, performed in schools and in public displays. Everyone learned and then knew by habit the gestures of selfless determination, the distant gaze into an eastern sunlit future, the indomitable fury of the downward gesture defeating enemies of the Chinese popular masses, and the ardent look toward the leadership of Mao and the Communist Party.

For the whole rural population there was also a short period when festival processions had been replaced by marching to work accompanied by such instruments of procession as drums, cymbals, red flags, and slogans: the Great Leap Forward in production and collectivisation, 1958–61. But then, temples and halls were in several places rebuilt or reactivated after 1961. According to Madsen (1984)'s careful study of political rituals in one, Pearl River Delta village, it was only in 1964 that the ideological effects of school and Party campaigns began to take effect in the village more generally. They were reinforced by the combined efforts of cadre work-teams and youth from towns and cities. Work-teams mobilised a tension between an egalitarian morality of selfless loyalty to the public good and a general acceptance that anyone in public office owes their first loyalty to their own families.

From this discord between a sense of public good without favouritism and expectations of reciprocity and human feeling came accusations of corruption. Sent from the town to clean up cadre corruption, the work-team members shared meals, for which they paid, and rented rooms from the poorest households, presenting to the villagers a living example of selfless asceticism for several months. Eventually they set up dramas of denunciation, led by the young and the poor. They recalled similar meetings for the denunciation of landlords and rich peasants and for the rectification of cadres in the 'forties and early 'fifties, where the denounced cadres on stage suffered blows and shouts of accusation from the assembled villagers.

Youth from the city had volunteered for immersion in the countryside to propagate devotion to Maoist socialism. They competed with each other for hard work in the fields and for being seen to be paragons of selflessness. They set up daily study sessions. In addition they broadcast several times a day from village loudspeakers to praise instances of good political attitude and work performance, and to criticise laggards. Production improved. So did material well-being, reduction of pilfering and respect for the idea of acting as part of a collective. Other meetings dramatised stories of the longer-distant past, before Land Reform, where those who had suffered most learned to recite their bitterness and bring tears to the eyes of listeners. As at the Jewish passover, all shared a meal of bitter herbs.

From interviews with villagers who had migrated to Hong Kong after the reforms of the early 'eighties, Madsen concludes that these political rituals

> did not result in a permanent commitment on their part to lives less devoted to private interests and more devoted to the collective, but it did develop a sufficient degree of emotion-laden respect for Mao's ethical ideas to make the peasants temporarily susceptible to the urgings of the work team (p. 137).

A few pages later, however, he provides a longer-term view of their effect:

> The Mao Study rituals in effect allowed the peasants to keep some of their old moral traditions – for instance [this is the most important instance, in fact], the idea that a good person was one who treated the entire village like his big family – and integrate them into some of Mao's teachings about the goodness of selflessly serving the people as a whole (p. 149).

In other words, they did not destroy older moral traditions but did modify them, adding collectivism to pseudo-kinship.

This combination is exemplified by Chen Wansheng in another village, Meifa, in the neighbouring province of Fujian. He was a commune cadre who in 1961 supported the rebuilding of his ancestral hall and the defence of his lineage village in a feud over theft with a neighbouring brigade and was later denounced and imprisoned in the factions which the fervour of Maoist politics and rituals threw up. In 1994, he said to my colleague Wang Mingming

> I tried to do my best to be good to the people as the Party taught me to be, and I did not do anything wrong according to the Party's principles. In the fifties, my good conduct was recognised by the Party and so I was promoted. Why should I be imprisoned?

In his view, loyalty to his fellow villagers was part of his revolutionary leadership. The focal symbols of the village's identity, its hall and its temple, and the sense of history and morality that they embodied, were not 'superstitions'. They were public works of the people whom he served. In the same spirit, continuing to profess service to the people and in turn respected precisely for this loyalty to his fellow villagers, it was he who organised the rebuilding of the village temple and his lineage hall in the 'eighties and 'nineties. Serving the people is what he said he had been doing and he has continued to do throughout.[4]

## POLITICAL RITUALS AND THEIR LASTING EFFECTS

Madsen's account is invaluable for enquiring in sufficient detail at village level into the effects of political rituals and what he calls their ascetic priests. But he relies on a conception of ritual and religion derived from Clifford Geertz which has rightly been criticised by Talal Asad. Geertz and Madsen assume without making explicit the derivation of what they mean by 'ritual' from a particular politics, which institutionally divides government from religion and is part of a larger division into 'public' institutions and the institutions of 'private' conscience. This division, and the Christian doctrine that encouraged it, made 'belief' into the essence of religion. In China, minus Christianity, a similar politics was asserted by both states in the twentieth century, but not with complete success. And then precisely in the political rituals that were becoming so universally effective in the 1960s, the distinction was dissolved. Instead, previous rituals (of religion and superstition) were not just institutionally divided off. Political rituals replaced them in their entirety and were themselves indistinguishable from government.

I think it is more instructive to think about 'ritual' using Talal Asad's criticisms, but in a way that goes against his genealogical grain. He places three different connotations of ritual in a chronological order, before the modern category of religion and its academic authority stamp onto it their own authoritative conceptions. I will instead treat them as four aspects of any ritual, considered to be at work simultaneously.[5] They are 1. ritual as a prescribed performance of divine service, 2. ritual as apt and disciplinary performance which forms virtue and desire, 3. ritual as dissembling and simulation, and 4. ritual as symbolic action (action which has multi-faceted meaning) and which, in Geertz's (1966: 7-8) words about religion, rehearses models of the world for action in the world. All are more or less applicable to the political rituals of mass mobilisation. The least applicable is 'divine service' – it has to be changed to a service of sacrifice to the greater revolutionary good, exemplified in figures of revolutionary leaders which are icons of an historical destination for a people rather than an eternal divinity. Ritual as dissembling and simulation characterised mass meetings, in which everyone knew how to perform, but many, perhaps most by the 'seventies, were bored with it.

What I most want to draw out from Asad's conception of ritual is its disciplinary and modelling effects. The rituals of revolution affected school children, students and military personnel most intensely and frequently, but not only them. From the mid-'sixties everyone was involved in study meetings that were organised in every work unit and rural production team. They included the ritual performance of reasoning with reference to citations from the writings of Mao, Lenin and Marx, and modelling posture and attitude on the posters of men, women and children produced by arts academies or the work units themselves (Evans and Donald 1999). Loyalty dances in front of pictures of Mao were performed daily.

In 1966–7, the mobilisation of youth into detachments of Red Guards in cities worked as a training for rituals of political possession which would be spread throughout the land. At rallies, the flourishing of red books and reciting from them in a high pitched tone, collecting and comparing badges, posting great character slogans and denouncing class enemies, led to organising and conducting struggle meetings against members of the bad classes bent, labelled, hatted and beaten as a public spectacle. All these were a performance and a carrying out of the mass struggle which had been learned in children's songs and dances. They made of their performers anonymous heroes of social and self-transformation, cultivating in them the emotions of ardent love for the future of the Chinese masses, hatred and fear of their enemies, abroad and within. These became personal as a fear of being exposed as an enemy and as a desire to be glorified as a revolutionary. Ardour of service to a public good and to an egalitarian comradeship, shaded by fear of exposure as selfish or revisionist, is the subject of a number of memoirs of the Cultural Revolution. Those years and their politics have officially, by the same party that led them, been designated excesses of enthusiasm and violence. At the time to be thoroughgoing (*chedi*) was praiseworthy. Now 'thoroughgoing' is reserved for the repudiation of the Cultural Revolution.

The Cultural Revolution was a culmination of decades of a kind of politics, with the same basic elements of mass mobilisation campaigns, using labels to separate the people into classes and the people from their enemies, and designating monitors for every member of the population. Lynn White III (1989) summarises his detailed study of mass political rituals thus:

> Mao and his high rivals were less effective as long-term egalitarian socialists than as short-term political strategists. These leaders were all passionately fascinated with techniques to inspire unified action in their big country, so long divided, and they found some applicable policies .... the three most important [labeling, monitoring and campaigning] all involve distinguishing "the enemy and ourselves." Seeing conspiracy, having an enemy, defining the clean people and the unsalvageably dirty ones, "dividing one into two", all became state policy. But that affected people not because it was psychology or ideology, but because it was policy. It meant labeling people with good and bad names, monitoring them so that the good ones might be nurtured and the bad restricted, and running campaigns to inspire some and scare others. The top PRC leaders (irrespective of their rivalries) were more political technicians than social philosophers. They had ideals, but their main problem was implementation' (p. 315).

His emphasis on 'policy' is based on an acceptance of politics being a top-down process. Given this emphasis on top-down strategy and an assumption of its effectiveness in other ways one must wonder why he underplays its ideological effects. It certainly was a politics of mobilisation techniques from the centre outwards. But since the politics of mobilisation had unified the mainland of China from the early 1950s onward, they were part of the childhood formation of two generations of schoolchildren. Their culmination was a paradox: the centre became a number of iconic figures (Mao and the models of Worker, Peasant and Soldier class and socialist transformation) created for and by the mobilised masses, while the apparatuses of administrative control were themselves dismantled or demobilised. Mao was a figure of authority for what was in fact for eighteen months in 1966–68 self-organised mass power, led by the young. Reassertion of Party political order was done through the formation of Revolutionary Committees in every work unit and at every administrative level. They re-instituted distinctions between political administration, the Party-Army-State, on the one hand and on the other the organisation of production, of education, and of the performative and representational arts. Ritual performance of revolution was now contained within mass meetings in production teams and work units, containing the memory of the period of self-organised movements with decreasing enthusiasm until the death of Mao in 1976.

In the Soviet bloc socialism was emptied by increasing state control, growing dissidence, and economic stagnation. In China it had been emptied by an opposite process: the Cultural Revolution was a peculiarly idealistic and mass-participatory saturation of the contradictions of state-led mass power and mobilisation for achieving egalitarian goals even if it also sanctified vengeance and envy. By means of a Party decision on history, the politics of mass mobilisation have now been replaced with 'market socialism'[6].

Unlike other interpretations of the memory of the era now declared past, which see it as a residue because it cannot be repeated, I see long-term effects.[7] I do not envisage the possibility of a renewal of the same political enthusiasm. The effects are double- or treble-edged with ironies. But collectivism has become a tradition and therefore a resource, a set of values and volitions which can be recalled and transmitted as a moral authority critical of present corruptions and uncertainties. For instance, the ex-cadre who still serves the people of his village by managing the reconstruction of its temple and ancestral hall was trusted against town cadres and the village party secretary whose road-building schemes were lining their pockets and providing pitiably inadequate compensations to villagers for their destroyed homes. He could use this authority and his own connections to curb their predatory exploitation of his fellow villagers.

The long-term effect of mass mobilisation rituals is evident in one participant's memories (Chen 1999). Chen Xiaomei volunteered for immersion in the far northern countryside. She is the daughter of a stage designer and an actress with the Chinese National Youth Theatre, and she recalls the years of mass campaigns in the countryside from her present position as an American academic and therefore in a language not available to her at the time. It is a language that shares some of the Foucauldian and other approaches which also inform Asad's reformulation of the concept of ritual. I think this helps her as well as us to understand the processes and effects of the political rituals in which she participated. So I have put into a chronological order quotations from the biographical parts of her article. In them she describes what I think will be acknowledged to be the effects of ritual images and actions upon her as a discipline, producing senses of self and others and her own volition. This is not a uniform effect. The images and actions were ambiguous and their ambiguity left her with a sense of ease and freedom of initiative:

> I grew up in a culture where posters remembered, talked back, and also constructed and reconstructed who I was and what was socially expected of me. Born into a family of theater artists, I believed that, following the example of my parents, who were devoted to representing workers, peasants, and soldiers on stage, I must learn from these same cultural models in order to reform myself into someone who was acceptable to them (p. 105).

> Beginning in the fourth grade [about 1963], for example, I would get up at 5.30am and hurry to school to light the coal stoves and clean the office for my teachers, who were striving so single-mindedly to turn us into worthy standard-bearers of the proletaria[n] cause. Many an afternoon after school did I linger at the New China Bookstore to admire the beautiful bodies on wall posters, and, spending what little pocket money I had, I would bring some posters to my classroom so that my classmates might be equally inspired by them, in our mutual exertion to gain the honorary title of "five-distinctions class" (*wu hao ban jiti*) . . . . I provided the posters for my class anonymously, in a manner that would have been approved by Uncle Lei Feng, the national hero from the People's Liberation Army who always urged us to do compassionate deeds for the people without seeking credit (pp 106–7).

> [P]ainting, poster, artifact, museum, and national identities and narratives all become blurred, coalescing into the most valued memories of my childhood. One of the highlights of that childhood was the role I played as the enterprising diminutive leader of the Young Pioneers. In this capacity, I remember taking my class on a weekend outing to Jingshan Park, where we reenacted an ambush [on] Japanese invaders. Our military strategy entailed a charge toward the top of the hill to take over the enemy's territory, in the course of which we acted out familiar images from a *lianhuanhua* (illustrated [comic] strip) book, *Railroad Guerillas* (1956–1958). This activity afforded us at once game, sport, theater, and the ritual observance of young pioneers day (*Dui ri*), whereby we could renew our pledge to the sacred revolutionary cause (pp 109–110).

226

She notes how cross-dressing in patched boy's clothes was praised and at the same time how this gave her a sense of pleasure, a sensual effect, and how rivalry to be admired and gain praise for service and selflessness was an enhancement of her sense of identity. Performing prettily to please parents and teachers was exciting and fun, another effect which Lynn White's account of the politics of mobilisation would not allow. But note that dissembling did not preclude a disciplinary effect on her own internal senses; role modelling worked in both ways, as performance and as ideal. When it came to the call to volunteer for service to peasants and agricultural labour

> it was inspiring to believe (as Mao had instructed us [through slogans and longer quoted texts]) that in the vast arena of the countryside, revolutionary youth could make full use of their talents and enhance their prospects. Picture books, posters, and newspaper stories all helped to bring home the message. Indeed, at the age of fifteen, a year younger than the minimum age required, I had to beg permission from my school to join my fellow classmates in what seemed their exciting collective journey to the countryside (p. 106).

It was with such a formation that she went north where she must have helped to organise the political rituals of struggle in the village where she settled for some years before returning to the city as a 'worker-peasant-soldier' student selected by the villagers. In the village, she would have transmitted her ardour in the same way that her equivalent, Ao Meihua did in the south before she went to Hong Kong and became Madsen's assistant for his village study.

Chen Xiaomei's years of political ritual are ironic and even fond memories which, according to her own account, still animate her. There were ironies in the ritual formation of mobilisation at the time, beside the pleasurable ones she mentions. The rituals of Maoism produced a three-way tension. They induced a sense of public good by which to judge officials and representatives of 'the people'. At the same time the definition of public and people could be calibrated by loyalties to own people, defined by kinship, the personalisation of relations, and by locality. On the other hand, class labelling had produced villagers who were children of fathers who were landlords and other bad classes or of Rightists and counter-revolutionaries who were the quota enemies of the people, brought out for struggle meetings. But a key ambivalence occurred in the very demonisation of these enemies of the people. It drew from an already existing exorcistic vocabulary, mixing it with a new vocabulary of blood.

'Blood' had entered republican and nationalist political discourse with translations of Western eugenic writing about the struggle for survival and population hygiene, turning the family into the breeding unit of a race and its bloodline (*xuetong*).[8] Communist leadership rejected this idea as reactionary but then introduced a divisor called a political bloodline (*zhengzhi xueyuan xian*)[9] between the 'people' and its enemies, categories identified during mass campaigns which resulted in verdicts passed to the children of the enemies on their identity cards. Further uncovering of 'bad' class status became a major activity of Red Guards during the Cultural Revolution. Those already labelled were reduced to beggary. Demons and beggars became the figures of danger below the political bloodline. In this imagery they were remnants from a time before revolution, according to an ideology of history which ties history to politics and inevitability to political movement. In this historicisation of a people and the defeat of its class enemies, the enemies are at once pitiful and dangerous. Alongside blood labels, campaign imagery included tiger demons, saviour stars, and snake women.[10] The Party newspaper urged red youth to 'sweep away all ox ghosts and snake spirits'. Consider Gao Yuan, who was a boarder at his middle school in Yizhen, and proud to have been elected to his class's Cultural Revolution Committee. When he came home one day he found posters denouncing his father, whom he had until then known to have had a reputation as a selfless head of a neighbouring county. On the posters his father's name Mountain Laurel (Shan'gui) had been rewritten with characters which had the same sound: Mountain Devil (1987: 128).

The old demon images retain a force of vivid evocation. That is why they were used in editorials and posters. But their force invaded the class rhetoric of socialist revolution and mass democratisation as reminders of the myths and rituals from which they were derived. During the mass mobilisation campaigns there was often an inversion of class rhetoric in the pursuit of rivalries between villages. Inter-lineage struggle was inextricably mixed with attacks on old customs. Jonathan Unger (1998: 95) provides an example, from rural Guangdong, in which the temple of a village was burned down by rival villagers in the name of an attack on feudal superstition. Red Guards of the temple village retaliated in kind, to combat superstition by destroying an ancient tree near the temple-burners' village. The temple was held to enhance the *fengshui* of the one village and the tree was held to enhance the fertility of brides who married into the other. The two villages had long been in violent dispute over water rights.

It should also be noted that dissent began immediately. But it was dissent in the same self-sacrificing revolutionary mode as was cultivated by the politics of revolutionary mobilisation themselves (Chen 1999: 115–117). Later, disillusion with those very politics set in, when the most ardent contrasted the careerism of dissembling performers and the realities of rural misery with the images of poster peasants and their cadres (Chen 1999: 106). But the disillusion has left a legacy of nostalgia for the time of Maoism, as well as a memory of its hypocrisy and hardship.

A memoir by another Red Guard, Ma Bo (1995), provides an example of this nostalgia, and I give it as a striking contrast with Chen Xiaomei's. The book is dedicated to 'the victims of the Cultural Revolution' and its racy tones are those of a hero-victim, a tough-guy, a *germen*[11]. Ma Bo had become writer in residence at Brown University by the time the English translation of his book appeared, but his hindsight attempts no academic analysis. Instead it combines rough tone with uneasy irony. Its swaggering tales of physical prowess and the ethic of loyalty to friends through thick and thin are not entirely artless.

His experiences seem to have left him with a persona still affected by enthusiastic support of revolutionary morality and its rituals, and an acute sense of their betrayal. The standard scenes of enthusiastic departure for the northern steppes of inner Mongolia are already tinged with the narrower loyalty to comrades-in-arms. Nevertheless, being steeled in the furnace of revolution merges easily with pride in his own strength of purpose in sticking both to his ideals and to his physically demanding tasks better than anyone else. Ten years later his shared mission to make history became, by his own account, the greatest wasted effort in history, the effort to construct towns in the wilderness and to convert steppes to arable land, an effort during which lives were sacrificed for nothing because they ended in a wasteland. An emblematic scene is the assault on a prairie fire in which nearly all the members of the student corps sent to put it out with misdirected ardour perish.

Ma Bo is prepared for self-seeking and corrupt cadres using revolutionary campaigns to get rid of those who might expose their hypocrisy. He is bitter about the incompetent student corps commander. But he remains more than willing to be self-reliant and to stand up for himself and his version of revolution. He is defeated when those who are honest, competent, and decent lack the power to support him or the will to prevent his being victimised for standing up for himself and the principles for which he volunteered to labour hard. Finally he decides to work out his exile as a hermit, working with a similar dedication at writing down his experiences in the derelict stone quarry in which he had laboured so hard and pointlessly.

Paradox and irony join in two vignettes that involve the killing of dogs. The first is the dog he kills in righteous fury when beating up a former herd-owner whom he and his closest comrade have picked out as an object for renewed class struggle in 1969. The second is a puppy Ma Bo himself adopts and loves but which kills sheep. It has to be shot, again to his fury. As he recounts this second killing of a dog there is no sympathetic reflection from the hurt he feels upon the first. But later, after his macho defiance of a corrupt political instructor gets him branded as a counter-revolutionary, he does describe his guilt about the old man. Later still, the same old man whose dog he had killed looks after him when he becomes ill in his quarry hermitage. What started as a complete split, preventing sympathetic reflection, becomes guilt and eventually fellow feeling and gratitude. In the same way, the irony of hindsight supplies a link between the after of remembering and writing and the during of revolutionary zeal. At the time he killed the ex-herd-owner's dog he probably did not connect the class enemy with a poor fellow human. The connection was there for the making, since one of his student comrades advised against this exercise in class struggle. Telling us how he and the others ignored the good advice also tells us of his formation at the time, a macho mix of brotherhood and comradeship which he had forged from childhood models, including his parents (both of whom were 1930s Communists) and more recent Red Guard factional battles.

What both Chen Xiaomei and Ma Bo convey as examples of formation by political rituals and performances of class struggle, is that they had an effect which lasted in memory through disillusion. It is a memory of youth, still treasured and available as a standard by which to judge the present.

As result of a similar formation, villagers asked about their experiences from land reform to the end of the Cultural Revolution decade speak of chaos, fear and hunger. But in relation to the present, the same speakers remember those years as a time of security, straight dealing and simplicity (*posu*), to be contrasted favourably with the self-seeking Party of the reform state and enviously as a self-description compared with the rich textures of city life (Liu 1995). Villagers add the ideals of the collective cultivated during the Mao years onto respect for the loyal defence of fellow villagers by non-Party leaders, whom they elect to replace a corrupt cadre (Ku 1999). Mao has become a means to criticise the present regime. Loyalty to fellow villagers can be associated with loyalty to revolutionary ideals, betrayed by present cadres extracting exorbitant local taxes from which no one but they benefit.

Another lasting effect of the political rituals of mass mobilisation is the habit of congregational participation with overtones of egalitarian comradeship and mutual support. Once again, like Ma Bo's brotherly loyalty overlaying a pre-Maoist tradition of honour, other traditions are taken into and transformed by the new tradition of congregational comradeship.

## COMMUNITIES OF FAITH AND LOCALITY

According to Madsen's informants women were more willing to participate in the singing of stories of Maoist virtue during village assemblies. This seems to me to echo older traditions. Women take an unusually prominent role in the communities of obedience to ascetic vows (*zhaijiao*) for lay Buddhists that grew prodigiously into a proliferation of branches from the sixteenth century onwards. They were deliberately independent of the tonsured Buddhist orders, who were accused of corruption and mocked in popular stories. Lay Buddhists met in congregations for the recital of memorised passages from both orthodox sutras and newly written precious scrolls. They made donations for the printing and distribution of the scrolls and the building of assembly halls, and they met in congregations of both women and men, which was a scandal for Confucian orthodoxy. More scandalous yet, they published biographies of model women who had renounced marriage. These and stories of female deities who had done the same encouraged a strand of this tradition, prominent where Madsen conducted his enquiries, in which women formed communities equivalent to nunneries except that they earned their own livelihood by silk manufacture.[12]

Some of these lay assemblies of ascetic Buddhists will have continued to practice behind closed doors during the years of mass mobilisation, just as others did. The attacks on religion produced in many places defiant assemblies of devotion behind closed doors.

Wang Mingming was told that some of the older villagers in Meifa continued to worship a rescued and preserved figure of the village god in this way. Christian, both Protestant and Catholic, house churches grew during the years of Cultural Revolution. But the main point I want to draw from these examples, is the effect upon them of the Maoist rituals themselves. Take one instance from Madsen's studies of Chinese Catholics since 1979. He attended the service of the Assumption in the Catholic cathedral of Tianjin, an officially registered meeting place. He first notes that 'in the early nineties, in spite of new and bitter divisions in the Church and in spite of ominous new government restrictions against religious practice, the liturgy seemed exuberant and joyous' (1998:3). Then he gives an example of the bitter divisions. Other Catholics considered the service to be a betrayal of the faith because it was carried out by a ministry under terms set by the state rather than by the Church. The issue is who appoints bishops, Rome or Beijing. Outside the cathedral those who refused the authority of the state over their faith chanted and knelt at a grotto of Our Lady of Lourdes. They had issued a pamphlet proclaiming their principled stand in terms curiously reminiscent of the language of the cultural revolution against revisionism: 'This is a "line question"' it proclaimed ' – a question of whether one does or does not believe in Jesus' (1998:7).

There are equivalents in Protestant Christianity, who refuse the authority of the official Chinese Christian Council. They retain a communal and egalitarian spirit, much like that fostered in collectivist days, but addressing each other as brothers and sisters, not as comrades. They stress lay leadership, participatory democracy and mutual support (Hunter and Chan 1993: 82 and other cases 185–218).

Beside these communities of faith, sometimes affected by a radical egalitarian defiance of Maoism, Chinese Christians transmit just as did production brigades a more widespread and local sense of community. Madsen reports that of all the ten Judeo-Christian commandments, the fourth honouring parents is held highest and that loyalty to the local Catholic community is added to it. As a practising Catholic he calls this a compromise with 'folk' culture and a 'vice' (p.80). Setting his orthodoxy aside, the observation confirms his older study of Maoism, that local loyalty is transmitted as a virtue even as it is translated into another faith.

In sum, I see two effects of the collectivised past on the definition of locality. One is the continuation of collectivist ideals as a memory, which is realised in other forms in the present. The other is household individuation as a basis for the definition of local community. The redistribution of collective or communal land, first that of ritual trusts by land reform and more recently the leasehold of land from the brigade, has meant that village funds depend on household contributions. Village funds of one kind come from household subscriptions to the rebuilding of temples or halls and collective ritual activities. The other kind are official funds which come from local taxes on households and fees from village-run and private enterprises, and they are administered by cadres of what is still called a 'collective'. The universality of the event named 'cultural revolution' and of the line which has been drawn politically to make it into a mistaken past, make both the temple and the brigade a memory revived in a new present. Before seeing how this revival has taken place, it is instructive to compare it with a similar revival in Taiwan.

## A COLONIAL HIATUS IN TAIWAN

In Taiwan there was an equivalent but earlier event which made local religion a past to be revived. It was the Japanese colonial regime's attempt to make Taiwanese religion entirely Japanese. This was preceded by a less strenuous system of control, just as the Cultural Revolution was preceded by a far longer period of similar but less strenuous politics of cultural change.

In the first two decades of Japanese occupation (from 1895), a number of serious incidents of armed resistance occurred. Among them, one was mounted by a religious association based on spirit-writing and a meeting hall of lay Buddhist ascetics (*zhaijiao*) in the city of Tainan which plotted to set up an independent Taiwanese state (Jordan and Overmyer 1986: 34 and Jones 1999: 65). All other lay Buddhist congregations came under suspicion. The only way in which they could remove suspicion and the harassment of police attention was to form a Patriotic (Japanese) Buddhist Association and place themselves under the Japanese Buddhist order of the Soto School (Jones 1999: 66). Spirit-writing on the other hand became an underground activity. All the temples and altars of the state cults in the imperial capital of the province were destroyed and other city temples were brought under Japanese control. Temples had to have registered committees called 'god associations' (*shenming hui*), on which local eminences trusted by the colonial government were placed. City temples and their festivals ceased to be centres of compatriot association and ethnolinguistic grouping, and instead became those of a Taiwanese colony. This was also true of rural local temples. Mountainstreet's registered temple committee members included none of the members of the spirit-writing association flourishing at the same time. It had added the hall for Xian Gong and constituted the temple's actual managers. Beneath the protection of their registered front, the association preserved what it considered to be a spiritual heritage (Feuchtwang and Wang forthcoming).

Local definition by territorial cults in networks of festivals and their deities had referred to places and temples of origin on the mainland. This continued, but it was now inflected by another orientation toward both Chinese and Taiwanese national identification counter-posed to the Japanese regime.

Taiwan was governed by reforming Japanese civilians from 1919 for whom their colony was to be integrated into the Japanese nation, which they could in turn develop economically and culturally along what they considered to be modern lines. Then in 1937 the government's policy changed. It was the year that Japanese forces invaded China proper from Manchuria. To clean up the wasteful, vulgar and disorderly states of temples and festivals, and to turn Taiwanese recruits into Japanese forces fighting on the mainland, the new policy was to turn colonial subjects into imperial citizens (*kominka undo*). Chinese languages and writing were forbidden. Japanese was made the language of teaching in schools. It was the 'language of state', using the same written characters which on the Nationalist mainland meant 'the Chinese national language', *guoyu*. Every administrative village (*zhuang*) had a primary school, for both girls and boys, and by the 1930s most children of school age did attend. The proportion of Taiwanese 'citizens' who spoke Japanese doubled to over 70% between 1936 and 1944 (Jones 1999: 82). All households were in addition supposed to replace their domestic altars with Japanese-style shrines, including amulets from imperial shrines in Japan. Temples were to be destroyed or transformed into Japanese-style Buddhist or state (Shinto) places of worship, and their land and other property confiscated. Local Japanese officials pursued the policy with varying degrees of vigour, in some places hardly at all, in others quite thoroughly (Jones 1999: 87).

The substitution of other rituals was sporadic and without intensity, nothing like the political rituals of mass mobilisation later on the mainland. So the campaign's lasting effect was mainly the learning of Japanese. But together with the enforced deprivations of a

234

war economy, territorial cults and their festivals went into abeyance and their temples into disrepair. Rebuilding them was therefore also a new beginning, after a universal event of destruction. In the case of Taiwan, it was a re-creation of a heritage, renewed under the new circumstances of Chinese nationalism and under the watchful eye of its state.

Revival after 1945 was gradual. Subscription funds were small because of abject poverty made worse by the depredations of the corrupt Nationalist government installed during the civil war on the mainland. Demonstrations in 1947 against that government included a more determined bid for an independent Taiwanese state than the incident of 1915, and its base was a secular movement led by intellectuals and members of the professions, not a religious organisation. The draconian suppression of the demonstrators, resulting in the killing or exile of tens of thousands, has since the 1990s become the key social memory for an independent Taiwanese political identity. But for the next 48 years, it was an undercurrent beneath an identification of 'China' to oppose and rival that of the People's Republic. During that time, local temples and their festivals were everywhere revived as income gradually grew. The only restraints were government reforms to keep them within limits which prevented a return to the territorial rivalry when neighbourhoods and villages competed in series of festival days and feasts such as those held during the seventh and tenth lunar months in Mountainstreet.

They were among a series of reforms instituted by the exiled and entrenched government of the Republic of China on Taiwan from 1949, commencing with redistribution of land, including that owned by local temples. Some Buddhist temples of retreat were exempt, but all other temples were left only with the land on which their buildings stood. As on the mainland every repair and rebuilding, and all festivals, had now to rely entirely on funding by subscription, donation, and the interest from the investment of donations and savings. It was not recovery from so complete a hiatus as the fourteen years of political rituals. But it was within the institutional separation of 'religion' and its registration by a secular state and it was recovery of a sense of local historical continuity in conscious juxtaposition to a school system which taught a Nationalist version of Chinese ethics and civilisation (Chun 1996).

In 1995 the President of the Taiwanese Republic of China apologised for the 1947 massacre, opened a memorial, and declared an official anniversary of the day when the first demonstrations were suppressed: February 28. At the same time, temples have been able to renew their links to root temples on the mainland. The orientation of local temples and festivals has become an aspiration to a distinctively Taiwanese Chinese character, within which ancestral links and networks are traced. It has built on the response to Japanese nationalist colonial rule, whereas revival of local temples on the mainland has built on local loyalty tinged with the disappointed ideals of collectivism. But a cultural politics of national formation is prominent in the secular states of both the PRC and Taiwan. Under both, the rebuilding of local temples is treated as a preservation of local culture, though the views of government and of participants do not necessarily coincide.

## POST-MAO AND POST-CHIANG KAISHEK

In both the mainland and Taiwan, the assertion of a centralised political order with unprecedented powers has given way to less direct though still powerful controls by central government. But in Taiwan the military garrison command of the Republic of China in 1987 became a civil government increasingly Taiwanese in its cultural identification and increasingly multi-party in its democracy. Nothing like the same loosening of political controls has taken place on the mainland. Yet there are a number of significant similarities. Under both regimes a conscious promotion of recreational and popular culture has become a major item of policy, politics, and patronage as the means of cultural mass production and communication have multiplied. Cultural policy has to a great though not a complete extent replaced ideological propaganda and censorship, in constant counterpoint and negotiation with commercial, profit-seeking organisations.

One big difference, though, is the preservation of local boundaries in the mainland. Urbanisation of work, economic wealth and organisation in Taiwan has brought rural residence firmly into the orbit of large cities. Because it is a prosperous and densely populated island, there are few intervening layers of mediation and communication between the most remote and the most central parts. Indeed, remoteness and wilderness are in Taiwan at a premium, and rural poverty hardly exists. All locations are near a centre in time, distance and employment. In this respect the contrast with any one of the provinces on the mainland is great. On the mainland there has also been a huge increase in migration, affecting even the most remote zones of mainland regions. But it is strictly layered. Most villagers are far from an easy travelling distance to a large city.

By the end of the 'eighties, more of the economically active people on the mainland were engaged in non-agricultural than in agricultural work, a turning point that had been reached more than twenty years earlier in Taiwan. In administrative terms most of mainland China's units of government come within areas, each with a small city at its centre, but large city employment is available only to a minority of households. Tens of millions of migrant workers are remote from their place of registration where the rest of their family lives, and are not able to pay them more frequent visits than once annually, at lunar new year. But a far larger number of rural-urban migrants are within shorter distances from their natal places. There has been urbanisation. Mobility between village and city has increased greatly. But so far the spread of the horizons of rural locality is to towns and small cities.

I will soon come to the uneven revival of territorial cults fostered by these conditions on the mainland. I want first to draw attention to the layers of religious activity which now surround them and which in some places have superseded them, both in the mainland and in Taiwan.

In both Taiwan and the mainland, the intensity of material incentives and of engagement in global economic competition has brought about a ruthless cynicism on one hand and a search for spiritual healing and justification on the other. Senses of moral regeneration in a chaotic and corrupt world are sought as before in local temples from responsive deities. But beside them, on the mainland millenarian teachings and leaders thrive, attracting those who have a sense of failure or of having been excluded from material advancement.[13] Other, new senses of religious community, less territorial but still bound to the public places where they are performed, have also emerged on the mainland. In cities, towns and villages, exercises for bodily elasticity and deep, circular breathing – such as *taijiquan* – are often performed in public places like parks, and very often following a more experienced practitioner. In the same way, retired men and women gather in the early mornings for ballroom dancing.

For instance, performers of the northern Chinese procession dance called the Yang'ge gather on their own initiative every evening for more than two hours in Chengfu, a neighbourhood of Beijing. They had been organised in 1996 by an 80–year-old woman who had learned the movements from a university student in the 1930s.[14] The

237

dancers also provided music and entertainment at local weddings and other festive occasions and formed an organisational focus for informal networks in the neighbourhood. But their main activity was the evening performance, which was for their own enjoyment as well as being a spectacle for local residents and passers-by. They were divided between two orientations. One was toward the ideals of collectivisation in which the dance had been taken out of village and town festivals and transformed into a celebration of the powers of solidarity. The other was to go back to the earlier tradition and its practitioners and to professionalize their performances. The collectivists were dominant, but they were not acting according to any external, let alone official, instruction. Indeed local officials watched them from a cautious distance, apprehensive about autonomous assembly. The collectivists had appropriated a form of display which in an earlier time of the history of the Chinese Communist revolution had been officially propagated, but is now their own choice of leisure activity. They dance at a time of day and of life (since many of the participants are retired) away from the organisation of work and outside the organised recreational activities of work units, but retain the collectivist spirit, enjoying a ritual discipline that binds them into a close network. The same distance from present Party leaders and work organisation enjoyed by the retired was evident in Shenyang city, in northeastern China where older, retired cadres met in parks and discussed local politics. They led peaceful and well-organised protests at the curtailing of their benefits by local party leaders who drove smart cars, seized farmer's land, and deprived thousands of their savings when a private bank collapsed due to cadre corruption (NY Times News Service 3.7.2000).

A more sectarian ritual discipline is that of *qigong*, the various ways of exercising *qi* energies by choreographed movement, meditation and breathing exercises. Since 1980 it has been one of the largest movements of spiritual and physical regeneration.[15] Masters or mistresses of these regenerative exercises, some professing amazing powers of healing and salvation, have attracted large congregational followings in halls or open spaces. But whatever mistress, master or method is followed, their bases are not such large congregations but smaller gatherings in open spaces, which the practitioners make their own for a certain time of day, and in which they create their own camaraderie, infused with the regenerative doctrines they have learned. At the end of the 'nineties, the most famous and notorious were the followers of a master called Li Hongzhi and his method of the Buddhist Wheel (Falun'gong), notorious because of its fierce official suppression. The sharp rise in its popularity since its foundation at the beginning of the 'nineties was matched by a growing number of official press criticisms that it was unscientific, dangerous and destabilising. Its practitioners countered by well-coordinated and well-disciplined, non-violent and silent protests and by objections to misrepresentation. They were well informed on the law and channels of grievance open to PRC citizens, determined to withstand the charges made against them and the physical suppression of their activities. They insisted that the method is both spiritually and physically good and that while it borrows from Buddhist, Confucian and Daoist wisdom their practice is not that of a sect but is a re-discovery of Chinese science (*kexue*, which includes both natural and historical sciences).[16]

Early in his own political development, Mao Zedong stressed the regenerative importance of group exercises. Government posters still advertise their importance for physical health. The Buddhist Wheel and other *qigong* methods have appropriated the same aim, including its collective spirit, and added elements from Chinese ritual, moral and cosmological teachings. Like the Beijing *yang'ge* dancers, a large number of practitioners are retired and have memories of the ideals of the collective. Buddhist Wheel practitioners have also been seen to act in a way similar to official condemnations of other ritual practices as less scientific. During the festival of Guan Di in the village of Ten Mile Inn, in the Taihang mountains of Hebei province, in 1999 Buddhist Method practitioners demonstrated the superiority and world recognition of their rituals. They performed their exercises as a counter-festival beneath banners with their insignia and lists in both English and Chinese of the countries in which the method is practised, despite there being no foreign tourists present.[17]

There is a tapping of religious traditions to re-assert and innovate alternative, transcendental authorities. It may be an authority within the cosmology of the Way of *qi*, Yin and Yang, and *ling*, or re-formulations of syncretic Buddhism, Daoism and neo-Confucianism. It may be the joining of new, transnational foundations of Buddhist, Christian or Muslim teachings. It may be the wish to escape all political involvement by withdrawal into communities of mutual spiritual support, such as house churches and meeting points.

Taiwan appears to be exceptional in the extraordinary wealth, influence and proliferation of Buddhist organisations from the 1970s onward, and particularly since the end of garrison rule in 1987.

During these years, a large number of Buddhist organisations broke the hold of the Buddhist Association, which was the official link to government and the establishment of monastic orders. They have become influential institutions of communication, education and welfare. Many are led by nuns. They emphasise lay Buddhism and action in the world.[18]

These then are the religious and political contexts in which local temples have been revived, the historicising context of a national story and its state, loose congregations of ritual discipline, and the local organisations of transcendental communities. None of these new religious institutions, in Taiwan and on the mainland, can escape some politicisation, because they are always subject to government and surveillance, or to sectarian opposition. And on the mainland they include the effects of the disciplines of collective political rituals.

## REVIVAL OF TERRITORIAL CULTS ON THE MAINLAND

The resurgence of religious activity on the mainland has been analysed by official commentators as filling an ideological vacuum. What is needed is better ideological work, but the problem is lack of a cadre to do it and too often Party members are themselves engaged in the construction of religious buildings (Zhou Ying 1988). The vacuum is blamed on the Cultural Revolution, which amounts to an admission that the Chinese Communist Party has not been able to regain the moral authority it lost then. Resurgence of religious activity forms other communities of faith, alternative sources of moral authority and senses of security.

For instance, increasingly recurrent crises of drought and flood are both a cause of great insecurity, threatening survival, and something for which government can be held responsible. While government officials blame farmers for being unscientific, for over-grazing or for stripping slopes of their vegetation and neglecting to plant trees, farmers can as justly blame the vacuum of governmental inaction where large-scale management of the environment is necessary. In worse cases they can blame dereliction of government officials, mismanagement of funds for environmental projects, or their being botched. How this has worked itself out can be illustrated from two quite different parts of China.

There is a political vacuum in the three-section administrative village of Yangjiagou in the far north of the northern province of Shaanxi. Its Party Secretary in the late 'nineties did no Party work, spending the whole of his time working in transport. The other leader of the collective, the village head, was disliked for suspected corruption. But villagers got on with subsistence and attempts to move beyond it until droughts became increasingly frequent in the 1990s. Until the 'sixties there had been a temple for three dragon kings in the mountains above the village. In cases of drought a rain-making procession of three days was added to his annual fair. The last time this happened was in the 1950s. Some thirty years later, the temple was rebuilt, its annual festival revived and a rain ceremony performed. Then in the three years of 1995, 1997 and 1999 there was drought. Rain ceremonies are as regular as droughts.[19] Farmers in Yangjiagou refer to themselves as *shoukouren* 'people who suffer bitterness'.

In 1999, the villagers elected a new village head, but by now their authority was also vested in the rebuilt Dragon Kings temple. The village is famous for having been a headquarters for the base area government of the Chinese Communist Party during the war against Japan and the civil war with the Nationalists. Mao's cave house is preserved in the village centre. In 1999, the township Party Secretary accompanied by county cadres was driving in a convoy of three cars to pay a ceremonial visit to Mao's cave. Outside the village he came upon a procession of the tablet of one of the Dragon Kings. He might have heard the shouts and responses which the men of the village perform to plead for rain, going up to the mountain temple to collect clouds and down to the river bed where the village is situated to receive water (*shangshan cai yun, yanhe qu shui*). He stopped the convoy and asked pleasantly what was happening. The village men told him about the drought. One of the county officials advised him to drive on and let them get on with their affairs. Later some villagers told the visiting researcher that cadres can do nothing to help them in the drought. 'When we farmers seek a bit of rain the government cadres are useless, they cannot give us any, so the Dragon King is the head of us who suffer bitterness. He is very effective (*tebie ling*)'. As it happens, a little rain has fallen after every rain ceremony, enough to sew at least some seed.

Far off to the southwest, in a mountainous township of Sichuan, in 1992 a severe flood and landslide destroyed several buildings and brought tensions between villagers and government to a head. They had already been simmering over falling prices for farm products, awareness of official corruption, and suppression of small revivals of the cult of an upright official in the ruins of a local temple. The villagers insisted on rebuilding the temple in 1992, but compromised with a new leader of the township, appointed in the same year, who was more tolerant than his predecessor. They added Buddhist elements to the cult, which fitted better with the government's recognition of religion (Flower and Leonard 1996 and 1998).

In some places, the ending of religious activities and the destruction or changed use of religious buildings occurred only twenty years before they were revived again. In such places revival is a realisation of what was still a detailed schema in living recall. In other places destruction and elimination had occurred more than three generations before it became possible to reconstruct what could, in gazetteers and other records but not in living memory, have been known as part of their history. In many of these places there has been no revival, despite vague living recall. I shall choose instances from the two provinces of Hebei and Jiangsu, close to the two most important centres of the People's Republic, Beijing and Shanghai, just to demonstrate the fact that no province has been immune to the resurgence of religious activities.[20]

No temples have been rebuilt in the township (*zhen*) of Baigou in northern Hebei province. The revival and prosperity of its famous market for bags and cases has fostered no temples, just the mosque of Hui traders and a government-sponsored annual fair without religious rituals. In one of its villages, Xiaoying, an old man who was 82 years old in 1997 and who had been a teacher before 1949 could remember from his childhood three temples and their festivals.[21] None of them have been revived. By contrast in another part of the same province, the temple fair of Fanzhuang thrives. Every year for the three days of 18th-20th of the third lunar month, a huge marquee is erected at one end of an open market space.[22] A long, red cloth banner across its front proclaims it to be the 'Great Assembly of the Dragon Tablet Transmitted down the Ages whose Awesome Fame Shakes the Four Quarters'. The tablet, tall and heavy by now after a number of ever-larger renewals over fifteen years, has inscribed on it 'Seat of the Spirit of the Dragon, True Commander of the Ten Sections and the Three Regions of the Universe'. Accompanied by dramatic tableaux of mythical scenes, by drum bands, music bands, and martial arts bands, and by explosions of firecrackers, it is carried out of the house in which it has been kept for the past year, and is taken in procession to be installed in the place of honour within the marquee.

Baigou, the township where no revival had occured, was in an area which had been particularly fiercely contested between Communist,

Nationalist, and Japanese forces. The front-line between them kept shifting. Communist land reform campaigns there were particularly violent. Perhaps because of these prominent memorial scars, there was no move in the sixty following years to reconstruct an earlier historical sense of the place, either at village or at township level. Whereas in Fanzhuang township, the memory of temples was comparatively recent, since they were finally destroyed only in the 1960s.[23] Unlike Baigou, between 1945 and 1949 Fanzhuang's landlords and lineage chiefs were courted by both sides, the Nationalist and the Communist.

At present the dragon tablet is housed in the home of the head of the Dragon festival assembly (the *huitou*). The festival is a great outdoor carnival for performers of many kinds, as well as for more elite cultural activities such as the composition of calligraphic scrolls, and within the marquee women chant Buddhist scriptures, all of which in 1996 drew the attentions of local television, and could be interpreted as the various things the permitting authorities can tolerate: traditional custom, religion, and culture. With greater wealth some of the many destroyed temples, in particular a Dragon temple, will probably be rebuilt by permission of the township culture office.

Another but quite different example of a place where remembered temples and festivals have not yet been revived is Jinxing and its township Zhenze, in southern Jiangsu province. Villagers in Jinxing over 50 years old could recall with great certainty where the three temples of the village had been. The old trees by which they stood are still living. Two of them were for women Buddhists, the third for a feast of the wealthy elite of the village who were also the chief donors to an annual harvest procession festival. The trees remain, one shading a factory, another what had been a school and is now a warehouse, and the third an unused warehouse.[24] The only sign of revival is a small side building leaning against the warehouse. It is an unregistered temple, but only a few old people go to burn incense in it. In the town of Zhenze, a large church has been built. Many men and women from Jinxing attend its services. For funerals, Jinxing villagers cannot call in Buddhist practitioners because cadres stop them, considering the rituals of merit-making to be superstitious. So increasing numbers have taken up the permitted and registered Christianity, giving as their reasons the usual ones that they do not now have to worship gods, fear ghosts or go to the expense and bother of burning incense, spirit money and firecrackers. They summarise all this in the way missionaries would have done and now the non-religious government does: that Christianity is not superstition.

Within the same county of Wujiang, in Miaogang township not many minutes away by bicycle, there is a gingko tree, more than three hundred and sixty years old, and next to it a temple of Old Tai (Lao Tai miao), named after the nearby lake Tai, where thousands come on the night of the turn of the year to offer the first stick of incense. It has no procession festival, but the gathering there on the night of the new year by villagers from the whole township makes it the territorial cult of the township. This temple has been rebuilt twice since 1979. It was still a substantial building of several halls around a yard at the beginning of the Cultural Revolution and was completely destroyed as were all other temples in the following years. Rebuilt on a smaller scale in the early nineties, it was destroyed again in spring 1996 along with all the other rebuilt temples of the eighteen villages of the township.

Alarmed by the size of temples and the numbers of people who gathered for festivals in Wenzhou, in the neighbouring province of Zhejiang, the highest officials of Jiangsu sought to reinforce their reputation for retaining a strong collective leadership which had brought about great industrialisation and prosperity in their province. They arranged meetings of cadres in every township. In Miaogang, village loudspeakers broadcast a denunciation of superstition by the township Party Secretary, warning of the danger to spiritual civilisation. A coordinated set of teams was organised comprising workers from collective enterprises and cadres from each village, and in one morning they pulverised all the temples which had been rebuilt in the past two or three years. But people continued to place incense on the 1st and 15th of the lunar months at the ruins of the temples. Villagers in one Miaogang village, Kaixiangong, said it was customary to burn incense in a public temple for the last four of the five 7–day periods of mourning after burial, and that the temple gods were greater and of more use than their domestic god, the Stove God. In the same year, 1996, a Christian woman who attends services in Zhenze from Kaixiangong was helped by her Zhenze congregation to hold a funeral in the village. They came in large numbers, with a priest and a band and performed to an interested public of her village neighbours. Christianity could become attractive to them, but so far it has apparently not attracted as many households as in Jinxing.

In 1999 the Old Tai Temple, but none of the others, was rebuilt. The recalling of old temples is equally possible in both villages; it has even resulted in one minor revival in Jinxing. But why in Kaixiangong and not in Jinxing are villagers more insistent on reviving activities at the sites of their temples? In this case I think the key factor was the success or failure of the new institutions of local prosperity and security, and their leadership. In both villages, throughout the 1980s and the first half of the 1990s, when the village Party Secretary and its head retained considerable powers over appointment of enterprise managers, their enterprises grew and prospered. A large fraction of their profits went into infrastructure, utilities, schools and social insurance benefiting all the villagers, as well as providing them with work in the enterprises and a secure income. In Jinxing this continued until 1999. Large amounts of income from fees and retained profits were spent on road building, laying a TV cable, cheap loans for the repair and maintenance of homes, as well as the supply of basic utilities (gas, electricity and water) and an insurance scheme against fire and accident, a medical clinic, school, and nursery, and pensions available to all households. Kaixiangong had received less collective benefits, and then during the mid-'nineties in the whole of Miaogang township collective enterprises began to falter. In addition, it became increasingly apparent to villagers that they were being run for the benefit of village and township cadres and not for their welfare. In one village, the Party Secretary was withdrawn because of his corruption and was not replaced. Instead a popular villager who runs a private business was elected to the position of village head and took charge of the village's administration. The electorate of that village and probably most of the others evidently favoured something much closer to the Wenzhou model of development in which villagers form their own enterprises. They could no longer entrust the security of their future to the so-called 'collective' leadership of enterprises. So in Miaogang many villagers re-established a non-governmental author-ity by the burning of incense, the offering of petitions to the gods and divination for their response, and in the organisation which is required to build temples and hold festivals. They are an older and remembered form of collective village institution. In this they anticipated and perhaps drove a comprehensive change of provincial policy.

The year in which the Old Tai temple was rebuilt, 1999, the whole collective policy in Jiangsu was reversed. The provincial authorities decided that privatisation is after all the best road to future prosperity. Jinxing's collective enterprises became private corporations. Accord-ing to the man who had been its village head and is now retired, people feel less secure having to make their own arrangements and payments for the utilities and other benefits formerly arranged by the village administration for them. We shall have to see whether this brings about a religious revival, and if so whether it is a revival of temples or the spread of Christianity.

In Miaogang, the Old Tai temple had been rebuilt and protected because of an investment by a Taiwanese businessman. His business, to construct a plant for vegetable pickling, could not be refused by Miaogang officials presiding over a faltering local economy. Insistent worshippers at the destroyed temple went to him for a donation towards the rebuilding of the temple, and he made acceptance of the reconstruction part of the condition for investing in Miaogang. Supporters of the rebuilding also suggested to the township that reconstruction was justified as a tourist attraction. The township government did apply to higher authorities for endorsement, but the rebuilding went ahead anyway before any response was received. The rebuilding fund came from contributions by worshippers in the surrounding villages and in effect by builders who worked without charge.

What have not been revived are the more distinctly agriculture-based festivals. In Kaixiangong, which is next to the town of Miaogang, neighbourhood sections had each kept a figure of Emperor Liu (Liu Huang), a military deity who was a protector against drought, flood and locusts.[25] In case of drought, flood or plague villagers would go to Miaogang for a Liu Huang parade, but this has not been revived. Already in the 1920s the Wujiang county magistrate had condemned superstition and refused to endorse a parade which would have been his responsibility in imperial times (Fei 1939: 169). Neither has there been a revival in Kaixiangong of the gathering of neighbourhood sections with their figures of Liu Huang for a harvest thanksgiving theatrical performance. It had already ceased in the 1930s (Fei 1939:103–4).

In the revived Old Tai Temple itself there has been a change of emphasis. In the 1930s there was still the one main deity for whom the temple had been founded in the Ming dynasty, the Old Man of Lake Tai, whose family name is Qiu and whose title is Monarch of the Pacified State (Pingguo Wang). His figure with a long white beard stood in the main hall, and in side halls there were figures of his son and grandson, and the wives of all three. A wooden model of a boat from the old temple remains. When storms brewed up on the lake, boatmen called out the old man's name for protection. In the 1990s. the name of the temple was often interpreted by villagers, not as the temple of the old man of lake Tai but as the old woman (*lao taitai*) temple because the main altar table is filled with six small ceramic, glazed figures of the bodhisattva known locally as Guanyin Niangniang. There is a figure of an old man, but it is even smaller and on a side table.

There has been a turn toward domestic concerns from agriculture and fishing on Lake Tai. The other major change is protection by the Miaogang culture office. To the protection provided by the overseas investor, a further layer of protection is provided by the promotion of local heritage, immensely influenced by the work of the anthropologist and senior politician Fei Xiaotong as the most famous native of the county. They offer a way out of condemnation of the temple as superstitious and into negotiating a compromise with villagers' religious practices. Similarly, in a village in Shanxi a Niangniang temple has been rebuilt under the joint authority of the local tourist department, the village administration and various local groups.[26]

One last example of the revival of temples will help to underline a last and crucial point about the changes included in the revival of territorial cults on the mainland. It comes from the village of Ten Mile Inn, which is in the borderland between Shanxi and Hebei provinces, in the Taihang mountains where the Chinese Communist forces established their largest and most elaborate administration in the late 1940s before transferring it to Beijing. It was first studied during that time by David and Isabel Crook, participants in the revolution who later made the PRC their home. The base was like a small kingdom sealed off from both the Nationalists and the Japanese. At the time of the Crooks' first study there were many temples in Ten Mile Inn. A number of Daoist temples were situated by a hill to the north of the village. They are now the site of a school. In each of the corners of the village, there were territorial temples that served not only as *she* (community) temples but also as sacred guards against outsiders. The sponsors of these four temples were kinship groups known as *men* (gates), such as 'Fumen' or the gate of the Fus. Some of the other temples were like those of state cults in the county seat, including a Dragon King, Guandi, and the Three Officials (Sanguan), commanding the upper, intermediate and lower levels of the world, though they lacked a City God Temple. Some were local versions of regional cults such as Nuwa, popular along the Yellow River.

By the 'nineties three temples had been rebuilt, in three of the four quarters of the village, one for the goddess Nuwa, one for the Ninth Lord (Jiu Ye), and one for Guan Di. An old cadre who had assisted

247

the Crooks in their study was planning the reconstruction of the fourth, a second temple for Guan Di. Telling Wang Mingming about it, he reflected on how serving the people had changed. In earlier times he would have proved his leadership by organising and participating in the building of irrigation canals and ponds to retain rain water. Now he did the same by managing the rebuilding of a temple.[27] In other words, he is serving the wishes of fellow villagers and conceives of a temple as a public good, just as Chen Wansheng does in Meifa, southern Fujian.

This example of socialist ideals of leadership in the management of local temples emphasises a major change in the nature of temples.

## CONCLUSION

At the beginning of the century temples and their organisation were a form of village government by land-owners, managers of temple land holdings in southeastern China or an elite of patrons who organised crop-watching and irrigation in northern Chinese villages. They were centres of what Duara (1988: 15) calls a cultural nexus, linking villagers to higher-status scholar-gentry in the township and county seats. But during the first half-century of republican rule they were alienated, destroyed or replaced by reformers and by more predatory agents of the state. The new cultural entrepreneurs of the 1990s revival are represented in my examples by the retired and honourable cadres of Ten Mile Inn and Meifa and by the businessman head of the Miaogang village. They should also include cadres who gain their authority with villagers from the organising of ancestral halls and local temples rather than from the Party while retaining their official political positions as Party Secretary or as elected village leaders.[28]

A nexus with popular cultural institutions in small towns and villages, which Duara calls 'local society', is both a node which structures villagers' access to power and resources and an arena for contests of leadership. At the beginning of the century the nexus was a basic articulation of local society with what Tang Tsou has succintly described as the organic ruling class of landlords, scholars and officials of imperial China (2000: 207), though he should have included merchants and their guilds. I have already, in chapter 7, pointed out the multiplicity of centres of territorial cults. Long before that Skinner had pointed out the multi-centred marketing hierarchy (1964–5, reprinted 1993). As I have already emphasised, they do not exactly map onto each other, and neither do they map onto the single-centred hierarchy of the republican state. But the network linking managers and leaders of temples and lineages to local merchants, scholars and landlords, and of these to officials of the imperial regime, did articulate the variously centred hierarchies with each other. It was a *base* nexus, which existed under and was essential to the maintenance of the administrative hierarchy. But the establishing of a republican state, pushing out from its centres the institutions and ideologies of schooling, taxation, military recruitment, electoral and mass mobilisation, destroyed that nexus. Local temples were disarticulated. Then, as I have described, in the second half of the century with land reform and collectivisation, temples and festivals were deprived of resources and eventually destroyed.

Networks in the collective decades worked within and between a single set of institutions superimposed on one another, teams superimposed on local lineages, brigades on temple areas, both deprived of further centres in their hierarchies (clan associations and pilgrimage temples). Village administration is still tightly linked to township government, and constitutes a distinct node with central government. So today's linkers who work through local temples and ancestral halls are not basic. They form a *parallel* nexus, *next* to and not beneath governmental structures.

Temples and ancestral halls are a public property of villagers, but outside the combined private-and-governmental ownership of land and enterprises and beyond the politics of the governing party. They represent a sense of public good, informed by a recent past of collectivism. The Party in the mainland governs through a mix of collective management, regulated market forces, state cadres as entrepreneurs using their licensing powers to anchor enterprises to their offices, and an official ideology of Chinese market socialism. Villagers' assertions of their own public authority by subscribing to the building of temples and ancestral halls and by adding their memory of the ideals of the collective, cross into the official ideology's mix of Chinese socialism with private enterprise. At the same time, however, their authority is a basis for criticising and opposing cadres for being predatory in ways quite similar to the state agents of the Nationalist republican era (Duara 1988: 250–253).

Local cults combine a local sense of history with the transcendental authority of responsive gods. It may be that congregational forms of gathering prevail. New and larger, evangelical and worldly versions of Buddhism and Daoism have emerged in Taiwan, and may do so in the mainland. So might shrines and temples of healing and spirit-

249

communication, which have proliferated around Mountainstreet and elsewhere in Taiwan. Both the large organisations and the healing shrines attract followers, rather than involving everyone in a locality. But the same people can be followers of these as well as contributing and participating in local, territorial cults and their carnivalesque displays of autonomy. All provide public spaces by a self-conscious resort to 'pre-modern' popular culture, but the local temples by their territorial nature do so with most relevance to a state and with more layers of recent political history built into them. With their own authority and territorial hierarchies, they are at once a resource for local politicians and a basis for autonomous moral judgement.

# Notes

## PREFACE

1 Two in particular: Ahern (1981a), and Sangren (1987).

## 1 HISTORY, IDENTIFICATION AND BELIEF

1 The concept of collective representations is developed and used in several works by Durkheim and Mauss, in particular Durkheim (1982) and Mauss (1979).
2 On Sangren see Feuchtwang and Wang Mingming (1990). On Freedman see Feuchtwang (1991).
3 Apart from the stress on the mythical character of this theory, all the other elements of its exposition are given at greater length and in finer detail by Gane (1983).
4 My principal reference is to Derrida (1977: part 2).

## 3 OFFICIAL AND LOCAL CULTS

1 Many thanks to Steve Jones for making this article available to me, and for many other sights and sounds of Chinese villages.
2 See Feuchtwang (1977), the accounts of the cult of Mazu by Watson (1985) and Sangren (1988).

## 4 LOCAL FESTIVALS AND THEIR CULTS

1 For another version of the story of Hou Tu see Schipper (1977: 661), and for a version which identifies Tudi Ma as the malicious one who insists the bones remain as bones see Ahern (1973: 203).
2 This day is better known in the literature as the Dragon Boat Festival, when rival groups race on waterways and the search for the virtuous official who drowned himself (Chu Yuan in most accounts) is recalled. There is no boat race in Mountainstreet, but most households make the traditional sticky rice cakes wrapped in bamboo leaves, and many put up on their doors and altars sprigs of greenery for protection and strength, as in other parts of China. According to the accompanying myth the sprigs

251

were a sign of salvation. The rebel scourge Huang Chao had told a widow fleeing from him burdened with her husband's brother's sons as well as her own that as a reward for her filial piety she should return to her home and put on the door a sprig of green so that he would know not to destroy it. Also on the fifth day of the fifth month wine is mixed with a yellow ochre powder and sprinkled on the threshold as a safeguard against, according to the accompanying myth some told, the beautiful woman who turned back to her true form, a white snake, when fed the yellow powder.

3 Although they continue to care for graves on Qing Ming and to make dumplings on the winter solstice, some families choose alternative dates, in spring and autumn, for the worship of their ancestors because, they said, an ancestor had died (some used the formula 'been eaten by a tiger') on Qing Ming or the winter solstice.

4 In addition, the first and fifteenth of the sixth month are also devoted to the Bed Mother or Guan Yin and prayers for children, easy birth, and the preservation of infants.

## 5 THE INCENSE-BURNER: COMMUNICATION AND DEFERENCE

1 An incense-burner association is a formal bond for many kinds of grouping. I have records of mutual savings circles, of a renunciation of gambling circle, of mutual assistance at funerals, as well as sworn brotherhoods, groups of compatriots, surname groups and trade associations being organised formally around an incense-burner and a patron deity in Taiwan.

2 Of the remaining four patrons, one was the deceased chairman of the committee. Both he and his son and their successor's names recur as donors. Two of the four had moved out of Mountainstreet. As for the last, I can only guess why he was not included on the committee. He was resident in Mountainstreet, but in the recent past he had speculated heavily in investments outside the town, mainly in Taibei city. If they had been successful investments they would increasingly have drawn his interests and activities away from Mountainstreet. But they collapsed.

3 Ch'en Cheng-hsiang 1959 includes maps showing the concentrations of the main groups of compatriots as they stood in 1926. The area of concentration of Anxi compatriots in the Taibei basin coincides with the distribution there of temples dedicated to Bao Yi Zun Wang (Ang Gong) as recorded in the register of temples compiled by Liu Jiwan (1960).

4 I was told the names by a Mountainstreet man of over 60 years who was himself told them by his father.

## 6 DAOISM AND ITS CLIENTS

1 I should like to thank Arthur Wolf, who had lived and studied in this town and township, for introducing me to one of his informants there.

## 7 ANG GONG, OR THE TRUTH OF PUPPETS

1 As for temples to these two in Fujian province, Chen Xidong (1991: 367) has found references in the Quanzhou prefectural record of the Qianlong reign period (1736–96) to two temples to Zhang Xun and Xu Yuan to whom Guan Gong, the most famous god general, is added to make a trio of Loyal Ones. One was in the Shengde district (*pu*) to the southwest of Quanzhou city and the other at the foot of Fengshan to the east of the city, constructed in the period 1139–63. Chen adds that Zhang and Xu are honoured as a pair called Civil and Military Venerable Kings (Wen Wu Zun Wang) in temples all over the Quanzhou region, but not elsewhere in Fujian.

2 This and all the other titles, names and characters, mentioned here, except for 'red' and 'old man', are recorded by Liu Jiwan (1960) under Bao Yi Zun Wang.

3 These thoughts were inspired by conclusions drawn from Judith Farquhar 1989. My warmest thanks to her for sending me a copy of this paper.

## 8 THE POLITICS OF RELIGION AND POLITICAL RITUAL

1 It also includes a number of lesser autonomies, of people assigned minority nationality status which are becoming ethnicised while the majority nationality is promoted by government as an ethnic nation. See Naran Bilik (1998) and Cong Dachang (1997)

2 On the Muslim rebellions Gladney (1991: 351 fn 117) recommends Chu (1955 but see also Lipman (1990)); see Spence (1997) for the Taiping, and Cohen on the Boxers (1997)

3 On campaigns against both religion and superstition under the pre-1949 republican government, see Duara 1995: pp 98–110

4 For much more on the story of this man and his village see Feuchtwang and Wang (forthcoming).

5 Asad's genealogy goes against any such universalisation of a concept of ritual. To do what I suggest is to court the accusation he makes of Geertz, to turn an historical concept of religion (or ritual in this case) into a transhistorical one, by essentialising it. My defense is that I am using it pragmatically. If I find it to be helpful in the descriptive analysis which follows, then to that extent it is applicable to another history. Where the materials to which it leads me force me to return to the concept to modify it, or to state its lack of applicability, there the distinctiveness of its genealogy and of a concept of ritual more appropriate to a Chinese history begins to make itself known. The first modification is to put together into one time in China what he took to be a series of definitions of ritual in Euro-American thought, with Geertz's coming at the end of the genealogy.

6 In 1981, its sixtieth year and five years after Mao's death, the Communist Party of China ceremonially delivered its historical verdict: 'Comrade Mao Zedong was a great Marxist and a great proletarian revolutionary, strategist and theorist. It is true that he made gross

253

mistakes during the "cultural revolution", but, if we judge his activities as a whole, his contributions to the Chinese revolution far outweigh his mistakes. His merits are primary and his errors are secondary' (FLP 1981: 56). Quite unlike the ending of 'actually existing socialism' in the east European bloc, and also quite unlike the ending of the Brezhnev era of stagnation in the Soviet Union, the Chinese was an ending of what had been first a renewal and then a routinisation of popular revolution.

7  For instance Lydia Liu (2000: 768) picks out from the immensely popular TV serialisation of a novel, Beijing Sojourner in New York, a scene in which the immigrant entrepreneur quarrels with his daughter and she blurts out 'You are a stinking capitalist' – the return of a fierce cultural revolution denunciation. It must have been entirely familiar to its Chinese mainland audience, and funny because it had become an anachronism, especially in the context of a story which, Lydia Liu points out, promotes the reform ideology that the success of the new rich is not because of their privileges and connections but because of their entrepreneurial spirit and efforts. But is she right to say that 'it brings back a history, only to bury it deeper in the collective memory'?

8  Dikotter (1992: 175–195 and 1998: 104–114 and 142–146) discusses the Republican and the Communist mixes of population eugenics and class analysis, the Republicans stressing the superiority of intellectual and artistic bloodlines, the Communists stressing worker and poor peasant origin.

9  Dutton (2000: 8–9). Between March 1966 and early 1968 Red Guard groups and high political leaders fought for and against so-called blood theory, stressing class origin, and the opposite theory of socially acquired capacity for continuing revolution tested and proved in performance. By 1968 the battles had been resolved into a compromise which continued to lay emphasis on the inheritance of class identity, but qualified it with the possibility of proof by performance (White 1976).

10 A policy of transformation and cleansing from within the songs and dances collected by folklorists and troupes of revolutionary performers had been implemented since it was established in the Yan'an revolutionary base area in the early 'forties. Some folk theatre was ready made. One such, the Red Lantern Dance, had from long before the Communist revolution had a rebellious song to accompany it, containing the lines: 'With one blow I chop to bits the Demons' Gate./Don't pay rent, don't make contributions,/Don't give them hay, don't hand over money' (Holm 1991:201). But, as David Holm nicely points out, rebelliousness could not be left as such. It had to be turned into celebration of a successfully complete revolution. And anyway something had to be done with the 'Demons' gate'. It became the gate of the class enemy. Of the most celebratory anthem, Holm observes that The East is Red (Dongfang Hong) calls Mao the star of salvation (*jiuxing*) which 'implied exactly the kind of connection between earthly emperors and astral deities' such as the north pole star (1991:333).

Bad class elements and their children, carrying the labels given them in land reform or assigned to them in campaigns to weed out Rightists, had by the mid-sixties become the celebratory opposite. They were the rubble of the Demons' Gate, but were still portrayed as threatening. In otherwise close-knit villages, they were avoided by their neighbours for fear of being contaminated since they were bound to be the target of the next campaign of class struggle in which village officials could deflect accusations of political backsliding by viciously attacking these outcasts. A woman who was at the time a teenager was interviewed by Jonathan Unger, and even in the safety of more than a decade after the events she provides a vivid glimpse of a demonic imagery of fear: 'I was scared of class enemies. It seemed as if they would harm us, would poison us, kill us and eat us. I took them as horrible, fierce. I dared not talk to them in case I got muddled up' (1998: 98). Mao in particular used demonic figures to describe hidden bad class elements in the 1960s. For instance he described them as snakes who can assume the guise of a beautiful young woman. A children's book of the same years pictures a hero killing just such a female snake demon (Unger 1998:97).

These are examples of concerted incorporation of popular religious symbols into a centralised interpretative community. But they are also examples of the power of the images of popular religion in the service of resolutely non-religious political mobilisation.

11  For the first Chinese edition, in 1988, the author of *Xuese Huanghun* gave his name as Lao Gui. Jenner 1992: 206 mentions it as a prime example of the honour of tough-guys called *germen* (brothers) in Chinese slang, and which he nicely translates as 'mateship'. Jenner is much more dismissive of the book than is its due. He simply despairs of its ethic as a continuation of two thousand years of stories of *hao han* 'good men' who were knights errant seeking out injustice and imposing their own justice by physical prowess, an ethic debased by criminal gangs of the republican period. I think it tells us much more, and in particular it tells us about the ironic heritage of the Cultural Revolution.

12  For the history of precious scrolls, see Overmyer (1985), and for the silk women see Topley (1975).

13  For examples of these cults, of what Ann Anagnost calls imperial imposters and which Barend ter Haar identifies as a demonic paradigm, see Anagnost (1985, 1987 and 1997: chapter 2) and ter Haar (1996).

14  I saw this group performing on two evenings myself, but all the information in this paragraph is based on the research of Florence Graezer (1999).

15  For the 1980s boom in *qigong*, see Zhu and Penny (eds) (1994).

16  At the time of writing, no-one in the mainland of China dares to practice *qigong* in groups in the open in any way resembling the Buddhist Wheel method for fear of police action. But dedicated practitioners do still mount protests and allow themselves to be arrested. The best sources of documentation, discussion and news about the Buddhist Wheel method are on the web. Start from the page maintained by Barend ter Haar (http://www.let.leidenuniv.nl/bth/index.html).

17  This was witnessed and reported to me by my colleague Wang Mingming.

18  As before, I am relying on Jones' (1999) excellent history of Taiwanese Buddhism, which culminates with descriptions of this extraordinary and innovative growth.

19 At the time of writing (2000) there is even more severe drought and I fully expect another rain ceremony, later, in the Sixth lunar month when it is (now) normal to hold one. All the information on Yangjiagou comes from Guo Yuhua, a colleague for whose generosity with her field data from repeated and lengthy visits to the village I am deeply grateful. Thanks too to Luo Hong'guang whose earlier and continuing fieldwork in Yangjiagou has informed Guo Yuhua.

Of the four temples which had existed in the village in the 1930s, only the temple to the three dragon kings and a temple to Guanyin have been revived. In addition, a new temple, which had not existed, was built around the figure of the Efficaceous Offical of the Black Tiger (Hei Hu Ling Guan) invoked by a spirit medium from his root temple on Baiyun mountain in another part of the province. But after the death of the medium in 1996, the Black Tiger's annual festival ceased and his celebration was joined with the annual festival of the Dragon Kings. In other words, the Dragon Kings have obvious priority, not only for personal petitions but for collective village affairs. The effective manager of the committee, which organises the collection of money for repairs of both village temples and from every household for annual festival theatre, musicians and offerings, had been the village secretary (*shuji*). Villagers respect him, and compare his public service favourably with the suspected village head. In addition to him, the annual festival of the Dragon Kings is organised by six 'gatherers' (*jiushou*), two from each of the three sections of the village, each appointing his successor after one or two years from people willing to take on the task of 'organising for everybody' (*ge dajia banshe*).

20 In addition, Feuchtwang and Wang (forthcoming) provide an extended case study from Meifa, southern Fujian, which I have already mentioned. Among many other local studies which mention the rebuilding of temples, the most extended instances from other provinces are Flower and Leonard (1998) in Sichuan, Jing Jun (1996) in Gansu, Luo Hongguang (1998) for another village in northern Shaanxi beside Yangjiagou, and Siu (1990) in Guangdong.

21 For Tudi Gong, for Guandi and for a Niangniang, who is a goddess protecting childbirth. For all the information on Xiaoying and Baigou, I am again indebted to Guo Yuhua who, together with Luo Hongguang and other fellows of the Institute of Sociology of the Central Academy of Social Sciences, conducted surveys in the township and all its villages.

22 The following description is how I saw it in March 1996, in the company of members of the Chinese Folklore Association.

23 As the centre of a flourishing market, beside a Dragon God temple its elites had sponsored the building of a set of temples similar to those in the county capital – for the City God, for the God of Literary Accomplishment, for Guandi, and a great number of others on a smaller scale. There were also three Catholic churches, and there are now more than three Catholic study rooms. This information comes from Wang Mingming, to whom I am indebted for this as for so much else.

24 For most of this and the following information on Jinxing, Zhenze, Kaixiangong and Miaogang I am indebted to Chang Xiangqun, and her amazingly thorough field research for a Ph D at City University, London.

A little is derived from my own, short field trips and interviews in 1990 and 1995.

25  According to Xu Wenchu (1996). The story of Liu Huang which Fei tells seems to refer to a different Liu (Fei 1939: 168).

26  According to Wang Mingming, whose student Tian Qing wrote a dissertation on this village in Beijing University 1999.

27  Wang Mingming was accompanied by his student Hu Zongze, who had completed a preliminary re-study of Ten Mile Inn as an MA dissertation at Beijing University

28  An example of cadres managing public works such as road-building and schools from the base of lineage organisation in a village see Feuchtwang 1998: 68, and for an elected village leader who is a key organiser of the new ancestral hall and opposed to all the appointed cadres see Ku 1999: 310–319.

# References

Ahern, E. Martin (1973) *The Cult of the Dead in a Chinese Village*, Stanford: Stanford University Press.

—— (1981a) *Chinese Ritual and Politics*, Cambridge: Cambridge University Press.

—— (1981b) 'The Thai Ti Kong festival', in Ahern, E.M. and Gates, H. (eds) *The Anthropology of Taiwanese Society*, Stanford: Stanford University Press.

Allio, F. (2000) 'Spatial organisation in a ritual context: a preliminary analysis of the *Koah-hiu* processional system of a Tainan county region and its social significance' paper presented to the Third International Conference on Sinology, Academia Sinica: Nankang, Taipei.

Anagnost, A. (1985) 'The beginning and end of an emperor: a counter-representation of the state' *Modern China* vol 11 no 2 pp 147–176.

—— (1987) 'Politics and magic in contemporary China' *Modern China* vol 13 no 1 pp 40–62.

—— (1997) *National Past-times; Narrative, Representation and Power in Modern China*. Durham and London: Duke University Press.

Asad, T. (1993) *Genealogies of Religion: Discipline and Reasons of Power in Christianity and Islam*. Baltimore: Johns Hopkins University Press.

Balazs, E. (1965) *Political Theory and Administrative Reality in Traditional China*, London: Luzack.

Bilik, N. (1998) 'Language education, intellectuals, and symbolic representation: being an urban Mongolian in a new configuration of social evolution' in William Safran (ed), *Nationalism and Ethnoregional Identities in China*. London: Frank Cass. pp 47–67.

Bolz, J. (1987) *A Survey of Taoist Literature; Tenth to Seventeenth Centuries*, Institute of East Asian Studies China Research Monograph 32, Berkeley: University of California.

Bourdieu, P. (1977) *Outline of a Theory of Practice*, Cambridge: Cambridge University Press.

Bredon, J. and Mitrophanow, I. (1927) *The Moon Year*, Hong Kong: Oxford University Press, 1982 edition.

Brim, J. (1970) *Local Systems and Modernising Change in the New Territories of Hong Kong*, unpublished PhD thesis, Stanford University.

Chard, R. (1990) 'Folktales on the God of the Stove', *Chinese Studies*, 12:1, Taibei.

258

Ch'en Cheng-hsiang (1959) *Geographical Atlas of Taiwan*, Research Report 93, Taibei: Fu-min Geographical Institute of Economic Development.

Chen Xiaomei (1999) 'Growing up with posters in the Maoist era' in H.Evans and S.Donald (eds), *Picturing Power in the People's Republic of China*. Lanham, Maryland: Rowman and Littlefield Publishers.

Chen Xidong (1991) 'Quanzhou haiwai jiaotong yu haishen xiying (Quanzhou overseas communication and belief in ocean gods)', in UNESCO Quanzhou International Seminar, *Zhongguo yu Haishang Xizhou Zhilu* (China's Maritime Silk Route), Fujian People's Publishing House.

Chu Wen-djang (1955) *Ch'ing Policy Towards the Muslims in the Northwest*, Ph D dissertation, University of Washington.

Chun, A. (1996) 'From nationalism to nationalising: cultural imagination and state formation in postwar Taiwan' in J. Unger (ed) *Chinese Nationalism*. Armonk: M.E.Sharpe pp 126–147.

'Ciji' (shrines and sacrifices), 'Jisi' (sacrifices and offerings), and 'Cijisi' (shrines and offerings), in *Da Qing Huidian: Li Bu* (The statutes of the Qing dynasty: Board of Rites) (1690).

Cohen, P. (1997) *History in Three Keys; The Boxers as Event, Experience and Myth*. New York: Columbia University Press.

Cong Dachang (1997), *When Heroes Pass Away*. Lanham: University Press of America.

Cormack, J.G. (1935) *Everyday Customs in China*, London.

Day, C.B. (1974) *Chinese Peasant Cults*, Taibei: Ch'eng Wen Publishing Company.

Dean, K. (1988) *Taoism and Popular Religion in Southeast China: History and Revival*, PhD dissertation, Stanford University.

—— (2000) 'Lineage and territorial cults: Transformations and interactions in the irrigated Putian plains' paper presented to the Third International Conference on Sinology, Academia Sinica: Nankang, Taipei.

Derrida, J. (trans. Spivak, G.) (1977) *Of Grammatology*, Baltimore and London: Johns Hopkins Press.

Dikotter, F. (1998) *Imperfect Conceptions; Medical Knowledge, Birth Defects and Eugenics in China*. London: Hurst & Co.

Douglas, Rev. Carstairs, with a supplement by Barclay, Rev. T. (1899) *Chinese–English Dictionary of the Vernacular or Spoken Language of Amoy*, London.

Duara, P. (1988) *Culture, Power, and the State: Rural North China, 1900–1942*, Stanford: Stanford University Press.

—— (1995) *Rescuing History from the Nation: Questioning Narratives of Modern China*. Chicago: University of Chicago Press.

Durkheim, E. (1982) *The Rules of Sociological Method*, London: Macmillan.

Dutton, M. (1988) 'Policing the Chinese household', *Economy and Society* 17:2.

—— (2000) 'Inflections of the sacred: mango Mao and other stories', paper presented to the conference on *Diasporas of Mind/Dilemmas of Culture/Diverging Identities: New Directions in Contemporary Chinese Cultural Studies*, London: University of Westminster.

Eberhard, W. (1958) *Chinese Festivals*, London and New York: Abelard Schurnan.

Farquhar, J. (1989) 'Multiplicity, point of view and responsibility in traditional Chinese healing', paper presented to the American Sociological Association.

—— (1991) 'Time and text: approaching contemporary Chinese medical practice through analysis of a published case', in Young, A. (ed) *Paths of Asian Medicine*, Dordrecht D. ReideL.

Fei Hsiao-tung (1939) *Peasant Life in China*, London: Routledge & Kegan Paul.

Feuchtwang, S. (1974a) *An Anthropological Analysis of Chinese Geomancy*, Vientiane and Paris: Vithagna.

—— (1974b) 'City temples in Taibei under three regimes', in Elvin, M. and Skinner, G.W. (eds) *The Chinese City Between Two Worlds*, Stanford: Stanford University Press.

—— (1975) 'Investigating religion', in Bloch, M. (ed.) *Marxist Analyses and Social Anthropology*, London: Malaby.

—— (1977) 'School temple and City God', in Skinner, G.W. (ed.) *The City in Late Imperial China*, Stanford: Stanford University Press.

—— (1989a) 'The problem of "superstition" in the People's Republic of China', in Benavides, G. and Daly, M.W. (eds) *Religion and Political Power*, Albany: State University of New York Press.

—— (1989b) 'The study of Chinese popular religion', *Revue Europeenne des Sciences Sociales* 27:84, Geneva.

—— (1991) 'A Chinese religion exists', in Baker, H. and Feuchtwang, S. (eds) *An Old State in New Settings: Studies in the Social Anthropology of China in Memory of Maurice Freedman*, Oxford: Journal of the Anthropological Society of Oxford.

—— (1998) 'What is a village?' in Edward Vermeer, Frank Pieke and Woei Lien Chong (eds), *Cooperative and Collective in China's Rural Development; Between State and Private Interests*. Armonk and London: M.E.Sharpe.

Feuchtwang, S. and Wang Mingming (1991) 'The politics of culture, or a contest of histories; representations of Chinese popular religion', *Dialectical Anthropology*, 1:1.

—— (forthcoming), *Grassroots Charisma in China*. London and New York: Routledge.

FLP (Foreign Languages Press) (1981) *Resolution on CPC History (1949–81)*. Beijing.

Flower, J. and Leonard, P. (1996) 'Community values and state cooptation; civil society in the Sichuan countryside', in Chris Hann and Elizabeth Dunn (eds), *Civil Society; Challenging Western Models*. London and New York: Routledge.

—— (1998) 'Defining cultural life in the Chinese countryside: the case of the Chuan Zhu temple' in Edward Vermeer, Frank Pieke and Woei Lien Chong (eds), *Cooperative and Collective in China's Rural Development; Between State and Private Interests*. Armonk and London: M.E. Sharpe.

Gane, M. (1983) 'Durkheim: the sacred language', *Economy and Society* 12:1.

Gao Yuan (1987) *Born Red*. Stanford, California: Stanford University Press.

Geertz, C. (1966) 'Religion as a cultural system' in Michael Banton (ed) *Anthropological Approaches to the Study of Religion*. London: Tavistock Publications.

Gladney, D. (1991) *Muslim Chinese; Ethnic Nationalism in the People's Republic*. Cambridge (Mass): Harvard University Press.

Graezer, F. (1999) 'Le "yangge" en Chine contemporaine; pratique populaire quotidienne et vie associative de quartier', *Perspectives Chinoises* 53, pp 31–43.

Granet, M. (1925) 'Remarques sur le Taoisme ancien', in Stein, R. (ed.) (1953), *Etudes Sociologiques sur la Chine*, Paris: PUF.

Guo Zhichao (1985) 'Minnan nongcun yige shugu de minjian zongjiao chutan' (An enquiry into the popular religion of a community in rural southern Fujian), *Renleixue Yanjiu* (Anthropology Research), Xiamen: Xiamen University.

ter Haar, B. (1990) 'The genesis and spread of temple cults in Fukien', in E.B.Vermeer (ed) *Development and Decline of Fukien Province in the 17th and 18th Centuries*, Leiden: Brill.

—— (1996) 'China's inner demons; the political impact of the demonological paradigm' *China Information* vol 11 nos 2/3 pp 54–88.

Hamilton, G. (1989) 'Heaven is high and the emperor is far away; legitimacy and structure in the Chinese state', *Revue Europeenne des Sciences Sociales* 27:84, Geneva.

Harrell, S. (1974) 'When a ghost becomes a god' in Wolf, A.P. (ed.) *Religion and Ritual in Chinese Society*, Stanford: Stanford University Press.

Henderson, J. (1984) *The Development and Decline of Chinese Cosmology*, New York: Columbia University Press.

Holm, D. (1991) *Art and Ideology in Revolutionary China*. Oxford: Clarendon Press.

Hou Ching-lang (1979) 'The Chinese belief in baleful stars', in Seidel, A. and Welch, H. (eds) *Facets of Taoism*, New Haven and London: Yale University Press.

Hsiao Kung-chuan (1960) *Rural China: Imperial Control in the Nineteenth Century*, Seattle: University of Washington Press.

Jenner, W. (1992) *The Tyranny of History: The Roots of China's Crisis*. London: Allen Lane, The Penguin Press.

Jones, C. (1999) *Buddhism in Taiwan: Religion and the State 1660–1990*. Honolulu: University of Hawai'i Press.

Jing Jun (1996) *The Temple of Memories: History, Power, and Morality in a Chinese Village*. Stanford: Stanford University Press.

Jordan, D. and Overmyer, D. (1986) *The Flying Phoenix: Aspects of Chinese Sectarianism in Taiwan*, Princeton: Princeton University Press.

Ku Hok-bun (1999) *Defining Zeren; Cultural Politics in a Chinese Village*, University of London: unpublished PhD dissertation.

Lagerwey, J. (1987) *Taoist Ritual in Chinese Society and History*, London: Collier Macmillan.

Levenson, J. (1965) *Confucian China and its Modern Fate; a Trilogy, 3: The Problem of Historical Significance*, Berkeley: University of California Press.

Levi, J. (1989) *Les Fonctionnaires Divins; Politique, Despotisme, et Mystique en Chine Ancienne*, Paris: Editions du Seuil.

Li Yiyuan (1988) 'Taiwan minjian zongjiao de xiandai qushi' (Trends in Taiwanese popular religion), paper presented to the international conference on Chinese Religious Ethics and Modernization, University of Hong Kong.

Lin Meirong (1986) 'Yu jisituan lai kan caotunzhende difang zuzhi (From ritual sphere to grassroots local organisation)', *Minzuxue Yanjiusuo Jikan* 62: 53–114 (Taipei, Academia Sinica, Institute of Ethnology).

—— (1988) 'Yu jisituan dao xinyingtuan, Taiwan minjian shehuide dicheng hengcheng yu fazhan (From ritual sphere to organisation of believers, popular social extension and development of locality in Taiwan) *Zhongguo Haiyang Fazhanshilun Wenji* (Historical Papers on Chinese Coastal Development) 3: 95–125 (Taipei: Academia Sinica, Sun Yatsen Institute).

Liu Jiwan (1960) 'Taiwan sheng simiao jiatang diaocha biao' (A table of religious buildings in Taiwan province), *Taiwan Wenxian* (Taiwan Documents) 2:2.

Liu, L. (2000) '*Beijing Sojourners in New York*: postsocialism and the question of ideology in global media culture', *Positions* 7:3.

Liu Xin (1995) *Zhao Villagers – Everyday Practices in a Post-Reform Chinese Village*, University of London: unpublished Ph D dissertation.

Luo Hong'guang (1998) 'Quanli yu quanwei – Heilongtande fuhaotixi yu zhengze pinglun (Politics and authority – on the symbolic system and politics of Heilongtan)' in Wang Mingming and Wang Sifu (eds) *Xiangtu Shehuide Zhixu, Gongzheng, yu Quanwei (Order, Justice and Authority in Rural Chinese Society)*. Beijing: Zhongguo Zhengfadaxue Chubanshe (Press of the University of Government and Law) pp. 333–388.

Ma Bo (1995) *Blood Red Sunset; A Memoir of the Chinese Cultural Revolution*. New York: Penguin Books.

McCartee, Rev. (1869–70) article XI in *Journal of the North China Branch of the Royal Asiatic Society*.

Madsen, R. (1984) *Morality and Power in a Chinese Village*. Berkeley: University of California Press.

—— (1998) *China's Catholics; Tragedy and Hope in an Emerging Civil Society*. Berkeley, Los Angeles, London: University of California Press.

Major, J.S. (1987) 'The meaning of Hsing-te', in Le Blanc, C. and Blader, S. (eds), *Chinese Ideas about Nature and Society; Studies in Honour of Derk Bodde*, Hong Kong: Hong Kong University Press.

Mather, R.B. (1979) 'K'ou Ch'ien-chih and the Taoist theocracy', in Seidel, A. and Welch, H. (eds) *Facets of Taoism*, New Haven and London: Yale University Press.

Mathews, R.H. (1956) *Chinese–English · Dictionary*, Cambridge, Mass.: Harvard University Press.

Mauss, M. (1979) 'Some recent services of psychology to sociology', in *Sociology and Psychology; Essays by Marcel Mauss*, London: Routledge & Keg an Paul.

Menshikov, L., Petrov, V., and Rudova, M. (1988) *Chinese Popular Prints*, Leningrad: Aurora Art Publishers.

Naquin, S. (1985) 'The transmission of White Lotus sectarianism in late imperial China', in Johnson, D., Nathan, A., and Rawski, E. (eds) *Popular Culture in Late Imperial China*, Berkeley: University of California Press.

Needham, J. (1959) *Science and Civilisation in China, 3: Mathematics and the Sciences of the Heavens and the Earth*, Cambridge: Cambridge University Press.

—— (1965) *Time and Eastern Man*, Occasional Paper No. 21, London: Royal Anthropological Institute.

Needham, R. (1972) *Belief, Language, and Experience*, Oxford: Basil Blackwell.

Overmyer, D. (1985) 'Values in Chinese sectarian literature: Ming and Ch'ing *pao-chuan*', in Johnson, D., Nathan, A., and Rawski, E. (eds) *Popular Culture in Late Imperial China*, Berkeley: University of California Press.

Palmer, Martin (ed.) (1986) *T'ung Shu; the Ancient Chinese Almanac*, London: Rider.

Palmer, Michael (undated) 'Stone Lake Market in late imperial times', unpublished chapter of a PhD dissertation, University of London.

Perry, E. (1980) *Rebels and Revolutionaries in North China, 1845–1945*, Stanford: Stanford University Press.

Potter, S.H. and J.M. (1990) *China's Peasants; the Anthropology of a Revolution*, Cambridge: Cambridge University Press.

Rowe, W.T. (1990) 'The public sphere in modem China', *Modern China* 16:3.

Sangren, P.S. (1987) *History and Magical Power in a Chinese Community*, Stanford: Stanford University Press.

—— (1988) 'History and the rhetoric of legitimacy: the Ma Tsu cult of Taiwan', *Comparative Studies in Society and History* 30.

Saso, M. (1965) 'Chinese new year's customs in Taiwan', *Journal of the China Society* 4, Taibei.

—— (1972) *Taoism and the Rite of Cosmic Renewal*, Pullman: Washington State University Press.

Schipper, K. (1966) 'The divine jester; some remarks on the gods of the Chinese marionette theater', *Bulletin of the Institute of Ethnology*, Taibei: Academia Sinica, 21.

—— (1977) 'Neighbourhood cult associations in traditional Tainan' in G.William Skinner, *The City in Late Imperial China*. Stanford: Stanford University Press.

—— (1982) *Le Corps Taoiste*, Paris: Fayard.

—— (1985) 'Vernacular and classical ritual in Taoism', *Journal of Asian Studies* 45:1.

Seaman, G. (1978) *Temple Organisation in a Chinese Village*, Taibei: The Chinese Association for Folklore.

—— (1982) 'Spirit money: an interpretation', *Journal of Chinese Religions* 10.

Shahar, M. and Weller, R. (1996) *Unruly Gods; Divinity and society in China*, Honolulu: University of Hawai'i Press.

'Shidian xu' (The order of the rites of *shidian*) (1686) in *Honggong Jing Shilu* (Record of paying respects in the school-temple), 1835 edition.

'Sidian' (ceremonial statutes) *Taiwan Xianzhi* (Area record of Taiwan county), 1721.

Siu, H. (1989) *Agents and Victims in South China; Accomplices in Rural Revolution*, New Haven and London: Yale University Press.

—— (1990) 'Recycling tradition: culture, history and political economy in the Chrysanthemum festivals of south China', *Comparative Study of Society and History*, pp 765–794.

Skinner, G. (1965) 'Marketing and social structure in rural China. Part2' *Journal of Asian Studies* 24: 2.

—— (1964–5, reprinted 1993), *Marketing and Social Structure in Rural China*. Ann Arbor: Association for Asian Studies.

—— (2000) 'Space and time in the analysis of Chinese society' paper presented to the Third International Conference on Sinology, Academia Sinica: Nankang, Taipei.

Spence, J. (1997) *God's Chinese Son; The Taiping Heavenly Kingdom of Hong Xiuquan*. London: Flamingo.

Skorupski, J. (1976) *Symbol and Theory: A Philosophical Study of Theories in Social Anthropology*, Cambridge: Cambridge University Press.

Stein, R. (1979) 'Religious Taoism and popular religion from the second to seventh centuries', in Seidel, A. and Welch, H. (eds) *Facets of Taoism*, New Haven and London: Yale University Press.

Strickmann, M. (1979) 'On the alchemy of T'ao Hung-ching', in Seidel, A. and Welch, H. (eds) *Facets of Taoism*, New Haven and London: Yale University Press.

Suzuki, S. (1934) (trans. Guo Xianzhi and Feng Zamin) *Taiwan Xian Guanxi Yu Xinyang* (Taiwanese Customs and Beliefs), Taibei.

'Tanmiao' (Temples), in *Ningbofuzhi* (Area record of Ningbo prefecture) (1560).

'Tanmiao' (Temples), in *Ningbofuzhi* (Area record of Ningbo prefecture) (1733).

'Tanmiao' (Temples), in *Yin xianzhi* (Area record of Yin [which is Ningbo] county) (1788).

Teiser, S.E. (1988) *The Ghost Festival in Medieval China*, Princeton: Princeton University Press.

Thaxton, R. (1983) *China Turned Rightside Up: Revolutionary Legitimacy in the Peasant World*, New Haven and London: Yale University Press.

Topley, M. (1975) 'Marriage resistance in rural Kuangtung' in Margery Wolf and Roxanne Witke (eds) *Women in Chinese Society. Stanford: Stanford University Press*, pp 71–76.

Tang Tsou (2000) 'Interpreting the revolution in China', *Modern China* 26: 2. pp 205–238.

Vandermeersch, L. (1985) 'An enquiry into the Chinese conception of the law', in Schram, S. (ed.) *The Scope of State Power in China*, London: School of Oriental and African Studies, University of London, and Hong Kong: Chinese University Press.

Vermander, B. (1999) 'La loi et la roue; l'irruption du mouvement *Falungong* et les avatars de la "civilisation spirituelle"', *Perspectives Chinoises* 53 pp 14–21.

Wang Shih-ch'ing (1974) 'Religious organisation in the history of a Chinese town', in Wolf, A.P. (ed.) *Religion and Ritual in Chinese Society*, Stanford: Stanford University Press.

Ward, B. (1979) 'Not merely players: drama, art, and ritual in traditional China', *Man* 14:1.

Watson, J. (1985) 'Standardising the gods: the promotions of T'ien Hou ('Empress of Heaven') along the South China Coast, 960–1960' in Johnson, D., Nathan, A. and Rawski, E. (eds) *Popular Culture in Late imperial China*, Berkeley: University of California Press.

—— (1991) 'Waking the dragon: visions of the Chinese imperial state in local myth', in Baker, H. and Feuchtwang, S. (eds) *An Old State in New Setting: Studies in the Social Anthropology of China in Memory of Maurice Freedman*, Oxford: Journal of the Anthropological Society of Oxford.

—— and Rawski, E. (eds) (1988) *Death Ritual in Late Imperial and Modern China*, Berkeley: University of California Press.

Welch, H. (1958) *The Parting of the Way*, London: Methuen.

Weller, R. (1987) *Unities and Diversities in Chinese Religion*, London: Macmillan.

White, G. (1976) *The Politics of Class and Class Origin: The Case of the Cultural Revolution*. Canberra: Australian National University Contemporary China Centre.

White, L. (1989) *Policies of Chaos; The Organizational Causes of Violence in China's Cultural Revolution*. Princeton, New Jersey: Princeton University Press.

Wilkerson, J. (1994) 'The "ritual master" and his "temple corporation" rituals', a contribution to *Minjian Xinying yu Zhongguo Wenhua Guoji Yantaohui Lunwenji* (Collected papers of the international conference on popular beliefs and Chinese culture), Taibei: Sinology Research Centre Publications.

Wilson, S. (ed.) (1983) *Saints and their Cults; Studies in Religious Sociology, Folklore and History*, Cambridge: Cambridge University Press.

Wolf, A. (1974) 'Gods, ghosts and ancestors' in Wolf, A.P. (ed.) *Religion and Ritual in Chinese Society*, Stanford: Stanford University Press.

Wu Cheng-han (1988) *The Temple Fairs in Late Imperial China*, PhD dissertation, Princeton University.

Xu Wenchu (1996) 'Jiangcun – Jiangzhen; Miaogang fazhande jiaobu (Jiang village – Jiang town; the steps of Miaogang's development)' in Wujiang Shizheng Xie (People's Consultative Conference of Wujiang City) (ed), *Wenhua* (Culture). Beijing: Zhongguo Wenhua Chubanshe (Chinese Culture Press).

Xue Yibing and Wu Ben (1987) 'Qu Jia Ying "yinyue hui" de diaocha yu yanjiu' (Investigation and research into the 'music society' of Qu Jia Ying), *Zhongguo Yinyuexue* (Musicology in China) 2.

Yang, C.K. (1961) *Religion in Chinese Society*, Berkeley: University of California Press.

Zhou Ying (1988) 'Fengjian mixin yu qunzhong wenhua...' (Feudal superstitions and mass culture...), *Qunzhong Wenhua* (Mass Culture) 5.

Zhu Xiaoyang and Benjamin Perry (eds) (1994), 'The *qigong* boom', *Chinese Sociology and Anthropology* 27:1. Armonk: M.E.Sharpe.

Zito, A.R. (1987) 'City gods, filiality, hegemony', *Modern China* 13:3.

# Glossary

(not including personal and place names, nor titles of Chinese publications)

| | | |
|---|---|---|
| An Lung Song Hu | 安龙送虎 | Pacify the Dragon and Send Off the Tiger |
| *ang* (Taiwanese) | 翁 红 | old man or god, or red figure |
| *anwei* | 安慰 | find consolation |
| *anping* | 安平 | secure peace |
| *bai* | 拜 | pay respect, obeisance |
| Bai Hu | 白虎 | White Tiger |
| *baibai* | 拜拜 | pay respect, a festival |
| *bao* | 报 | reciprocal return |
| *baojia* | 保甲 | a system of mutual surveillance |
| Bao Sheng Da Di | 保圣大帝 | The Great Emperor who Protects Life |
| Baoyi Dafu | 保仪大夫 | The Great Minister who Protects the Rules of Propriety |
| Baoyi Zunwang | 保仪尊王 | The Venerable King who Protects the Rules of Propriety |
| *biao* | 表 | memorial |
| *bing* | 丙 | 3rd of the ten celestial stems |
| Cai Lun | 蔡伦 | the inventor of paper |
| Cao Kun (Taiwanese) | 灶君 | Stove God |
| Chan | 禅 | the Daoist-influenced school of Buddhism founded in China |
| *chang* | 场 | area |
| *chedi* | 彻底 | thorough |
| Che Gong | 车公 | Vehicle God |
| *chen* | 沈 | perish |
| Cheng Huang | 城隍 | Walls and Moats, City |
| *chong* | 冲 | clash |
| *chuantong* | 统通 | tradition |
| *ci* | 祠 | Hall |
| Ciouq-thao Kong (Taiwanese) | 石头公 | God of the Rock |
| *cun* | 村 | village |
| *cun nei* | 村内 | village |
| Da Fu | 大夫 | Great Minister |
| Da Mu Gong | 大墓公 | Mass Grave Shrine |

| | | |
|---|---|---|
| Da Shi Ye | 大士爷 | the Militant Guan Yin |
| Da Zhong Ye | 大众爷 | General in Charge of the Mass Dead |
| *dagu* (Taiwanese) | 大龟 | great turtle or tortoise bun |
| *dantian* | 丹田 | Cinnebar Field, crucible |
| Dao Fa Er Men | 道法二门 | Two Gates of Daoist Method (sect) |
| *daochang* | 道场 | the Daoists' area |
| *daoshi* | 道士 | Daoist priest |
| *deng* | 灯 | lantern |
| Dengzhen Yinjue | 登真隐诀 | Concealed Instructions for Ascent to Perfection |
| Di | 地 | the Terranean (or lower) region of the cosmological triad |
| *di* | 地 | earth |
| Di sha | 地煞 | Malign Earthly Emanations |
| *difang* | 地方 | place, locality |
| Diji Zhu | 地基主 | God or Ancestor of the Foundations |
| *dilong* | 地龙 | dragon of the locality |
| Dizang Wang | 地臧王 | the *bodhisattva* who looks after the dead |
| *ding* | 丁 | 4th of the ten celestial stems |
| *ding qian* | 丁钱 | collection of festival tax from households for every male member |
| *dongnei* | 洞内 | within/this side of the tunnel |
| *dongwai* | 洞外 | beyond the tunnel |
| *dou* | 斗 | dipper |
| *dou deng* | 斗灯 | dipper lantern |
| *duiri* | 队日 | Young Pioneers Day |
| *duoxing* | 惰性 | inertia |
| Enzhu Gong | 恩主公 | Merciful Lords |
| *fa* | 法 | law, doctrine, method, magic |
| *fa biao* | 发表 | send a memorial |
| *fa huo* | 发火 | flaring fire |
| *falun'gong* | 法纶功，法纶大发 | or *falundafa* The Method of the Buddhist Wheel of Law |
| *fa lu* | 发炉 | flaring incense |
| Fa Zhu Gong | 法主公 | God of Ritual Method |
| *fang* | 房 | sublineage |
| *fang jun* | 放军 | dispose troops |
| *fangzhi* | 方志 | local gazateer |
| *fashi* | 法士 | Daoist practitioner, magician |
| *fen deng* | 分灯 | ritual of dividing fire or lanterns |
| *fenxiang* | 分香 | division of incense from a root temple |
| *fengshen* | 风神 | appearance |
| *fengshui* | 风水 | the art of siting and timing |
| *fengse* | 风色 | countenance |
| *fengsu* | 风俗 | custom |
| *fu* | 符 | talisman, or charm |
| *fu* | 福 | good fortune |
| Fude Zhengshen | 福德正神 | Correct Spirit of Luck and Virtue, title of the Locality God |

| | | |
|---|---|---|
| Fuyou Dijun | 孚佑帝君 | Lord Emperor of Widespread Protection, title of the deified Lü Dongbin |
| *fu lu zhu* | 副炉主 | deputy master of the incense burner |
| *fu qi* | 福气 | energies of good fortune |
| *fuyue* | 副约 | deputy head of a pact |
| *gan* | 感 | responsiveness |
| Gao Gong Fashi | 高功法士 | Magician of High Merit |
| *ge* | 格 | control, correct, influence |
| *gei dajia banshe* | 给大家办事 | organise for everyone |
| *geng* | 庚 | 7th of the ten celestial stems |
| *germen* | 哥儿门 | 'brothers', male buddies |
| *gongde* | 功德 | merit |
| *gonghe* | 恭和 | mutual congratulations |
| *gongqi* | 公启 | public notice |
| *gongxi* | 恭喜 | congratulations |
| *gu* | 孤 | orphan |
| *gu hun* | 孤魂 | orphan souls |
| *guqi* | 古气 | old and fading energies |
| Guan Di | 关帝 | Emperor Guan, the god of military and strategic prowess |
| Guan Yin | 观音 | *bodhisattva* Avalokitesvara, Goddess of Mercy |
| Guan (Shi) Yin | 观世音 | the *bodhisattva* of Mercy |
| Guan Yin Niangniang | 观音娘娘 | Goddess of Mercy |
| *gui* | 鬼 | ghosts, demons |
| *gui* | 癸 | 10th of the ten celestial stems |
| *guishen* | 鬼神 | spirits |
| *guonian* | 过年 | new year |
| *guoyu* | 国语 | national language |
| *haohan* | 好汉 | good men, knights (samurai) |
| *hao xiongdi* | 好兄弟 | the good brothers, euphemism for ghosts |
| *haokan* | 好看 | attractive, entertaining |
| *haoxin* | 好心 | a good heart |
| *hejia* | 合家 | the whole family |
| *heping* | 和平 | peace |
| Hei Hu Ling Guan | 黑虎灵官 | Black Tiger Efficaceous Official |
| *hong* | 红 | red |
| *honggui* | 红龟 | red turtle bun |
| Hou Deng Shen | 猴灯神 | Monkey Lamp Spirit |
| Hou Tu | 后土 | tomb guardian |
| *houqi* | 候气 | watching for the pneumas |
| *hu* | 笏 | a ceremonial tablet of deferential reverence, a ritual tablet held by a Daoist practitioner |
| Hu Ye | 虎爷 | Tiger General |
| *huai* | 坏 | wicked |
| *huan-a* (Taiwanese) | 番子 | barbarian |
| *hui* | 会 | meeting, assembly |
| *huitou* | 会头 | head of the assembly |

| | | |
|---|---|---|
| *hun* | 魂 | soul |
| *hundun* | 混沌 | primal chaos |
| Ia Iu Sin (Taiwanese) | 夜游神 | Night Wandering Soul |
| Ia Kui (Taiwanese) | 野鬼 | Wilderness Demon |
| *ji* | 祭 | sacrifice |
| *ji* | 己 | 6th of the ten celestial stems |
| *ji dian bu* | 祭典部 | office of sacrificial ceremonies |
| *jia* | 甲 | 1st of the ten celestial stems |
| *jianei* | 家内 | household, family |
| *jianmin* | 贱民 | mean people |
| *jiao* | 醮 | the great offering and rite for cosmic readjustment |
| *jiaoju* | 醮局 | office of the organisation of the *jiao* ceremony |
| *jin* | 金 | gold |
| Jin Guang Ming Chang Zhai Tian | 金光明长齐天 | Golden Light Perpetual Penance for Heaven |
| *jin xiang* | 近香 | offer incense, procession |
| *jinian* | 纪念 | commemoration |
| *jing* | 敬 | honour, pay respect |
| *jing* | 经 | classic |
| *jisi* | 祭祀 | sacrifices and offerings – section of local gazeteers |
| *jiushou* | 纠手 | organisers, hands to bring people together |
| *jiuxing* | 救星 | saviour, emancipator |
| *jun* | 军 | troops |
| *kai guang* | 开光 | opening the light or eyes of an image |
| *kao jun* | 犒军 | feeding the troops |
| *kexue* | 科学 | scientific knowledge |
| *keyi* | 科仪 | liturgy |
| *ke* | 科 | performance |
| *la* | 腊 | a set of annual rites |
| *lang jun ye* | 郎君爷 | the young gentleman |
| Lao Tai *miao* | 老太庙 | temple of Old Tai |
| *lao taitai* | 老太太 | old lady or ladies |
| *lao tong* | 老童 | the old boy |
| Lao Zi | 老子 | the author of the Daoist classic, the Way and Its Power; old infant; old master |
| *li* | 理 | ordering principles |
| *li* | 礼 | rites, propriety |
| *li* | 里 | neighbourhood |
| *li* | 厉 | unworshipped ghosts |
| Li Chun | 立春 | the solar period of the Establishing of Spring |
| *li dou fa hui* | 礼斗法会 | assembly for the ritual of the Dipper |
| Li Nuojia or Li Nazha | 李那吒 | a powerful and unruly boy god |
| Li Shimin | 李世民 | the first Tang emperor |
| Li Tan | 厉坛 | Altar for Those-who-died-without-a-future |

269

| | | |
|---|---|---|
| Lie Shen | 烈神 | Eminent Gods |
| *lieng sia:* (Taiwanese) | 灵圣 | numinous power |
| *lin* | 临 | neighbourhood |
| *ling* | 灵 | uncanny intelligence, effectivity |
| *ling* | 令 | command |
| Ling Bao Pai | 灵宝派 | Efficacious Treasure Sect (of Daoism) |
| *linggan* | 灵感 | efficacious response |
| *lianhuanhua* | 连环画 | comic strip |
| *linghun* | 灵魂 | soul |
| Liu Huang | 刘皇 | Emperor Huang |
| *liumang* | 流氓 | brigand, gangster |
| *lu* | 律 | law |
| Lü Dongbin | 吕洞宾 | a Daoist celebrated as one of the Eight Immortals |
| *lu zhu* | 炉主 | master of the incense burner |
| *luan* | 乱 | disorder |
| Long Shan Si | 龙山寺 | The Temple of Dragon Mountain (Mengjia, Taipei) |
| Luo Shu | 洛书 | the River Diagram |
| Ma Zu | 妈祖 | Ancestral Goddess |
| Mang Shen | 芒神 | the Spring Ox driver |
| *mi* | 迷 | confused |
| *mianzi* | 面子 | face |
| *miao* | 庙 | temple |
| *miaohui* | 庙会 | temple fairs |
| *ming* | 命 | fate |
| Ming Tang | 明堂 | Hall for Clarification |
| *minjian guanxi* (or *xiguan*) | 民间惯习 | popular custom |
| *mixin* | 迷信 | superstition |
| *moshu* | 魔术 | perform conjuring magic |
| *mogui* | 魔鬼 | malign demons |
| *nian* | 年 | year |
| *nian li* | 年礼 | annual ritual occasions |
| *nian tou* | 年头 | beginning of the year |
| *nian wei* | 年尾 | end of the year |
| Niangniang | 娘娘 | female goddess |
| *pai* | 牌 | tablet |
| *pingan* | 平安 | peace |
| *pingan hejing* | 平安合境 | peace in the whole region |
| Pingguo Wang | 平国王 | Monarch of a Peaceful (Pacified) Country |
| *pu* | 堡 | military garrison, small area of military command |
| *pu du* | 普度 | general salvation |
| *pusu* | 朴素 | simple, plain |
| *qi* | 气 | pneuma, breaths, energies |
| *qigong* | 气动 | exercises for the cultivation of breaths, or energies |
| Qi Nü | 七女 | the Seventh Woman |
| *qian* | 钱 | money |

270

| | | |
|---|---|---|
| *qian* | 签 | divination lot |
| *qing* | 清 | pure |
| Qing Ming | 清明 | Pure and Bright, the occasion for tomb cleaning and veneration of ancestors |
| Qingshui Zushi Gong | 清水祖师公 | Ancestral Master of the Clear Water (Rock) |
| *qiu* | 求 | plead |
| Ren | 人 | the Human (Middle) region of the cosmological triad |
| *ren* | 人 | human |
| *ren* | 壬 | 9th of the ten celestial stems |
| *renao* | 热闹 | heat and noise |
| San Guan Da Di | 三官大帝 | Supreme Rulers of the Three Offices |
| San Jie Gong | 三界公 | The Offices of the Three Regions |
| *sanjue li* | 三爵礼 | the rite of the three libations |
| Sannai | 三奶 | The Third Matriarch (school of Daoism) |
| Seng-ong Ia (Taiwanese) | | see Cheng Huang |
| *sha* | 刹 | kill |
| Shan'gui | 山桂，山鬼 | Mountain Laurel or Mountain Demon |
| Shang Di | 上帝 | Supreme Ruler |
| *shangshan caiyun, yanhe qushui* | 上山采云，沿河取水 | going up to the mountain to collect clouds and down to the river to fetch water |
| *shang yuan* | 上元 | the first or upper primordial |
| *shanshu* | 善书 | good books |
| *shao lao* | 少牢 | lesser meat offerings |
| *she* | 社 | locality |
| She Ji Tan | 社稷坛 | Altar for Land and Grain |
| *shen* | 神 | spirit, god |
| *shen e* | 神额 | the spirit's sum |
| Shen Nong | 神农 | patron deity of agriculture |
| Sheng Ma | 圣妈 | Saintly Woman |
| *shenling* | 神灵 | spiritual power |
| *shenming* | 神明 | god |
| *shenminghui* | 神明会 | religious association |
| *sheng* | 圣 | saint, sage |
| *sheng dan* | 圣诞 | birthday |
| *shen'gui* | 神鬼 | spirit |
| *shengli* | 牲礼 | the offering of three or five meats |
| *shicai* | 释菜 | minor offerings |
| *shidian* | 释奠 | ceremony of veneration and recompense |
| *shoukuren* | 收苦人 | reapers of bitterness, farmers |
| *shoukurende tou* | 收苦人的头 | head of farmers |
| *shuangxi* | 双喜 | double luck |
| *shu ren bu shu zhen* | 输人不输阵 | spend men not to lose the front or battle-line |
| Si Da Zhu | 四大柱 | the Four Great Pillars |
| Si Ling | 四灵 | the Four Potentates |
| Si Sheng | 四圣 | the Four Saints/Sages |
| *sidian* | 祀典 | ceremonial statutes |

| | | |
|---|---|---|
| *song xiong xing* | 送凶星 | seeing off the baleful star |
| *suona* | 唢呐 | wind instrument like a shawm |
| *taijiquan* | 太极拳 | slow exercises of fighting or strategic movements |
| *tai lao* | 太牢 | great meat offering |
| Tai Sui | 太岁 | the Great Year, 12–year cycle of the planet Jupiter |
| Tai Yi | 太一 | Great Unity |
| *tan* | 坛 | altar |
| *tang* | 堂 | Hall |
| *tebie ling* | 特别灵 | exceptionally efficaceous |
| *te hng* (Taiwanese) | 地方 | area |
| *tham ci:* (Taiwanese) | 贪钱 | covet money, take bribes |
| Thai Pe Kim Sien (Taiwanese) | 太白金仙 | Great White and Gold Immortal |
| *Thi: Kong, Te Kong, Bin-cng kha, Sai-thang-a Ong* (Twns) | 天公地公 xxx 屎桶子王 | God of heaven, god of earth, under the bed, the god of the shit bucket |
| Thote Ma (Taiwanese) | 土地妈 | wife of the Locality God |
| Thote Kong (Taiwanese) | 土地公 | the Locality God |
| Tian | 天 | Heaven, the upper region of the cosmological triad |
| Tian Gang | 天罡 | the bowl of the Dipper constellation |
| Tian Gong | 天公 | God(s) of Heaven |
| Tian Gou | 天狗 | Celestial Dog |
| Tian Hou | 天后 | Celestial Consort (Ma Zu) |
| Tian Zun | 天尊 | Venerable Celestial |
| Tianmen Hui | 天门会 | Heavengate Association |
| Tian Shi | 天师 | Celestial Master |
| Tian Xuan Yuanshuai | 天玄元帅 | Celestial and Mysterious Marshal |
| *Tiandi shenming jigan fadu* | 天地神明基于法度 | The Cardinal Principles of the Bright Spirits (Gods) of the Universe |
| *tishen* | 替身 | replacement body |
| *tongji* | 童乩 | spirit medium |
| *toujia* | 头家 | head household |
| *tuanlian* | 团练 | militia band |
| Tudi Gong | 土地公 | Locality God |
| *tugu shen* | 土毂神 | soil and grain spirit |
| *waishen* | 外神 | outside spirit |
| Wan Xi Tong Gui | 万喜同归 | Ten Thousand Joys for Those Gathered Here |
| Wangye | 王爷 | Kings |
| *wen* | 文 | literary accomplishment |
| Wen'ge | 文革 | Cultural Revolution |
| *wenhua* | 文化 | culture |
| Wen Miao | 文庙 | Temple of Civil or Literary Accomplishment |
| Wen Wu Zun Wang | 文武尊王 | Civil and Military Venerable Kings |
| *weng* | 翁 | old man |

| | | |
|---|---|---|
| *wenming* | 文明 | civilisation |
| *wu* | 武 | military accomplishment |
| *wu* | 戊 | 5th of the ten celestial stems |
| *wuhaoban jiti* | 五好班集体 | school class of five distinctions |
| Wu Miao | 武庙 | Temple of Military Accomplishment |
| Wu Sha | 五煞 | Five Malign Influences |
| *wudao* | 舞蹈 | dance |
| *Wu men* | 午门 | central southern gate |
| *wu xing* | 五行 | the five phases or elements |
| *xi xin* | 喜心 | a good heart |
| *xiayuan* | 下愿 | to make a pledge and state a wish |
| *xian* | 县 | a county |
| *xian* | 仙 | immortal |
| *Xian Gong* | 仙公 | the Immortal God |
| *xiang* | 乡 | a rural township or administrative area |
| *xiang pian* | 香片 | incense, or fragrant, wafer |
| *xiangyue* | 乡约 | village pact |
| *xiao* | 孝 | filial duty |
| *xiao jin* | 消金 | to consume or burn gold |
| *xiao fashi* | 小法师 | a minor magician or Daoist practitioner |
| *xiao guonian* | 小过年 | minor new year |
| *xie* | 邪 | incorrect, aberrant, heterodox |
| *xin* | 辛 | 8th of the ten celestial stems |
| *xin mixin* | 信米信 | believe in superstition |
| *xing* | 形 | forms |
| *xiu* or *su* | 宿 | stellar mansion |
| *xiu shen* | 羞神 | malign spirits |
| Xu Yuan | 许远 | a Tang dynasty general, loyal to the emperor against the usurper An Lushan |
| Xuan Tian Shang Di | 玄天上帝 | Supreme Ruler of Obscure Heaven |
| *xuetong* | 血统 | blood line |
| *yamen* | 衙门 | imperial magistrate's office and court |
| *yang* | 阳 | one of the dual principles of cosmological generation |
| *yang'ge* | 秧歌 | a ritual dance, short dramatic tableau |
| *yi* | 谊 | correct, rule |
| *yi* | 乙 | 2nd of the ten celestial stems |
| *yin* | 阴 | one of the dual principles of cosmological generation |
| *yin* | 淫 | excessive, depraved |
| *yinsi* | 淫祀 | excessive cults |
| *yinshen* | 隐神 | dark gods |
| *ying'gan* | 应感 | responsiveness |
| *ying xiang* | 迎香 | to welcome incense, procession |
| *yingshen saihui* | 迎神赛会 | competitive procession assemblies for greeting spirits |
| *yinyang* | 阴阳 | the paired principles of cosmological generation |
| *yiwen ji* | 仪文集 | collection of rites and petitions |

273

| You Ying Gong | 有应公 | God(s) who Respond |
|---|---|---|
| *you qiu bi ying* | 有求必应 | to plead is to gain response |
| *youjing* | 游境 | tour of the boundaries |
| *youmin* | 游民 | vagrants |
| Yu | 禹 | the legendary tamer of waters |
| Yu Huang Shang Di | 玉皇上帝 | the Jade Emperor, Supreme Ruler |
| *yuan* | 元 | primordial |
| *yuan* | 圆 | round |
| Yuanshuai | 元帅 | Marshal |
| *yuan chen* | 元辰 | original conjunction |
| *yuanzi* | 圆子 | dumplings |
| Yue Ling | 月令 | Monthly Commands |
| *yuezheng* | 约正 | head of a pact |
| *yundong* | 运动 | mobilised movement, exercises |
| *zhaijiao* | 祭教 | lay ascetic Buddhist teachings |
| Zhang Xun | 张巡 | Tang dynasty general, loyal to the emperor against the usurper An Lushan |
| *zhen* | 镇 | township |
| *zheng* | 正 | correct |
| *zhengzhi xueyuan xian* | 政治血管线 | political bloodline |
| Zheng Chenggong | 郑成功 | Koxinga, the Ming patriot |
| *zhengshen* | 正神 | correct, upright gods |
| *zhengxin* | 正信 | sincere belief |
| *zhengyi* | 正义 | rectitude |
| Zheng Yi | 正一 | Orthodox Unity (school of Daoism) |
| Zhi Nan Gong | 指南宫 | The Southpointing Palace |
| *zhiyue* | 志约 | recorder of a pact |
| Zhong Kui | 钟馗 | the great exorciser and door guardian |
| Zhong Zun | 中尊 | Venerable of the Centre |
| *zhongxin* | 中心 | centre |
| *zhongyuan* | 中元 | the central primordial |
| *zhu hui* | 主会 | host of the assembly |
| *zhu jiao* | 主醮 | host of the great offering |
| *zhu pu* | 主普 | host of the general salvation |
| *zhu tan* | 主坛 | host of the altars |
| *zhuang* | 庄 | administrative rural area |
| *zhuangtou* | 庄头 | village |
| Zit Iu Sin (Taiwanese) | 日淤神 | Day Wandering Spirit |
| *zongjiao* | 宗教 | religion |
| *zu* | 祖 | ancestral |
| *zu de liu fang* | 祖德流芳 | ancestral virtue, flowing and fragrant |
| *zu fu* | 祖福 | ancestors from Fujian |
| Zu Shi Gong | 祖师公 | Honoured Ancestral Master, also short for Qingshui Zushi Gong |
| *zun jing* | 尊敬 | pay respects |
| Zun Wang | 尊王 | Venerated King |

# Index